# COPYRIGHT
## FOR ACADEMIC
### LIBRARIANS AND PROFESSIONALS

ALA Editions purchases fund advocacy, awareness, and accreditation programs
for library professionals worldwide.

# COPYRIGHT
## FOR ACADEMIC
### LIBRARIANS AND PROFESSIONALS

REBECCA P. BUTLER

An imprint of the American Library Association
Chicago   2014

REBECCA P. BUTLER is a Presidential Teaching Professor in the Department of Educational Technology, Research, and Assessment, College of Education, at Northern Illinois University (NIU) in DeKalb, Illinois. At NIU, she teaches graduate (master's and doctoral) students in school library media and instructional technology. Prior to moving to NIU in 1998, she was an assistant professor in the Department of Curriculum and Instruction at East Tennessee State University (ETSU). While a faculty member at NIU and ETSU, she has conducted a variety of workshops, conferences, and graduate classes on the topic of copyright. Butler has written numerous articles and columns on copyright for library and technology professional journals. She has also written three books, *Copyright for Teachers & Librarians in the 21st Century* (2011), *Smart Copyright Compliance for Schools: A How-to-Do-It Manual* (2009), and *Copyright for Teachers and Librarians* (2004). She currently belongs to three national professional organizations' committees concerned with copyright issues.

Butler earned a B.A. in library science from the University of Northern Iowa in 1972; an M.S.L.S. from the University of Kentucky in 1978; and a Ph.D. in educational technology/curriculum and instruction from the University of Wisconsin-Madison in 1995. She has worked in a variety of library positions, including several years as a school librarian and library media specialist in public schools (K–12) in Fort Dodge, Dubuque, and Scott County, Iowa, and in a private school in Caracas, Venezuela; as a reference and young adult public librarian in Naperville, Illinois; as a medical librarian in Aurora, Illinois; and as a historian/special librarian in Coshocton, Ohio.

© 2014 by the American Library Association

Printed in the United States of America
18  17  16  15  14      5  4  3  2  1

Extensive effort has gone into ensuring the reliability of the information in this book; however, the publisher makes no warranty, express or implied, with respect to the material contained herein.

ISBN: 978-0-8389-1214-0 (paper).

**Library of Congress Cataloging-in-Publication Data**
Butler, Rebecca P., author.
    Copyright for academic librarians and professionals / Rebecca P. Butler.
        pages cm
    Includes bibliographical references and index.
    ISBN 978-0-8389-1214-0 (softcover : alk. paper)
    1. Copyright—United States. 2. Academic librarians—United States—Handbooks, manuals, etc. I. Title.
KF2995.B875 2014
346.7304'82—dc23                                              2014000997

Book design in the Adobe Caslon Pro and Univers typefaces by Alejandra Diaz.
⊗ This paper meets the requirements of ANSI/NISO Z39.48-1992 (Permanence of Paper).

*To Tom and Benj, you are the lights of my life!*

# CONTENTS

## PART II    SPECIFIC APPLICATIONS OF COPYRIGHT LAW

# LIST OF FIGURES

# PREFACE

Over the past seventeen years, I have conducted copyright workshops, classes, and presentations for college and university librarians and faculty; K–12 teachers and school librarians; public, medical, and other librarians; technology coordinators; school administrators; higher education students; and other interested parties. They came to these sessions for much the same reason that you picked up this book—they realized the importance and complexity of copyright issues in education – and beyond – and wanted help. *Copyright for Academic Librarians and Professionals* is largely based on the questions and concerns raised by those in my workshops, presentations, and classes, as it speaks to the needs of college and university librarians, technology specialists, and faculty, and it recognizes how copyright fits into your professional lives. In this book (similar in theme, concept, and format to that of my books written for K–12 educators), I have included copyright information and flow charts relevant in today's world, as well as addressed new and upcoming mediums in terms of copyright law.

*Copyright for Academic Librarians and Professionals* is, first and foremost, a handbook on copyright law for college and university librarians, faculty, technology specialists, and more who work in higher education environments. In addition, the information included in this book can be used by, or taught to, undergraduate and graduate students, as well as used by others in need of copyright advice. I have chosen to use realistic examples with interpretations of the law from copyright experts in the field. Although reading and interpreting the United States Copyright Law for oneself would be one approach, librarians and faculty may choose to use the interpretations from copyright experts given in the book, so that they don't have to wade through the law on their own. Because copyright law leaves some gray areas, there may be more than one interpretation to any one question. Since that is the case, I have chosen to give the readers the answer I consider most practical and most applicable in a college or university setting. For other concerns, or for further information, you may refer to the law itself, at www.copyright.gov/title17/.

This book is divided into two practical and necessary parts. Part I introduces the general concepts associated with copyright law. Part II describes the specific applications of copyright law as they affect nine different formats. It is important to use and understand both parts of this book, as they speak to each other. Knowing the general concepts will help your understanding and use of the specific applications. In the same way, knowing how copyright applies to your position in education will help you better understand and read the copyright legislation and literature you encounter in your day-to-day work. While you may refer to the chapters of part II more frequently than part I, you won't completely understand the information in part II without having first read part I.

Through the five chapters of part I, readers will develop a basic knowledge of the language and provisions of copyright law. Chapter 1, "Introduction to Copyright Law: What Is It and Why Is It Important in Higher Education?" provides a basic explanation of copyright, a history of legislation, its importance, how it affects media, and the policies and ethics associated with copyrighted materials. Chapter 2, "Fair Use: Is It Necessary to Ask for Permission?" introduces readers to the four factors of fair use that will help them make the best decisions for using materials, as well as to other parts of the law specifically of importance to educators: the classroom, handicap, and library exemptions. This chapter also provides some information on state copyright laws and on guidelines for the popular educational multimedia materials faculty and librarians often use. Chapter 3, "Public Domain: Is Anything Really Free?" answers questions concerning one of the most speculated-about aspects of copyright—public domain materials. This chapter explains public domain, including how something becomes public domain; identifies what media are in the public domain, as well as the relation of government documents to public domain; and discusses how you can identify public domain works. Chapter 4, "Obtaining Permission: In What Ways Can We Legally Obtain Permission to Use Others' Works?" gets to the core and function of this book. This chapter outlines permissions (what are they and how they work) and helps you understand their relationship to clearinghouses and licenses. Chapter 4 also explains how to write a permission letter, what goes in it, and an example of an effective letter. Chapter 5, "Other Important Copyright Information: What Else Do We Need to Know in Order to Function Legally within Copyright Law?" explains some of the remaining issues including international copyright law, plagiarism and citation, open-sourcing/Creative Commons, and violations and penalties.

Chapters 6 through 12 in part II cover specific applications of copyright law to the Internet, including blogs/vlogs, podcasts, wikis, social networking tools, and more; movies, DVDs, CDs, and television; computer and gaming software; music and audio; multimedia; and print works. Although librarians and other higher education personnel are familiar with terms such as *media* and *mediums*, for the purpose of this book, I have chosen to use the word *work* to represent these items as it is the more common term used with copyright law. Each chapter explains fair use, public domain, documentation and licenses, permissions, creation and ownership, violations and penalties, international copyright law, and avoiding copyright problems as they relate to the specific works. These are chapters that you can consult as the issues arise or read over to become more familiar with the formats you use most often. Chapter 13, "Distance Learning and Copyright Law: This Is Confusing! How Can We Share Materials with Our Students and Still Comply with the Law?" also covers the points found in chapters 6 through 12. In addition, it discusses the Digital Millennium Copyright Act (DMCA) and the Technology, Education, and Copyright Harmonization (TEACH) Act and how these relate to the many aspects of distance education. Chapter 14, "Conclusion: What Does All of This Mean for Librarians and Other Higher Education Professionals?" brings it all together and provides some last-minute advice for avoiding problems, how to deal with pressure to break the law, and how and why to teach students and faculty the importance of copyright law.

Copyright law is something that you have probably always been aware of, but that perhaps you have never closely examined or understood. The truth is that copyright is an everyday part of your function as a college/university librarian, technology specialist, or faculty member, and it requires your full attention and knowledge. This guide is meant to be a quick and thorough look into the implications of copyright in higher education. In it, I have answered many of the common questions I have encountered in my classes, presentations, and workshops, while still expanding and fleshing out this source so that it anticipates even the questions that were not asked. In truth, copyright should be a part of education. Thus, it is necessary to be aware of the various facets of copyright and use them to your own and your students' advantage. Please be aware that I am a university professor who researches, writes, and presents in the area of copyright law, and that the information in this book does not substitute for advice from an attorney.

# ACKNOWLEDGMENTS

I would like to thank the college and university librarians and interested faculty and staff whose requests for information on copyright in a "non-legalese" manner have culminated in this book. Additionally, I would like to thank my library information specialist and instructional technology students, other interested master's and doctoral students, and graduate assistants at Northern Illinois University and East Tennessee State University who have participated in my copyright classes and workshops over the past fifteen years and asked insightful questions on the subject. Lastly, I wish to express my appreciation for the support of family and friends, especially my husband, Tom, and my son, Benjamin, who read over drafts, made comments, and helped create flow charts. I cannot thank you enough!

# PART I

Copyright Fundamentals

# 1

# Introduction to Copyright Law
## What Is It and Why Is It Important in Higher Education?

Copyright is a very confusing area of U.S. law—one that can be argued to have an ethical component, since it is possible that the only person who knows whether copyright law is being violated is the individual copying or borrowing the work. Because it is written in a manner that opens it to many interpretations, copyright law is especially of concern in a college or university setting, where librarians, professors, instructors, administrators, technology coordinators, students, and others may think, "We can copy all we want, because it's for education." If the copyright owner has granted consent for use of his or her work, then there is no problem. Frequently, however, the dilemma is that the borrower does not have the time or inclination (or is unable) to locate the owner in order to determine if desired use of a work is legal.

Often, in the world of academia we tend to think that we will not get caught if we borrow without obtaining permission from the work's owner. After all, academics "push the envelope" often, it takes time we do not have to research for copyright permissions, and who has really heard of copyright police? There is also the opposite approach, for example, when a department chair may demand that absolutely no copying occur in his or her division. Here, the misconception is that all copying is illegal. In actuality the answer lies somewhere in between. As faculty and librarians, we deal with communication technologies in a wide variety of formats, from books to movies and music to the Internet. We are usually busy and often searching for something to use at the last minute. Borrowing a few pages out of a textbook for a math class to take home over the weekend, copying another piece of music for the drum section, or using a popular song for a vocal podcast may seem the easiest ways to go. After all, who is going to know? That the owner of the copyrighted work may lose money or control over his or her product is not our concern. Below are some of the questions that we should ask as we go about our daily responsibilities as academics.

Can you change a digitized image so that using it is not a copyright infringement? What can you legally put on a wiki? Are there copyright concerns when you use a social network, like Shelfari or Facebook, for a class communication tool? Do you need special permission from Internet authors to use their works? Can you print anything you want off a CD-ROM? Is it okay to copy a television program and use it as part of a class unit? Legally, is it possible to show a DVD rented from a video store/vendor in a face-to-face class? Can an instructor lawfully retain students' completed assignments to use in future classes or to show as "best examples"? If you want to copy a magazine article thirty times for a reading assignment, can you do this under copyright law? College and university educators often ask such questions as they develop curriculum, prepare lessons, and otherwise go about their daily teaching duties. In addition, they ask questions dealing with research as well. Examples of this might be: can we borrow videos from another person's project to analyze for our research? Who owns our research, if we get a grant? Can we change the format of old interviews from reel-to-reel tapes to digital so that we can study them easier? All of these questions deal with copyright, perhaps the most well known of our intellectual property rights. These questions and more will be asked and answered in the next few chapters, along with other copyright topics.

As you use this book, please note that there are three similar terms: U.S. Code, U.S. Copyright Law, and the U.S. Copyright Act. Although they are all related, each one is somewhat different from the other two. The U.S. Code "is the codification by subject matter of the general and permanent laws of the United States." It is divided by broad subjects into fifty titles and published by the Office of the Law Revision Counsel of the U.S. House of Representatives (U.S. Code 2009, 1). One part of the U.S. Code is Title 17. Chapters 1–8 and 10–12 of Title 17 contain the United States Copyright Law. This is the U.S. law that is concerned with copyright and, thus, the one we use in this book to interpret our copyright questions. ("Chapters 9 and 13 of title 17 contain statutory design protection that is independent of copyright protection" [U.S. Copyright Office 2010c: Preface].) The Copyright Act is part of the U.S. Copyright Law. Passed in 1976, the Copyright Act "provides the basic framework for the current copyright law" (U.S. Copyright Law 2002: 1). In broad terms, this means that the Copyright Act is a piece of U.S. Copyright Law, which is one part of the U.S. Code (all the laws of the United States). For the purposes of this book, we focus on U.S. Copyright Law. Please note that the complete Copyright Law is available in a variety of places, including the United States Copyright office's website (www.copyright.gov), and in print for $32.00, from the U.S. Government Bookstore (U.S. Copyright Office 2011).

## COPYRIGHT DEFINED AND EXPLAINED

Below is a brief definition of copyright and what it means to those of us in higher education.

### Definition

"Copyright is a statutory privilege extended to creators of works that are fixed in a tangible medium of expression" (Bruwelheide 1995, 4). Owners of copyrighted works have the exclusive right, by law, to

- reproduce or copy;
- distribute;
- publicly perform;
- publicly display, and
- create derivatives.

Copyright law violations occur when someone other than the owner attempts to use works in one of the manners described above (Butler 2000).

### Things That Can Be Copyrighted

Almost anything originally created is copyrightable, that is, it can be or is registered with the U.S. Copyright Office. Figure 1-1 below lists examples of works that can be copyrighted.

A note worth mentioning concerning the concept of "originality" is that the perception of an original work is that it "reflects the personality of the maker" (Ploman and Hamilton 1980, 31). Thus, two different people may write stories about voice classes at the Peking Opera School, and both stories can be copyrighted—assuming that each story is sufficiently unique. Because this can be confusing, sometimes courts make the decision as to whether or not a work is "truly" an original (Ploman and Hamilton 1980).

### Automatic Copyright

Under current copyright law, almost anything a person creates is automatically copyright-protected, whether it is officially registered or not. Thus, every e-mail you send, every paper your students write, or every digital picture you take is protected. What this means for college and university educators is that if the football coach creates a blog to supplement football practice, a student writes an original paper on John Brown, or an art professor films a video of his or her students' artwork, all have created copyrightable works. If you like, you may put a © on everything you or your students create. This shows those who view/listen/use your work that it is copyright-protected, whether officially registered with the U.S. Copyright Office or not. (Official registration of copyright is addressed later in this chapter.) Remember: in the instance of a lawsuit, those items registered with the U.S. Copyright Office have a stronger chance of winning than do those that have only been "unofficially" copyrighted; that is, not recorded with the U.S. Copyright Office (Bruwelheide 1995).

## FIGURE 1-1

**Works That Can Be Copyright-Protected**

| PRINT | NONPRINT | INTERNET |
|---|---|---|
| Articles | Architecture | Blogs/Vlogs |
| Books | Audio Recordings | Digitized Graphics, Movies, and Advertisements |
| Letters | CD-ROMs | |
| Newsletters | Computer Software | E-Mails |
| Newspapers | DVDs | Nings |
| Plays and Musicals | Games | Podcasts |
| Poems | Modern Dance and Other Public Performances, including Pantomimes and Choreography | Social Networks |
| Sheet Music | | Web Pages |
| Other Print Works | | Wikis |
| | Multimedia | Other Digitized Works Available on the World Wide Web |
| | Paintings | |
| | Photographs | |
| | Statues | |
| | Television Programs | |
| | Videos | |
| | Other Nonprint Works | |

## Who Owns the Copyrighted Work?

Usually the person or group who creates a work owns the copyright; for example, a student who digitizes a series of stories that he has written for English class would probably own the rights to his stories. However, it is possible for individuals or companies to own works they did not create. This can occur in one of two ways. The first is when the creator transfers or assigns copyright ownership to a third party. Thus, it is possible for a technology coordinator to create a web page about child care among penguins on his or her own time and sell the copyright to an educational Internet company. The second way is "work for hire." This is when work is considered the property of the organization that hired the individual or group to do the work. For example, a reference librarian uses his free time for several weeks to write up a new policy on student reference interviews. He was asked to create this policy by the library dean, he is doing it on university time, and he uses a university computer. Such a situation may be considered "work for hire." Another example is if a mathematics professor, at home, creates a digital math game for an educational software company. If she signs a contract with the company stating that it is "work for hire," the professor does not own what she has created. Instead, she is paid a fee by the company, which then may register the game with the U.S. Copyright Office.

## Derivative Works

Derivative works are items created by changing an already existing work. The extent of change to the work can be slight, moderate, or a great deal. Take a graphic of an elephant, for example. A web designer has created an elephant for her website. A technology student finds the elephant graphic and borrows it, adding a red hat to its head. The elephant with a red hat is an example of a derivative work. Another example of a derivative work is when a dance class instructor takes a set of original dance moves borrowed from a musical and changes them slightly to fit a dance number that her class is presenting at a workshop. When works are changed somewhat—but not completely—a derivative work is the result. When derivative works are created from copyrighted works, without the proper permissions or licenses, this is an infringement of copyright law.

## What Copyright Law Is Not

Copyright is only one of several intellectual property rights addressed in a general manner, in the U.S. Constitution: "exclusive rights to . . . respective writings and discoveries" (1788). Other intellectual property in the United States includes (1) patents (issued by the government, for a specific period of time, in order to monopolize an invention); (2) trademarks (logos, symbols, sounds, etc., which distinguish products from one another); and (3) trade secrets (information that makes an item competitive). (Silver 2003; Wherry 2008)

# HISTORY OF COPYRIGHT

Those not interested in history might wonder, "Why is the history of copyright important to my students and me?" Most librarians and many university faculty have their eyes on the future, on new technologies and how to use them in the classroom. As will be seen from the discussion below, however, while copyright is often seen as a relatively new concern, especially with new technologies, it has, in fact, been around for some time. Understanding where it has been before can help with thinking about where it will go in the future. "One way we have of sensing the future is to look back into the past" (Saltrick 1995, 1).

Copyright in the United States is greatly influenced by English common law. For example, the Statute of Anne of 1710, noted as the beginning of contemporary copyright law, provided for protecting authors' literary property for a limited number of years (Tryon 1994). Notions of copyright in the future United States are seen as early as 1672, when bookseller John Usher's petition to the General Court of the Massachusetts Bay Colony resulted in a private copyright for his revised edition of *The General Laws and Liberties of the*

*Massachusetts Colony* (Bettig 1996; Usher's Printing Privilege 1672). About 100 years later, such prominent citizens of the fledging United States as Noah Webster and Thomas Paine worked to promote state copyright law. (In the 1780s, state copyright laws were passed by all thirteen original colonies as a result of Noah Webster's work to protect his writings. This was necessary because the Articles of Confederation did not provide federal copyright protection [Bettig 1996; Peterson 2003].) The first federal copyright legislation was signed in 1790 by President George Washington. Congress was given the power to "promote the progress of science and useful arts, by securing for limited times to authors and inventors the exclusive right to their respective writings and discoveries" (U.S. Const., art. I, sec. 8). This law was later expanded and revised in 1831, 1879, 1909, 1976, and 1998. It is the basis of intellectual property rights in our country today, and continues to be modified. At any given point in time, a number of bills dealing in some way with copyright sit in our nation's House and Senate awaiting action (Butler 2003). Many new bills cover digital works, including Internet applications, television broadcasting, DVDs, and more. Indeed in the 21st century, "one of the primary reasons for copyright law is . . . the protection of the owners and creators to earn money and recognition for those things that they own or create" (Butler 2003, 39).

## WHY COPYRIGHT LAW IS IMPORTANT

Copyright is important in that it protects creators and owners' rights to their works. Copyright legislation grants the owner the "exclusive right to reproduce, prepare derivative works, distribute, perform and display the work publicly. Exclusive means only the creator of such work, not anybody who has access to it and decides to grab it" (Whatiscopyright .org 2010, 1). However, copyright law also helps the user of the work, in that the owners' rights are limited (see chapters 2 and 3). As such, this law actually represents both the owners and the users of works.

It is helpful here to look briefly at owners and users of works—usually two distinctive groups. Owners are those individuals or groups who either created a work or obtained the copyright for it. Usually, owners are looking for assurance that the rights they own are not being infringed upon. Users of works are those individuals or groups who wish to borrow all or part of a work for their own employ. For example, suppose you are a library instruction librarian and you wish to borrow a series of research activities from a workbook for use with the freshman class. In addition, you plan to photocopy these activities and share them with colleagues who also do library instruction. It is very possible that in pursuing either activity, you would be violating the rights of those who own the copyright to the workbook activities. These two distinct groups (owners and users) are what keep the issue of copyright going, year after year, generation after generation. Next, you will learn how to officially register a work you have created with the U.S. Copyright Office.

## HOW TO REGISTER WORKS WITH THE U.S. COPYRIGHT OFFICE

Usually when you think of copyright, you think in terms of how much you can borrow without getting permission from the owner or creator of the book, movie, audio file, web page, or whatever it is that you want to copy. However, look at this subject from a different approach—how can you obtain an official copyright for something you have created?

Assume that you are a retired professor with a hobby in astronomy. As a former professor, you have decided to try your hand at creating units on astronomy for undergraduate and graduate students. You have written a number of units, created on your own time, at home, with your own software and computer. These have not been used in the classroom. You compile the units into manuscript form, with the idea that perhaps an educational publishing firm would be interested in them. Before you send them out for review, you would like to obtain official copyright registration for your work. How do you go about doing this?

### Contacting the Copyright Office

Your first step is to contact the U.S. Copyright Office at the Library of Congress. They can be reached online, by phone, or through the U.S. Postal Service. If you are contacting them by phone or mail, tell them that you want to register your manuscript with their office, and they will send you the materials you need via snail mail. Online forms and application instructions, as well as other copyright information, are also available on the Internet at (www.loc.gov/copyright).

### Registering Your Work

Be aware that any kind of work that can be copyright-protected can be registered with the U.S. Copyright Office. While print forms, such as TX (literary works), VA (visual arts works), SR (sound recordings), and more are still available via mail from the U.S. Copyright Office, it is easier and cheaper to register a work online. Go to the Electronic Copyright Office at (www.copyright.gov/eco) and access the detailed PowerPoint, tutorial (PDF format), and/or online tip sections for all instructions and materials.

Concerning the example above, where you are a retired professor who has created astronomy units in manuscript form for publication, you could file online at any time of the day or night (except Sunday from midnight to 6 a.m. Eastern time) for a $35.00 fee, or receive the TX form by mail for $65.00 (Electronic Copyright Office 2012). Other works that can be assigned copyright registration include lyrics, music, plays, movies, scripts, pantomimes, choreography, sound recordings, cartoons, comic strips, photographs, architectural works, games, multimedia works, various digital formats (for example, wikis, podcasts, and so on), and recipes.

Note that there are some works that cannot be registered by the Copyright Office. Such works include those protected by another intellectual property, such as a patent or those that are not entitled to protection, for example works that are not set in a fixed form (Torrans 2003). In addition, works that cannot be copyrighted include ideas, methods, blank forms, names, titles, slogans, short phrases and "works that consist entirely of information that is common property and containing no original authorship"; among these are "standard calendars, height and weight charts, tape measures and rules, and lists of tables taken from public documents or other common sources . . . mere listings of ingredients or contents, procedures, systems, processes, concepts, principles, discoveries, or devices" (Torrans 2003, 40).

Information needed by the U.S. Copyright Office, in order to register a work, includes such things as title, name and address of author, name and address of owner, year of creation, publication date (if applicable), type of authorship, name and address of permission contact person, format of the item, and where the copyright certificate is to be sent (U.S. Copyright Office 2010).

### When Does Your Work Receive Copyright Registration?

"Whatever time is needed to issue a certificate, the effective date of registration is the day the Copyright Office receives a complete submission in acceptable form. You do not need to wait for a certificate to proceed with publication" (U.S. Copyright Office 2010). Therefore, if your work can be registered for copyright protection, it will be protected immediately upon all required information and materials being received by the U.S. Copyright Office.

### When Will You Find Out If Your Work Received Copyright Registration?

Normally, the person(s) requesting copyright registration will receive an e-mail notice of receipt of materials from the U.S. Copyright Office, if applying online, with the registration certificate arriving in approximately nine months. If applying with paper forms, no receipt will be sent and the registration certificate, which the work's owner would take delivery of, could be sent up to twenty-two months after the first contact with the U.S. Copyright Office (U.S. Copyright Office 2010).

### U.S. Copyright Office Contact Information

U.S. Copyright Office
101 Independence Ave. S.E.
Washington, D.C. 20559-6000
(202) 707-3000
Internet: www.copyright.gov

## CONCLUSION

Have you ever infringed on someone's copyright while pursuing your teaching activities, researching, or doing library work? Have your colleagues? If you and those that you work with are completely honest, undoubtedly the answer is "yes." Let's take a look at some of the ways that you might infringe on an individual or group/organization/company's copyright in your professional lives. Have you or a colleague:

- added part of a commercial video, which supported a particular curricular unit, to an online educational site, such as TeacherTube?
- loaded a piece of computer software that a student brought in onto more than one classroom computer at the same time (without reading the documentation, which might state that such use is illegal)?
- burned a music CD to several blank CDs, so that students could listen to it in small groups while working on group projects?
- "borrowed" liberally from a web page that you liked to create one of your own?
- copied an extra script of a play for the new student director?
- scanned and posted an entire book on your Blackboard site? (You really wanted everyone to read it, and you only had your own copy.)
- "borrowed" a survey from a dissertation to use in your own research?

This list could go on and on. Without proper permissions or other exemptions, all of these points above and more could be considered copyright infringements. Indeed, abuse of U.S. copyright law probably occurs every day in higher education. Whatever the case, it does not mean that you need to continue along such lines—there is hope! Using this book, it is possible to follow the law, rather than rationalize reasons for not doing so. Now, continue on to chapter 2, for a discussion of fair use, one of the areas of copyright law of most importance to education.

## REFERENCES

Bettig, Ronald V. 1996. *Copyrighting Culture: The Political Economy of Intellectual Property*. Boulder, CO: Westview.

Bruwelheide, Janis H. 1995. *The Copyright Primer for Librarians and Educators*. 2nd ed. Chicago: American Library Association.

Butler, Rebecca P. 2000. "Copyright as a Social Responsibility—Don't Shoot the Messenger." *Knowledge Quest* 29, no. 2 (November/December): 48–49.

———. 2003. "Copyright Law in the United States . . . and How It Got That Way." *Knowledge Quest* 31, no. 4 (March/April): 39–40.

Electronic Copyright Office. 2012. eCO Online system. www.copyright.gov/eco.

Peterson, Dennis L. 2003. "The Enduring Legacy of Noah Webster." www.homeschoolingtoday .com/Articles/DPJF03.htm.

Ploman, Edward W., and L. Clark Hamilton. 1980. *Copyright: Intellectual Property in the Information Age*. Boston: Routledge and Kegan Paul.

Saltrick, Susan. 1995. "The Pearl of Great Price: Copyright and Authorship from the Middle Ages to the Digital Age." *Educom Review* 30, no. 3 (May/June): 44–46.

Silver, Judith A. 2003. "What Is Intellectual Property? Trade Secret Law." http://library.findlaw.com/2003/May/15/132743.html.

Torrans, Lee Ann. 2003. *Law for K-12 Libraries and Librarians.* Westport, CT: Libraries Unlimited.

Tryon, Jonathan S. 1994. *The Librarian's Legal Companion.* New York: G. K. Hall.

U.S. Code. 2009. "Office of the Law Revision Counsel of the U.S. House of Representatives." www.gpoaccess.gov/uscode.

U.S. Constitution. 1788. Article 1, section 8.

U.S. Copyright Office, Library of Congress. 2009. "What Does Copyright Protect?" www.copyright.gov/help/faq/faq-protect.html#title.

U.S. Copyright Office, Library of Congress. 2010. Copyright.www.loc.gov/copyright.

———. 2010b. "I've Submitted My Application, Fee, and Copy of My Work to the Copyright Office. Now What?" www.copyright.gov/help/faq/faq-what.html#certificate.

U.S. Copyright Office, Library of Congress. 2011. "Copyright Law of the United States of America and Related Laws Contained in Title 17 of the United States Code, Circular 92, Preface." http://www.copyright.gov/title17.

Usher's Printing Privilege. 1672. "Introduction." www.copyrighthistory.org.

Whatiscopyright.org. 2010. "What Is Copyright Protection?" www.whatiscopyright.org.

Wherry, Timothy Lee. 2008. *Intellectual Property: Everything the Digital-Age Librarian Needs to Know.* Chicago: American Library Association.

# 2

# Fair Use
## Is It Necessary to Ask for Permission?

Walk into a college or university library or classroom in the United States and ask a librarian, professor, administrator, or technology person what he or she knows about copyright. In all likelihood, one of the first things that these individuals will mention is the term *fair use*. Now, ask these people what "fair use" means. After a pause, you may get either a scattered answer containing half-truths about fair use and how it can be used in an educational setting or (in some cases) perhaps a brief summary. This chapter focuses on clarifying the idea of fair use, one of the most important concepts in copyright for education.

## FAIR USE DEFINED AND EXPLAINED

Probably one of the handiest and yet most easily misinterpreted copyright principles deals with fair use. Fair use "limits copyright holders' exclusive rights" (Butler 2001a, 35). There are four fair use factors: "(1) the purpose and character of the use, including whether such use is of a commercial nature or is for nonprofit educational purposes; (2) the nature of the copyrighted work; (3) the amount and substantiality of the portion used in relation to the copyrighted work as a whole; and (4) the effect of the use upon the potential market for or value of the copyrighted work" (Lawrence and Timberg 1989, 380). These fair use principles, which are found in section 107 of the Copyright Act (1976), are explained below.

## FAIR USE FACTOR 1: PURPOSE AND CHARACTER OF USE

The first fair use factor, purpose and character of use, looks at how those copying the work are going to use it. Works copied for educational, nonprofit, or personal purposes are much more likely to be considered within fair use than are those items that are copied with the intention of earning money. Thus, an associate professor of kinesiology may be able to copy an article on exercise science for a class but not for the purpose of selling the article. A good question for you to ask yourself here is, "What do I want to do with the materials I plan to copy?"

Parodies and other transformative uses, such as commentaries, fit under the first fair use factor. Such use of works is allowed "for purposes such as criticism [or] comment" (U.S. Copyright Law 1976, Section 107, 16). This means that, for the kinesiology class above, an associate professor may assign the students to take a television advertisement that demonstrates exercise science principles, and write a skit transforming the ad content into a criticism of said principles.

## FAIR USE FACTOR 2: NATURE OF THE WORK

The second fair use factor, the nature of the work, deals with the work's characteristics: is the work fact or fiction, published or unpublished? Works most usable under fair use factor #2 are nonfiction published pieces. Therefore, a travel magazine article about the Pocahontas statue in Pocahontas, Iowa, might be copy-able for a social studies class that future teachers are attending, while a handwritten fictionalized story about Pocahontas and John Rolfe—just found in someone's attic—and dated 1801 might not be. Good questions for you to ask yourself here are, "Is this work fact or fiction? Has this work been published or not?"

## FAIR USE FACTOR 3: AMOUNT TO BE BORROWED

The third fair use factor covers the quantity of work one plans to borrow. For example, do you want to use an entire hour-long movie or just five minutes of it? Are you interested in copying the Beatles' song "Hard Day's Night" in its entirety or just a small part of it? With this fair use factor, the smallest amount borrowed is usually the best. This factor is measured two ways: quantitatively and qualitatively. "Quantity considers the amount copied relative to the whole original as well as the amount needed to achieve the objective of the copying. Qualitative measurement is more creative. It involves the concept of substantiality, whereby copying the "heart" of the work—no matter how small—is too much" (Butler 2001a, 35). Thus, five minutes of an hour-long movie about computer science hackers would fit into this factor—unless that particular five minutes was the heart of the recording; that is, showing exactly how the hacking was accomplished. Good questions for you to ask yourself here are, "How much do I need to borrow? Is this the heart of the work?"

## FAIR USE FACTOR 4: MARKETABILITY OF THE WORK

The fourth fair use factor features the marketability of the work. In essence, this means that if this work were to be copied and sold, either as part of a newly created item or by itself, would such a sale affect the amount of money that the owner or creator of the original work could earn from it? For instance, if copying an extra script of a play means that the publisher who owns the rights to that play does not get royalties, then such copying is in violation of the law. Another example is that dealing with sheet music. Here we will use an orchestra director as the case in point. Perhaps the director finds that there is one student too many in the violin section for the available music. That student needs a copy of the second violin part for the concert coming up in two weeks. The director decides to make one copy—after all, the music selection was purchased for the whole orchestra! Unfortunately, unless there is no other way to get the violin part before the concert, such copying may be in violation. In addition, if the concert is imminent and a copy is made, that copy needs to be destroyed right after the concert, unless the copyright holder granted permission. A good question to ask here is, "Will my copying this item mean that the copyright holder will earn less money?" (Since the mid-1990s, the licensing of works is now also being considered in evaluating this factor with "for-profit organizations"—which could include some private colleges and universities. This is a result of *American Geophysical Union et al. v. Texaco Inc.* [1992] in which several Texaco scientists were found to have violated copyright law by copying a number of scientific journal articles without paying royalties to the publishers [*American Geophysical Union* 1992].)

There are exceptions to almost every rule, and the fair use factors are not exempt. For example, copying, in excess of the four fair use factors, is allowed at times for disabled users, depending on the disability and how the copying is made and used. Such exemptions are addressed in more depth in later chapters. Internet sites that support fair use determination include a Fair Use Check List (http://www.usg.edu/copyright/fair_use_checklist), a fair use flow chart (www.benedict.com/Info/FairUse/FairUse.aspx), and a fair use evaluator tool (http://librarycopyright.net/resources/fairuse).

## COPYRIGHT GUIDELINES FOR EDUCATIONAL MULTIMEDIA

The four "fair use factors" discussed above are very important to libraries and librarians, as well as higher education professors and instructors, as they work with new and old technologies, with students and colleagues. However, these four factors were purposefully written so they are vague (Rose 1993) in order to permit flexibility in their use—which makes many educators uncomfortable when they are trying to use all or part of a copyrighted work. Thus, users of works may want to have an exact amount in mind when considering how much they can and can't copy without permission. This is where directives such as the Fair Use/Copyright Guidelines for Educational Multimedia come into play.

Guidelines are far more rigid than the fair use factors discussed above, are not binding under the law, and represent minimum amounts rather than maximums. Basically, when used by the borrower of a work, it means that the borrower is trying to act in good faith. Because of this, many copyright experts do not encourage their use. They are covered here because, while they do not have the power of law, "they give the courts a sense of how . . . fair use (is) to be interpreted" (Butler 2001b, 34).

One well-known set of copyright guidelines, the Copyright Guidelines for Educational Multimedia, was originally developed by the Consortium of College and University Media Centers (CCUMC) (2002), when this organization participated in the Conference on Fair Use (CONFU). (These guidelines have since been retired by the CCUMC [ARL Policy Notes 2014, 1].) These guidelines were solely applied to the creation and use of educational multimedia; thus, when creating a multimedia presentation for a class with excerpts from a video, CD, digitized music, televised cartoon, book, and so on, the numbers in figure 2-1 (see below) could be applied. Moreover two copies, one for viewing and one for reserve, in addition to one for each of the creators of the multimedia presentation, could be made and kept. While these copies could be kept and used for two years, if you wanted to keep using the project after that time period, then you would need to obtain permissions from the owners of the original works borrowed. These permissions would have to be obtained from everyone from whom you borrowed, whether the borrowing originally fit under the fair use guidelines or not. However, the multimedia project could be kept intact after the two years, without obtaining permissions, if used by the creator(s) for a portfolio, (unpaid) workshop, or presentation for peers (Lehman 1996).

## FIGURE 2-1

**Quantities of Media Recommended for Borrowing under the Fair Use Guidelines for Educational Multimedia**

| MEDIUMS | AMOUNTS |
|---|---|
| Motion Media | 10 percent or three minutes |
| Text | 10 percent or 1,000 words |
| Poems of Less Than 250 Words | three poems |
| Poems over 250 Words up to 250 Words | three excerpts by a poet, five excerpts by different poets in same collection |
| Music, Lyrics, Music Video | up to 10 percent or 30 seconds |
| Illustrations and Photographs | five by the same artist or photographer - 10 percent or 15 images from one published work |
| Numerical Data Sets | 10 percent or 2,500 fields or cells (Fair Use Guidelines for Educational Multimedia 2007) |

Be aware that CONFU, discussed above, first convened in 1994. It was composed of a number of individuals representing such user organizations as the American Library Association and the National Education Association and such owner groups as the Motion Picture Association of America and the Software Publishers Association. The purpose of CONFU was to talk about fair use and develop guidelines for librarians and educators to use when working with copyrighted works. The CONFU concept was that such guidelines would be agreeable to both users and owners (Lehman 1996, 2). As one might have expected, representatives of the two groups found it difficult to agree on copyright guidelines; while user groups tended to feel that the suggested guidelines were too stringent, owner groups felt that the same guidelines were not strong enough.

Furthermore, often colleges and universities post their own copyright guidelines. Thus, in addition to what is written in this book, it is helpful to check your particular school's policies and procedures. For more on copyright guidelines, see chapter 5 of this book.

## CONCLUSION

If copyright law were a color, it would be seen in shades of gray. Oftentimes, there is no one answer to a copyright question. Instead, there are any numbers of points that a borrower must consider when using a work owned by someone else. This also means that those interpreting the four fair use factors may not always agree on interpretations. (Illustrative examples of variances within understandings of fair use include discussions found in current copyright books, professional periodical articles, and websites (Aufderheide et al. 2007; Center for Digital Research and Scholarship 2009; Greenhow et al. 2008; Hobbs 2010; McLeod 2005; Reyman 2010; and Young 2011). Because such lack of agreement is often the case, it is important to remember that all four of the fair use factors need to be followed; "none in theory is given more weight than another, as fair use is an equitable concept" (Lipinski 2005, 156). Another good point to keep in mind is that, whether using copyright law or guidelines, when borrowing without permission from copyrighted works, always use the smallest quantity that you can.

## REFERENCES

*American Geophysical Union et al. v. Texaco Inc.* 1992. 802 F. (S.D.N.Y.).

ARL Policy Notes. 2014. "CCUMC Endorses #Librarianscode, Retires Guidelines."
      http://policynotes.arl.org/post/42434587912/ccumc-endorses-librarianscode-retires-guidelines.

Aufderheide, Pat, et al. 2007. "Media Literacy Educators Need Clarity about Copyright and Fair Use." *Journal of Media Literacy* 54, no. 2 and 3: 41–44.

Brewer, Michael, 2008. "Fair Use Evaluator." http://librarycopyright.net/resources/fairuse.

Butler, Rebecca P. 2001a. "Copyright as a Social Responsibility—Fair Use: I Need It Now!" *Knowledge Quest* 29, no. 3 (January/February): 35–36.

———. 2001b. "Fair Use Guidelines for Educational Multimedia." *Knowledge Quest* 29, no. 4 (March/April): 34–35.

Center for Digital Research and Scholarship. 2009. Revamped Copyright Web Site from Columbia University. http://cdrs.columbia.edu/cdrsmain/?p=732.

Copyright Website. 2010. "The Law: Fair Use: Coming Out." www.benedict.com/Info/FairUse/FairUse.aspx.

Davidson, Hall. 2002. "The Educator's Guide to Copyright and Fair Use." www.mediafestival.org/old_site/copyright_chart.pdf.

Fair Use Checklist. 2012. http://www.usg.edu/copyright/fair_use_checklist.

Fair Use Guidelines for Educational Multimedia. 2007. http://ccumc.org/node/210.

Greenhow, Christine, et al. 2008. "Fair Use Education for the Twenty-First Century: A Comparative Study of Students' Use of an Interactive Tool to Guide Decision Making." *Innovate* 4, no. 2: unp.

Hobbs, Renee. 2010. *Copyright Clarity: How Fair Use Supports Digital Learning.* Thousand Oaks, CA: Corwin.

Illinois General Assembly. 2009. Public Act 095-0869. www.ilga.gov/legislation/publicacts/fulltext.asp?Name=095-0869.

Lawrence, John S., and Bernard Timberg. 1989. *Fair Use and Free Inquiry: Copyright Law and the New Media.* 2nd ed. Norwood, NJ: Ablex.

Lehman, Bruce A. 1996. *The Conference on Fair Use: An Interim Report to the Commissioner.* Washington, DC: U.S. Patent and Trademark Office.

Lipinski, Tomas A. 2005. *Copyright Law and the Distance Education Classroom.* Lanham, MD: The Scarecrow Press.

Mcleod, Kembrew. 2005. *Freedom of Expression: Overzealous Copyright Bozos and Other Enemies of Creativity.* New York, NY: Doubleday.

Radcliffe, Mark F., and Diane Brinson. 2010. "Copyright Law." http://library.findlaw.com/1999/Jan/1/241476.html.

Reyman, Jessica. 2010. *The Rhetoric of Intellectual Property: Copyright Law and the Regulation of Digital Culture.* New York, NY: Routledge.

Rose, Mark. 1993. *Authors and Owners: The Invention of Copyright.* Cambridge, MA: Harvard University Press.

U.S. Copyright Law. 1976. Public Law 94-553, sec. 107, 16.

Young, Jeffrey R. 2011. "Pushing Back against Legal Threats by Putting Fair Use Forward." *Chronicle of Higher Education* (June 3, 2011): A8 and A11.

# 3

## Public Domain
### Is Anything Really Free?

As the Internet rapidly expands, digital overload is a common complaint; masses of material exist at our fingertips. It is easy to assume, since the information is all "right in front of us," that it is also free for us to use in any way that we want. In actuality, the Web, like any other medium, may be or may not be copyright-protected; that depends on the whims of the owner(s) of the works. In addition, many college and university educators use any number of rationalizations for borrowing all sorts of material without permission, including: (1) we are a nonprofit educational institution, so it's OK; (2) no one will know anyway; and (3) it's for the students, they need it, and we can't afford to purchase it. Such arguments are often in direct contrast to copyright law. However, at times there is free material—on the Web or otherwise. Such material is in the public domain.

### PUBLIC DOMAIN DEFINED AND EXPLAINED

Essentially, works in the public domain are free to use any way that you want. For example, Grimm's fairy tales, including "Cinderella" and "Snow White," are in the public domain. This means that you can create a wiki where your students rewrite these stories into new ones, based on modern times; print out the new stories for all students in your class; even sell copies of these stories at a professional conference. Thus, public domain also encourages the creation of new works. What is not in the public domain is a revised fairy tale (one that someone else has already changed). Thus, while "Cinderella" is in the public domain, the

Disney version of it (whether book or movie) is not. This is because derivatives of the original piece are protected under copyright law. Consequently, while the story of "Cinderella"
remains in the public domain, a cartoon version, or any other revision of the story, may be
copyright-protected.

When using public domain materials, you can borrow all or part of a work—print or
nonprint, fiction or nonfiction—and not worry about copyright infringement. The idea
behind public domain is that the copyright owner has given up, to the public at large, all of
his or her original rights to the work (see chapter 1 for the list of original rights).

## WORKS IN THE PUBLIC DOMAIN

Works in the public domain include:

- most federal documents (See the section in this chapter entitled "The Public Domain
  and Federal Government Documents" for discussion on which federal documents
  are in the public domain and which are not.);
- phone books;
- works with expired copyrights;
- works for which creators/owners have chosen to give up their copyrights;
- freeware;
- some open-source documents;
- works registered with Creative Commons and similar organizations;
- things that cannot be copyrighted, for example, names, short phrases, titles, ideas,
  and facts;
- some clip art (Internet and print);
- works published in 1923 or before; and
- some works published between 1923 and 1963 (Gasaway 2003).

Do you have to purchase public domain material or is it free? Because educators are
often on tight budgets and looking to cut costs, this question can be critical to college and
university personnel. Therefore, it is important to note that public domain materials, just
like other works, may be free, as in the cases of an Internet site that states it is in the public
domain or free software found on the Web. Public domain materials may also be sold, although the cost is usually not as much as works that carry copyright notices. For example,
someone could take the U.S. Constitution, Bill of Rights, and Declaration of Independence
and print them up in booklet form for purchase. While these three pieces of United States
history are in the public domain, a printed booklet containing them might be sold for
replication costs and whatever the printer thinks could be earned over and above that. No
royalty expenses need be figured into the cost.

Please note: it is also possible to copyright reprinted public domain materials if there
are any changes to the works; for example, if the materials were not originally packaged

together, there is a new collection title, there is a graphic added to the collection that was not available with the originals, and so on. (Again, be aware that in reality, only the revised sections of the public domain work are being copyrighted; that which remains original is still in the public domain.)

## LENGTH OF TIME IT TAKES A WORK
## TO BECOME PART OF THE PUBLIC DOMAIN

Public domain used to follow copyright law as it existed at the time of the creation or publication of the work. The Copyright Term Extension Act (CTEA) was passed in October 1998, and there are now exceptions to this rule. CTEA changes U.S. copyright law by extending the term of copyright protection for works created January 1, 1978, or after from the life of the author plus 50 years to the international criterion of life plus 70 years (and works for hire to 95 years from publication or 120 years after creation) (Torrans 2003; U.S. Copyright Office 2010c). In addition, the CTEA applies retrospectively as well as prospectively to all works still under copyright on the bill's effective date, October 27, 1998. This is very confusing, and is a result of U.S. Copyright Law being amended many times since its inception. Because of this, "no simple statement can be made to the effect that 'the term of protection for Y types of works is X years.' Rather, works of the same type but produced at different times will often have different terms of protection" (Karjala 2002, 1). Still, some rules (Gasaway 2003; Hirtle 2012; U.S. Copyright Office 2010) apply:

1. Works published before 1923 are in the public domain.
2. Works published between 1923 and 1963, when a copyright notice is attached, can have their copyright renewed for a total of 67 years beyond the date of publication. (However, if the copyright is not renewed or if the work originally had no official copyright notice, then the work is already in public domain.)
3. For works published from 1964 to 1977 with an official copyright notice attached, copyright is automatically renewed for a total of 95 years.
4. Works created but not published before January 1, 1978 (January 1, 1978, is the effective date of the 1976 Copyright Act [Butler 2001]), are legally copyrighted for the life of the owner plus 70 years.
5. All works published on or after January 1, 1978, are copyrighted for the lifetime of the creator/owner plus 70 years (Butler 2001: 47–48; Karjala 2002). (If there is more than one creator/owner, the 70-year rule applies based on the lifetime of the longest living copyright holder.) If works have a corporate author or are "work for hire," then works published on or after January 1, 1978, are copyrighted for 120 years after the date of creation or 95 years from publication, the lesser amount being the one that applies (Torrans 2003). The 70-year rule is a direct result of the Sonny Bono Copyright Term Extension Act of 1998 (Public Law Number 105–298) mentioned

above in this chapter. (The reasoning behind this act was to bring the U.S. copyright term of ownership under the same conditions as that of many European nations, thus giving U.S. owners of works the same protection as that afforded European owners [Sinofsky 2000].) Because the Sonny Bono Act is retroactive, this means that the earliest any work copyrighted after 1978 can come into the public domain is December 31, 2047.

### How Do We Know If a Copyright Has Been Renewed or Not?

Concerning rule #2 above, how would one know if a copyright had been renewed or not? Essentially, if renewed, the new copyright date would be listed on the verso page (back side of the title page) of a newer version of a book or in the area where copyright information is listed for other works. However, this would not answer the question for older works, which would only contain the original copyright date. For such older works, it is possible to obtain public domain information by contacting the U.S. Copyright Office. While the Copyright Office does not compile or maintain lists of public domain materials, it can conduct a search to find the answer (for a fee of $165 per hour/2 hour minimum), or you may search their records online yourself (without the fee) (U.S. Copyright Office 2010b).

### Are There Any Simple Strategies for Knowing What Is Definitely in the Public Domain at the Present?

While the terms *simple strategies* and *public domain* appear to be polar opposites, below are a few guidelines that apply. Works definitely in the public domain include those published:

1. before 1923;
2. between 1923 and 1963 with a copyright notice but no renewal of copyright;
3. between 1923 and 1977 with no copyright notice;
4. between 1978 and March 1, 1989, with no copyright notice and no registration; or
5. to which the author/owner has given up all rights. (Gasaway 2003; Hirtle 2012)

In addition, several colleges and universities have versions of public domain charts (Cornell, University of North Carolina, Vassar, Stanford, and more) (Gasaway 2003; Hirtle 2012; Vassar College Guide to Copyright). There is also a public domain flow chart (www .sunsteinlaw.com/practices/copyright-portfolio-development/flowchart.htm) developed by the Sunstein Copyright Practice Group. This flowchart takes the viewer from works published before 1923 on into the present. Another helpful public domain tool is the Digital Copyright Slider http://librarycopyright.net/resources/digitalslider/ (Brewer 2012).

## WHAT TO DO IF THERE IS NO COPYRIGHT DATE ON A WORK

Sometimes we can find a work that does not seem to have a copyright notice posted anywhere on it. While this is especially true of many web pages, it is also the case for various older works. Can we assume, if there is no copyright notice, that such works are in the public domain? As usual, the answer to this question depends—in this case on when the item in question was first published (see the public domain rules above). For example, works published between 1923 and 1963 with no official copyright notice are already in the public domain. However in our twenty-first-century world (since 1989, in fact [Bruwelheide1995]), all works are automatically copyright-protected, whether or not the authors and owners put a copyright notice on their creations. Thus, it is good to remember that many works in the public domain are there because their copyright term has expired.

## HOW TO DEAL WITH WORKS
## CREATED AS PART OF THE TERMS OF EMPLOYMENT

What is "work for hire?" "Section 101 of the copyright law defines a 'work made for hire' as . . . a work prepared by an employee within the scope of his or her employment or a work specially ordered or commissioned for use as a contribution to a collective work, as a part of a motion picture or other audiovisual work, as a translation, as a supplementary work, as a compilation, as an instructional text, as a test, as answer material for a test, or as an atlas, if the parties expressly agree in a written instrument signed by them that the work shall be considered a work made for hire" (U.S. Copyright Office 2010d, 1). Thus, when an archeology professor creates a vlog (video blog) of his students participating in fieldwork, that may be considered part of his job, thus work for hire. If he is hired by an educational design company to construct a unit on field archeology at home, during his time off from university work, and said work is not part of his university job description, that might also be considered "work for hire." In this second case, however, the hiring company is the educational design one, rather than the university.

If a work is created as part of an employee's job description or is work "for hire," then the organization that employs the creator owns the copyright for either the publication date plus 95 years or 120 years from the time of creation—the shorter term applying. After that, the work will be in the public domain. For example, this means that if you, a college librarian, created a web page for the library during your workday, using computers and software that the college owns, then your employer (the college) would own your work for 95–120 years. (Because the Internet is a relatively new phenomenon, the only way a website can be in the public domain is if the author/owner of the work chooses to place it there.) For those things published between 1923 and 1978, the term of copyright varies, based on what the copyright law stated at the time of publication (Gasaway 2003). A general rule is to assume that whatever you want to use is still under copyright, unless there is a statement on or near the item, clearly indicating that it is in the public domain. This includes the Internet. It is a misconception that the Internet, because it is so accessible, is free, that is, not copyrighted (Simpson 2001).

## THE PUBLIC DOMAIN AND FEDERAL GOVERNMENT DOCUMENTS

Federal government documents, created as work for hire, are not normally copyright-protected. As such, they are in the public domain. Examples of such documents are House and Senate legislation, texts of federal court decisions, agency circulars, and federal reports. However, if the federal government hires outside contractors to produce works, such works may or may not be copyrighted — depending on the contract between the government and the contracted individual/s or company. Say, for example, that the federal government hires a historian to write a definitive history of the House of Representatives. If the contract between the government and the historian says that copyright ownership is the historian's, or does not state who will own the copyright, then ownership stays with the historian. If this contract states, instead, that the work is for hire, then the government owns the copyright. In addition, the federal government can own the copyrights to works transferred to it. This means, if you transfer the copyright to an educational website on Alaskan king crabs— one you created as a class unit—to the Department of Education (DOE), then the DOE will own whatever copyrights came with your gift. (It is best to retain a record of all copyright transfers in print format.) There is a third instance in which federal government documents are not public domain material. This is when an individual or organization takes a federal government document in the public domain and adds original elements, such as critiques, indexing criteria, conclusions, summaries, or other original elements to it. In such a case, the individual or group creating the document derivative can claim copyright to the derivative parts. Since there is no specific rule to federal government documents and public domain, if you are unsure, it is best to contact the document author or issuing agency or department and inquire as to its copyright status.

## THE PUBLIC DOMAIN AND
## STATE AND LOCAL GOVERNMENT DOCUMENTS

For the purposes of copyright law, state and local government agencies—considered owners of works in much the same way as are individuals or companies—may choose the works (state and local government documents include state legislative materials, texts of state and local court cases, minutes of city council meetings, birth and death records, tax files, real estate transactions, county board proceedings, etc.) for which they want to own the copyright and the works they want to place in the public domain. Again, there is no one rule, guideline, or principle. Therefore, check with each particular agency for information as to what is in the public domain and what is not. Such information may be accessible from

1. state offices, such as the State Attorney's Office in your county seat;
2. the city manager's secretary; or
3. other state, county, and community offices.

Information may be just an e-mail or phone call away.

## INTERNATIONAL COPYRIGHT LAW AND THE PUBLIC DOMAIN

The United States is a member of a number of international treaties that cover or are concerned with copyright law. Generally, when a work is disseminated in the United States, U.S. law applies, and when an item is distributed overseas, the laws of the particular countries receiving the item apply. Therefore, it is possible for a work to be in the public domain in one country and copyright-protected in another.

## THE PUBLIC DOMAIN AND
## RETURNING WORKS TO COPYRIGHT PROTECTION

Copyright law, as written by our forebears and current lawmakers, is a very gray issue. Public domain is no exception. For example, the Uruguay Round Agreements Act of 1994 implements the General Agreement on Tariffs and Trade (GATT Treaty). One result of the GATT is that as of January 1, 1996, a number of foreign works, at that time in the public domain in the United States, were placed back under copyright protection. These works were from a number of countries, including Japan, Germany, and several Spanish-speaking countries, and titles varied from *Hipokuratesu-tachi* to *Echo der Heimat* to *Aguiluchos Mexicanos* (Federal Register 1998). Why? This was because they were still under copyright protection in their own countries (Sinofsky 2000). What this means for us as educators, is that how much of an artwork we can copy, put on a website, blow up for a bulletin board, or include in our class multimedia art project may depend on whether we are using a U.S. or another country's edition of the work. For more information on international copyright protection, see chapter 5.

## IDENTIFYING A WORK AS PART OF THE PUBLIC DOMAIN

One way for identifying public domain works is to find out when the item was first copyrighted. (The easiest way to determine the first copyright date is to look for the oldest of the copyright dates listed on the work in question. Remember: copyright can be registered from either the date of publication or the date of creation.) An easier approach is to look for a statement on the item in question or use a public domain chart (see examples above in this chapter). If an item says that it is public domain material, it probably is. Nonetheless, be aware that "probably in the public domain" is an operative phrase here, since hypothetically it is possible to label a work in the public domain when it is still under copyright. For example, a clip-art website owner may have a statement at the beginning or end of his or her web page stating that it is in the public domain. This means that you should be able to borrow any of the clip art from this site and use it in any manner that you wish. However, a site owner or administrator could feasibly take art from a copyrighted site and put it on his or her site without your knowledge. Thus, you could, in good faith, borrow a piece of copyrighted clip art from a site that supposedly was in the public domain. The best advice in cases like this is to make sure that graphics you use are from reputable sites. For instance, a trustworthy clip-art site might be one obtained from a prominent software company's web page.

## BORROWING WORKS IN THE PUBLIC DOMAIN

Since users or borrowers of works must often rely on media documentation that an item is in the public domain, the best solution is to choose public domain material from reputable sites (Internet); publishing companies (books, articles, recordings, software, etc.); or vendors.

While public domain material cannot be "re-copyrighted," except foreign works, it is possible to alter a public domain piece and create a derivative work. When this happens, as was discussed above in this chapter, the pieces of the public domain work that were changed can be placed back under copyright protection. A work by Shakespeare can serve as an example. Shakespeare's works are in the public domain. However, an artist may illustrate a copy of *Hamlet* by sketching scenes from the play in the margins or drawing beautiful curlicue letters to begin each act. If this artist wishes, she or he can then sell this newly illustrated copy of *Hamlet*, copy it, or display it in public. In other words, since original work has been added to alter *Hamlet*, the artist/creator now owns this particular version of the play and the copyright to it.

## CONCLUSION

In the current economic environment, educators often do not have the money to support their many needs. At such times, faculty, librarians, and others who work with them become creative at getting more for less. In such cases, public domain materials may help, for with such materials educators may copy, create derivatives, and, in essence, use these works any way they want as they strive to teach their students and better support their curriculums. Last, a quick piece of advice—if a work does not state it is in the public domain, assume it is copyright-protected, unless it was published before 1923 or you have been able to find out otherwise from the owners of the work.

# REFERENCES

Brewer, Michael, and the ALA Office for Information Technology Policy. 2012. "Digital Copyright Slider." http://librarycopyright.net/resources/digitalslider.

Bruwelheide, Janis H. 1995. *The Copyright Primer for Librarians and Educators*, 2nd ed. Chicago: American Library Association.

Butler, Rebecca P. 2001. "Public Domain: What It Is and How It Works." *Knowledge Quest* 29, no. 5 (May/June): 47–48.

Federal Register. 1998. Vol. 63, no. 157 (August 14): Docket No. 97-3E. www.copyright.gov/fedreg/1998/63fr43830.html.

Gasaway, Lolly. 2003. "When Works Pass into the Public Domain." www.unc.edu/~unclng/public-d.htm.

Hirtle, Peter B. 2012. "Copyright Term and the Public Domain in the United States." http://copyright.cornell.edu/resources/publicdomain.cfm.

Karjala, Dennis S. 2002. "Chart Showing Changes Made and the Degree of Harmonization Achieved and Disharmonization Exacerbated by the Sonny Bono Copyright Term Extension Act (CETA)." http://homepages.law.asu.edu/%7Edkarjala/OpposingCopyrightExtension/legmats/HarmonizationChartDSK.html.

Simpson, Carol. 2001. *Copyright for Schools: A Practical Guide*. 3rd ed. Worthington, OH: Linworth.

Sinofsky, Esther R. 2000. "The Privatization of Public Domain?" *TechTrends* 44, no. 2 (March): 11–13.

Sunstein, Kann, Myrphy, & Timbers LLP. 2002. "Flowchart for Determining When U.S. Copyrights in Fixed Works Expire." www.sunsteinlaw.com/practices/copyright-portfolio-development/flowchart.htm.

Torrans, Lee Ann. 2003. *Law for K-12 Libraries and Librarians*. Westport, CT: Libraries Unlimited.

U.S. Copyright Office, Library of Congress. 2010. Copyright law of the United States of America and related laws contained in title 17 of the United States code, circular 92, chapter 3, duration of copyright. www.copyright.gov/title17/92chap3.html.

———. 2010b. "Copyright: Search Request Estimate." http://www.copyright.gov/forms/search_estimate.html.

———. 2010c. "Frequently Asked Questions." www.copyright.gov/help/faq.

———. 2010d. "Circular 9: Works Made for Hire under the 1976 Copyright Act." www.copyright.gov/circs/circ09.pdf.

Vassar College Guide to Copyright. "When Works Pass into the Public Domain." http://copyright.vassar.edu/fairuse/publicdomain.html.

# 4

## Obtaining Permission

### In What Ways Can We Legally Obtain Permission to Use Others' Works?

L et's imagine that you are a film collection's librarian at your university. A campus student organization approaches you with a request: they want to take one of the films in the library's collection—Orson Welles's *Citizen Kane*—and show it for an all-campus outdoor movie night. You inform the student group, since the movie is going to be used for entertainment rather than an instructional purpose, that a license or permission to perform it in public is needed. A question to ask here is: does the library have or can it obtain the needed rights to show this movie as the student group wishes? This chapter will look at how to obtain permission from the author or owner of a work—the ideal way of making sure that you are following the law.

### PERMISSION DEFINED AND EXPLAINED

Sometimes, the owner of a work will state up front in the work that permission, that is, his or her consent, is being given to a user for certain rights. One example of this is from the Fair Use Evaluator created by Michael Brewer and the ALA Office for Information Technology Policy (http://www.librarycopyright.net/resources/fairuse). The main page of this Internet site sends the would-be user to a Creative Commons license called Attribution-NonCommercial-Share Alike 3.0 Unported (http://creativecommons.org/licenses/by-nc-sa/3.0), which informs you exactly what rights you have to the Fair Use Evaluator. In this case, the user is given the rights to "to copy, distribute and transmit the work . . . to adapt the work . . . Under the following conditions: Attribution—You must attribute the work in the manner specified by the author or licensor (but not in any way that suggests that they endorse you or your use of the work) . . . Noncommercial—You may not use this work for commercial purposes. . . . Share Alike—If you alter, transform, or build upon this work, you may distribute the resulting work only under the same or similar license to this one" (Creative Commons, 1). Another example can be found in the book *Freedom of Expression* by Kembrew McLeod. McLeod, the author and copyright holder of this book, states on p. 10 that "I thoroughly approve if you copy this book for noncommercial uses" (2005). A third case in point is on p. 19 of the *Code of Best Practices in Fair Use for Media Literacy Education:* "Feel free to reproduce this work in its entirety. For excerpts and quotations, depend upon fair use" (Hobbs 2010).

In such cases as the three above, the would-be user simply follows the copyright owner's specifications. But what happens when the owner has not placed any usage agreements, other than a copyright notice, on the product? Well, you ask for the rights that you need from the owner or obtain a license to use or copy the work. (How to find copyright owners and clearinghouses for copyrighted works will be addressed later in this chapter.) Remember that the copyright owner has the right to give, sell, or refuse your request to use the work.

## PERMISSION REQUESTS

It is always best to put requests in writing so that you have a record of the permission criteria, should any disagreements occur between you and the copyright owner or clearinghouse. If that is not possible, then take notes of your oral conversation with the copyright owner or clearinghouse and keep these on file for future reference. Once you have found the owner of the work, information that should be included in the permission request is as follows:

1. Identify what it is that you want permission to use by author, title, format, and other identifiers.
2. Determine what kind of permission you need; for example, how, where, how many times, and how long you are going to use this item. (For example, given your movie question above, you need permission to show in public a classic movie.)

Remember to request permission as early as possible. There is no time limit to replies, and just because you do not hear from an owner, it does not mean that she or he has tacitly agreed that you may use the work(s). Thus, you may find that you need to follow up on permission requests, or contact another source if you discover that the individual(s)/organization you originally contacted is not the owner. In addition, if the owner's reply is to the negative, you now have some time to find a substitute item.

## LICENSES

A license provides the user with the rights of the work that have been obtained from the owner, or an organization representing the owner. For example, the American Society of Composers, Authors and Publishers (ASCAP), which functions as a clearinghouse representing a large number of those who compose, write, and publish music, "protects the rights of its members by licensing and distributing royalties for the non-dramatic public performances of their copyrighted works. ASCAP's licensees encompass all who want to perform copyrighted music publicly. ASCAP makes giving and obtaining permission to perform music simple for both creators and users of music" (ASCAP 2012, 1). A group that could help with a movie use question would be the Motion Picture Licensing Corporation (MPLC; http://www.mplc.com/), whose umbrella license "grants permission to organizations and companies to show any legally obtained film without the need of reporting titles, dates or times of exhibition" (Motion Picture Licensing Corporation 2012, 1). What this means, for the problem posed at the beginning of this chapter, is if the library or university has an umbrella license with the MPLC, and *Citizen Kane* is under this umbrella license, then it will be possible to show the movie in a public (noneducational) performance for an all-campus outdoor movie night. (See Movies and Copyright box.)

---

### Movies and Copyright

Movie owners' copyrights are limited in that movies (DVDs, CDs, videos, and digital formats) used for instructional purposes in nonprofit educational institutions can be displayed without infringement (U.S. Copyright Law, Section 110(1) 1976). This means that whether you purchased the movie from a discount store or an educational company, whether it is marked "For Home Use Only" or not, if it is for use in a teaching situation, you may use it without obtaining the permission of the movies' owner/s. However, if you are using it for entertainment or reward, permission is needed. For more information on movies and copyright, see chapter 7: "DVDs, Video Streaming, On Demand, and Copyright Law: Are the Use of These and Other Movie Formats Legal in College and University Classrooms?"

---

## GIVE CREDIT WHERE CREDIT IS DUE

Payment is not necessarily required for permission. The owner or author may want nothing more than to be recognized for his or her work. Thus, always give credit to copyright owner(s) in a reference or citation section at either the beginning or end of the use or presentation of the work and follow any stipulations for the format of the citation. (Such citing does not replace the need to acquire permission, however.) Also, you should be aware that while technically payment is not required for permission, it is possible the work's owner(s) will request that you pay a fee or purchase a license before you are allowed to use the work.

## PERMISSION LETTERS

For the purposes of this exercise, assume you are requesting clearance to use a movie for a public showing. Formats other than DVDs, videos, and other movie formats may require different criteria and will be discussed below. (Criteria need to match the media format and type of request.) Sample general information includes the following:

- author, title, format;
- type of permission you are asking for (how often you will use the work, length of time of use, number of copies needed, intended audience, and whether or not you will be charging your audience for use of the work);
- your name, address, phone and fax numbers, e-mail;
- your signature; and
- a place for the copyright holder's signature.

The following format information should also be included in a letter requesting appropriate permission.

### Print
- volume number
- edition
- ISBN (book) or ISSN (magazine) number
- editor, compiler, or translator
- publisher
- place of publication
- copyright date
- page, figure, table, or illustration identifiers
- copy of what you want to borrow

### Nonprint
- how the borrowed item (multimedia project, online class, etc.) will be used
- distributor
- where you plan to use or market your creation
- expected date of publication or use (if appropriate)
- copyright date
- URL, site manager, name of site (if part or all of a website)
- footage amount (if a video, DVD, or television program)

You may also add a date by which you would like to hear back from the copyright owners. While they do not need to comply with your request, it may be an incentive to their granting permission information more quickly. In addition, you may wish to ask them to provide you with the correct copyright owner, if you have sent your permission request to the wrong place. It is also important to thank those from whom you are requesting permission for their time and effort in providing you with the use of their copyrighted item(s).

Remember, the more complete the information that you include in your request, the quicker the response time may be (Crews 2006).

Send the request-for-permission letter to the copyright owner, clearance center, distributor, or publisher of the work(s).

Including a stamped, self-addressed envelope (SASE) may speed up response time.

Make sure that the permission is both sent and received either in a letter, fax, or e-mail form. It is imperative that you have a written record of all copyright permissions granted. This way no one can come back at a later date and say, "I did not say that," or "That's not what I meant."

"Sample Request for Permission" is an example of a letter that you might use for the movie question from above. (See figure 4-1.)

## FIGURE 4-1

### Sample Request for Permission

Your name and address (letterhead)
Date
Name and address of copyright owner or publisher


Dear _____,

I would like to request permission to show the movie [citation: including such things as title, copyright date, distributor, publisher] to the students and guests of _____ university on [date] in the campus quad. This will be a one-time showing. The purpose of this showing is an all-campus outdoor movie night. If you are willing to grant this permission, would you please sign this letter below, and return to me by [date] or as soon as possible? Also, if I should be contacting someone other than you for this request, could you provide me with the name and address of the party to contact? I have included an SASE for your use. Thank you for considering my request.


Sincerely,
(Your name)


PERMISSION GIVEN FOR_____
TO USE MY Work, [title], ON [date specified above].

DATE:

SIGNATURE:
(Bellingham Public School 2003; Crews 2006)

## CLEARINGHOUSES AND OTHER ORGANIZATIONS

If you are unable to find the owners or authors of a work, where do you send your request for permission to use or copy their item(s)? Well, you can go to the publisher of the work for contact information. You can also go to an organization, such as an agency or royalty house, company, or clearinghouse that specializes in helping users obtain copyright clearance. Such a group, usually for a fee (clearinghouse fees are typically dependent on the nature of the use the borrower requests), will work with you to obtain the proper clearance or license that is needed. The type of work that you need permission to use or copy determines where you go to find permission or further information. Below are some of the places that you may go to online to obtain permissions.

### Cartoons, Columns, and Editorial Features

Featured in this section is an organization illustrative of those that provide permission, in the form of contracts and licenses, for the use of such things as newspaper cartoons and columns.

*Universal Uclick: (http://www.universaluclick.com/licensing_permissions)*
> For those users who want to place a published cartoon or editorial feature on a web page, in a multimedia production, and so on, Universal Uclick can provide permission and fee information. This company offers "long-term licensing programs as well as one-time rights and reprints for use of single comics and feature content" (Universal Uclick 2011, 1).

### DVDs, CDs, and Video

Yes, you *can* use motion pictures legally in higher education! Either follow the copyright law for classroom works or look to a movie clearinghouse.

*Motion Picture Licensing Corporation (MPLC; http://www.mplc.org/index)*
> "The Motion Picture Licensing Corporation (MPLC) provides Umbrella Licenses to nonprofit groups, businesses, and government organizations for the public performances of DVDs and home video cassettes" (Motion Picture Licensing Corporation 2012).

*Swank Motion Pictures Inc. (http://www.swank.com/about.html)*
> "Swank Motion Pictures provides both public performance licensing rights and licensed movies to numerous non-theatrical markets, including . . . U.S. colleges and universities" (Swank Motion Pictures Inc., 1)

### Images

Search online for a variety of image clearinghouses, many specializing in a particular kind of imagery, such as wildlife, space shuttle imagery/aerial photography, history, and more. Two such sites are listed next:

*Illinois Historical Aerial Photography 1938–1941: (www.isgs.uiuc.edu/nsdihome/webdocs/ilhap)*
> Aerial photographs of Illinois from 1938 to 1941, many of them digitized, are available free of charge from this site.

*Media Image Resource Alliance (MIRA; www.mira.com)*

Through MIRA, users may view stock photographs/images from a photographers' cooperative called the Creative Eye online and obtain permission to use/publish them.

## Music

For the purposes of this chapter, various music clearinghouses are grouped together. "There are three aspects of musical works that must be separately considered under the copyright laws. The first aspect is the sound recording itself. The sound recording embodies the actual sound of the music. The second is the visual transcription of the words and music involved in the musical work (the lyrics and sheet music). The third aspect is musical sound that is part of a motion picture or audiovisual work" (Digilaw 2008, 1). What this means is that there is a lot to consider when looking at music: (1) the formats to which music is recorded (CDs and other audio files, digitized materials for use with electronic devices such as iPads, etc.); (2) the originally written sheet music and lyrics; and (3) the musical performance or broadcasts. With these three aspects of musical works come a variety of licensing rights, among them: (1) mechanical rights, "permissions granted to mechanically reproduce music onto some type of media (e.g., CD, etc.) for public distribution"; (2) "print rights . . . based on sales of printed sheet music"; (3) "performance rights allow music to be performed live or broadcast"; and (4) "synchronization rights . . . needed for a song to be reproduced onto a television program, film, video, commercial, radio, or even an 800 number phone message. This type is so named because you are 'synchronizing' the composition, as it is performed on the audio recording, to a film, TV commercial, or spoken voice-over" (HowStuffWorks 2012, 1). More on licensing is discussed in chapter 5: "Other Important Copyright Issues: What Else Do We Need to Know in Order to Function Legally within Copyright Law?" and in chapter 10: "Music and Copyright Law: Who Will Know If You Copy It?" Discussed below are several music clearinghouses.

*American Society of Composers, Authors and Publishers (ASCAP; http://www.ascap.com/about)*

"ASCAP protects the rights of its members by licensing and distributing royalties for the non-dramatic public performances of their copyrighted works. ASCAP's licensees encompass all who want to perform copyrighted music publicly. ASCAP makes giving and obtaining permission to perform music simple for both creators and users of music" (American Society of Composers, Authors and Publishers 2012, 1).

*Broadcast Music, Inc. (BMI; http://www.bmi.com/about)*

BMI represents over 500,000 songwriters, composers, and music publishers and over 7.5 million works in all styles of music. "BMI . . . collects license fees on behalf of songwriters, composers, and music publishers and distributes them as royalties to those members whose works have been performed" (Broadcast Music, Inc. 2012, 1).

*Harry Fox Agency (http://www.harryfox.com/public/AboutHFA.jsp)*

"HFA licenses the largest percentage of the mechanical and digital uses of music in the United States on CDs, digital services, records, tapes and imported phonorecords" (Harry Fox Agency 2012, 1).

*The Music Bridge (http://www.themusicbridge.com)*
  "The Music Bridge is an independent music corporation . . . specializing in music clearance, music licensing & music supervision services" (The Music Bridge, 2013, 1).
*SESAC, Inc. (www.sesac.com)*
  SESAC is a "performing rights organization . . . designed to represent songwriters and publishers and their right to be compensated for having their music performed in public" (SESAC, 1). This organization is similar to ASCAP and BMI (see above).

## Print

Publishing companies often serve as a sort of clearinghouse for print materials. That said, the following agencies also address this issue.

*Authors Licensing and Collecting Society (ALCS; http://www.alcs.co.uk):*
  This British group states that they "protect and promote the rights of authors writing in all disciplines" and "ensure authors receive fair payment for the various uses of their work" (Authors Licensing and Collecting Society 2009, 1).
*Publications Rights Clearinghouse (PRC; https://nwu.org/publications-rights-clearinghouse):*
  Part of the National Writers Union, the PRC "is a collective licensing agency for writers. It collects royalties on behalf of writers from publishers with whom it has agreements for distributing such royalties" (National Writers Union, 1).

## Religious

Remember—even religious groups can infringe on someone's copyright ownership! Thus, using a religious clearinghouse can be important.

*Christian Copyright Licensing International (CCLI; www.ccli.com):*
  Christian Copyright Licensing International is an example of an organization that provides religious groups with licenses for congregational music and videos used in church and church-related settings.

## Theatrical Performances

Please note that theatrical performances' clearinghouses may charge licensing fees based on such things as the planned number of performances, the performance dates, the number of script copies needed, and sometimes even the number of rehearsals. An example is listed below.

*Musical Theatre International (MTI; www.mtishows.com):*
  MTI offers online applications to obtain licenses for many musicals (both professional and amateur performances).

## Other

There are clearinghouses for many media formats. If you cannot find what you are looking for, then it may be time to go to a more general clearinghouse for help.

*Copyright Clearance Center (CCC) www.copyright.com*
> This well-known copyright clearinghouse provides licensing agreements for a wide variety of both print and nonprint and electronic (digital and analog) works. For example, it assists college and university faculty, libraries, and bookstores when they are looking to create course-packs and post items to e-reserves and online learning (Copyright Clearance Center 2003; Copyright Clearance Center 2013). The CCC can also help users locate hard-to-find or unregistered copyright holders. The CCC focuses on serving such groups as higher education and the business world, as well as authors and publishers.

*U.S. Copyright Office (www.copyright.gov/forms/search_estimate.html)*
> "For a fee, of $165 per hour or fraction thereof (2 hour minimum)" the U.S. Copyright Office will search its records to find permission information/whether or not . . . a work is under copyright protection" (U.S. Copyright Office 2010, 1).

## CONCLUSION

When requesting permission for use of a work, obtain your license or user/borrower agreement in writing, and be sure to follow all stipulations of the agreement. Do not be discouraged if the first place you contact cannot help you. Instead, try another clearinghouse (the Internet has any number of these), the publisher, author, or even find another work to fit your needs.

---

Please note that chapter 4 is based, in part, on six copyright permission articles: Butler, Rebecca P. 2006–2007: "Obtaining Permission to Copy or Perform a Work," 2006, Parts I–III. *Knowledge Quest* 35, no. 2–4; and Butler, Rebecca P. 2001–2002: "Obtaining Permission to Copy or Perform a Work," Parts I–III. Knowledge Quest 30, no. 2–4.

## REFERENCES

American Society of Composers, Authors and Publishers (ASCAP). 2012. "About ASCAP."
http://www.ascap.com/about.

Authors Licensing and Collecting Society (ALCS). 2009. "Welcome." http://www.alcs.co.uk.

Brewer, Michael, and the ALA Office for Information Technology Policy. 2008. "Fair Use
Evaluator." http://www.librarycopyright.net/resources/fairuse.

Broadcast Music, Inc. (BMI). 2012. "About BMI." http://www.bmi.com/about.

Butler, Rebecca P. 2001. "Obtaining Permission to Copy or Perform a Work, Part I." *Knowledge
Quest* 30, no. 2 (November/December): 43–44.

————. 2002a. "Obtaining Permission to Copy or Perform a Work, Part II." *Knowledge Quest* 30, no. 3 (January/February): 32–33.

————. 2002b. "Obtaining Permission to Copy or Perform a Work, Part III." *Knowledge Quest* 30, no. 4 (March/April): 45–46.

————. 2006. "Obtaining Permission to Copy or Perform a Work, Part I." *Knowledge Quest, 35(2)*.

————. 2007a. "Obtaining Permission to Copy or Perform a Work, Part II." 2006. *Knowledge Quest, 35(3)*, 48-49.

————. 2007b. "Obtaining Permission to Copy or Perform a Work, Part III," 2006. *Knowledge Quest, 35(4)*.

Christian Copyright Licensing International (CCLI). 2012. What We Offer." www.ccli.com/WhatWeOffer.

Creative Commons. "Attribution-Noncommercial-Share Alike 3.0 Unported." http://creativecommons.org/licenses/by-nc-sa/3.0.

Copyright Clearance Center (CCC). 2003. *Copyright! Academic Permissions.* CD-ROM.

Copyright Clearance Center (CCC). 2013. "Get Permission." http://www.copyright.com/content/cc3/en/toolbar/getPermission.html.

Crews, Kenneth D. 2006. *Copyright Law for Librarians and Educators: Creative Strategies and Practical Solutions.* Chicago: American Library Association.

Digilaw. 2008. "Copyrighting Music." www.weblawresources.com/Copyright/copyrighting_music.htm.

Harry Fox Agency. 2012. "About HFA." http://www.harryfox.com/public/AboutHFA.jsp.

Hobbs, Renee. 2010. *Copyright Clarity: How Fair Use Supports Digital Learning.* Thousand Oaks, CA: Corwin and National Council of Teachers of English.

HowStuffWorks. 2012. "How Music Royalties Work." http://entertainment.howstuffworks.com/music-royalties4.htm.

Illinois Natural Resources Geospatial Data Clearinghouse. "Illinois Historical Aerial Photography 1938–1941." www.isgs.uiuc.edu/nsdihome/webdocs/ilhap.

McLeod, Kembrew. 2005. *Freedom of Expression: Overzealous Copyright Bozos and Other Enemies of Creativity.* New York: Doubleday.

Mira. "About Mira Images." http://library.mira.com.

Motion Picture Licensing Corporation. 2012. http://www.mplc.org/index.

The Music Bridge. 2013. http://www.themusicbridge.com/about-us.

Musical Theatre International (MTI). "About Us." http://www.mtishows.com/content.asp?id=1_0_0.

National Writers Union. "Publications Rights Clearinghouse." https://nwu.org/publications-rights-clearinghouse.

SESAC. "About SESAC." www.sesac.com/About/About.aspx.

Swank Motion Pictures Inc. http://www.swank.com/about.html.

U.S. Copyright Office. 2010. "Search Request Estimate." www.copyright.gov/forms/search_estimate.html.

Universal Uclick. 2011. "Licensing & Permissions." http://www.universaluclick.com/licensing_permissions.

# 5

# Other Important Copyright Information
## What Else Do We Need to Know in Order to Function Legally within Copyright Law?

T his chapter identifies a number of topics concerning or related to copyright, and defines and discusses them in a general manner. These subjects include licensing, interlibrary loan, selected areas of U.S. and state law, international treaties and organizations, future legislation, infringements and penalties, and plagiarism. Some of these subjects will also be mentioned in subsequent chapters. Others, which are covered only in this chapter, will give you a larger context in which to place copyright conversation.

## DOCUMENTATION AND LICENSES

### Documentation Defined and Explained
The term *documentation* is used here to cover those informational and identifying records that each work possesses. As such, the documentation is, at least partially, that information usually found in the reference section of a paper. The examples used here are a print item, a web item, and a piece of computer software. First, look at a book (print). The documentation for a book includes the author, title, copyright date, place of publication, publisher, and any special permissions that the copyright owner is willing to give the book owner or reader. Secondly, take a look at the Internet. Documentation for a website can vary somewhat from that for a print piece. It may also include the author, title, copyright date, place of publication, and publisher. In addition, it may include an e-mail link to the webmaster

or moderator of the site, the point of access to the site (URL), the date the site was last reorganized, agreements with which site users must abide, and so on. The third example is computer software. Software documentation also includes such basic things as author/creator, title, copyright date, publisher, and place of publication. It usually also includes a copy of the contractual agreement (license—see below) between the purchaser of the software and the software seller. It is always best to read the documentation of any work from which you plan to borrow before doing any copying.

## Licenses Defined and Explained

"A license is a physical or virtual document between two or more parties that allows an intellectual resource owned by one party (the licensor) to be used by another or multiple other parties (the licensees) for a fixed duration of time" (Rupp-Serrano, ed. 2005, 178). Licenses, which are legally binding contracts, are very important in the world of copyright. For users, they define the ways that a protected (copyrighted) work can be used. The owner of the copyright uses the license to delineate which exclusive rights in a work are granted to others for their use. Keep in mind that the rights granted to the user are limited and non-exclusive, and they only extend to using the work for specified purposes. Normally licenses for works are automatically purchased with handheld applications, computer software, sheet music, and theater scripts; as part of database documentation; involved in the rental of DVDs; and so on. For example, when considering computer software, there are three common types of licenses: shrinkwrap, clickwrap, and browsewrap. Shrinkwrap licenses are called such because they are located in plastic along with the software. Upon opening the plastic wrapping, the consumer is assumed to have agreed to the license—whether s/he has read it or not. With clickwrap licensing, the consumer has a chance to read the license online before installation, and before agreeing or not agreeing (through a click) to the license. The third type of computer license, browsewrap, is similar to the clickwrap license in that both are found online. However, with the browsewrap license, the user must go to a site identified online in order to obtain and read the license (Chilling Effects Clearinghouse, 1). The browsewrap license, itself, is not found "on the screen and the user is not compelled to accept or reject the terms as a condition of proceeding with further computer operations. Instead, a browsewrap agreement appears only as a hyperlink that is accessed by clicking on the link. It is optional, not required" (Kunkel 2002, 11). Thus, a user quickly moving through a site might not even realize that he or she has agreed to a contract via the browsewrap license.

Essentially licenses are a part of the package that buyers purchase in conjunction with most works. Licensing information is most often located near the front or beginning of a work's documentation. It is usually in fine print, and, often, online it can be something that the user can quickly click away. Be sure to read this fine print—you may be signing away rights that you need, or it is also possible that there will be rights that you can use, with which you would be unaware of otherwise. Suppose, for example, that your university purchases the license to place electronic publishing software on the computers in the English lab. The license is for 30 computers. If there are 31 computers in the lab, then legally either one computer may not have the software on its hard drive, or no more than 30 computers at a time may use the software, even if it is loaded on all 31 computers. Such actions depend on the contract between the purchaser and the seller.

Take a further example: you, a college reference librarian, are helping a biology instructor, who has brought his class to the library for research on a genetics unit. You inform him that the college has purchased two database licenses from companies dealing in undergraduate science. One database focuses on plant and animal genetics. With that particular license, your students may search the database and print out as many copies as they want of full-text articles on genetics. The second database also focuses on plant and animal genetics. However, that license only allows users to print out one copy of any full-text article, without permission from the publisher. In each case, you need to follow the license directions. Even though the databases may be similar in format and subject areas, their licenses are not necessarily the same.

As still another example, let's suppose that a history professor would like to use a particular popular movie in her class. She feels that it will illustrate, in an understandable manner, some of the influences of historical research. She checks out the movie at a video rental store and signs a form. With that form, she has essentially agreed to a license, or contract, and must abide by it. The form may be as simple as saying when the movie must be returned. It could also include penalties for destroying or losing the movie, returning it late, and so on.

Remember, a license is contract law, not copyright law. If you are dealing with both a license and copyrighted material, follow the licensing or contractual requirements. This works, because when you obtain a license—a contract—to use a copyrighted work, you are essentially contracting to use certain copyrights afforded that work. In addition to contracts/contract law, the last few years have found creators of works with another choice— that of creating their own licenses. The following sections address this issue.

## CREATIVE COMMONS

Creative Commons is a nonprofit organization that has developed a number of standardized copyright licenses that works' owners may use when licensing their creations. These copyright licenses have been written in such a way as to allow the owner(s) of a work to determine how others may use their work. As the reference source, the *Chicago Manual of Style,* says, "Creative Commons license throws any work subject to it open to public use of all kinds" (*Chicago Manual of Style* 2010, 178). While this sounds confusing, it means that an academic library consortium that develops a handbook on teen literacy may assign a Creative Commons license stating that colleges of education can take said handbook and modify it to fit the needs of the future teachers they are training. (Under the U.S. copyright law, such a modification could be a derivative work and a copyright infringement.) As Creative Commons states, their licenses define "the spectrum of possibilities between full copyright and the public domain. From all rights reserved to no rights reserved. Our licenses help you keep your copyright while allowing certain uses of your work— a 'some rights reserved' copyright" (Creative Commons, 1).

## OPEN-SOURCE SOFTWARE LICENSES

Open sourcing means that the software in question is free to be used and modified in any number of ways. This means that derivative works may be made without asking for permission from the copyright owner. Open sourcing, as a consequence, is more like a contract than part of copyright law. Thus, concerning the licensing of open-sourced software: (1) distribution is free (no royalties or other fees); (2) the software source code must be available or accessible via the Internet in a form usable by computer programmers; (3) the license must allow derivatives and modifications to the software as well as distribution of the modified work(s) under the same license as that of the original work; (4) the license can, at times, restrict source code modification, if "patch files" are acquired at build time; (5) the license cannot discriminate against any person or group; (6) the license cannot restrict the use of the software in a particular field; (7) program rights must apply to all who wish to use the software; (8) the license cannot be specific to a particular artifact; (9) no restrictions can be placed on other software that is distributed with the open-sourced software; and (10) the open-source license must be technology-neutral (Open Source Initiative, 1).

## GNU

The Free Software Foundation feels that all software should be free to use and modify, with free licenses. With this in mind, the organization often uses the "GNU General Public License" (GNU GPL) which states the following: "Nobody should be restricted by the software they use. There are four freedoms that every user should have: * the freedom to use the software for any purpose,* the freedom to change the software to suit your needs,* the freedom to share the software with your friends and neighbors, and* the freedom to share the changes you make. When a program offers users all of these freedoms, we call it free software. Developers who write software can release it under the terms of the GNU GPL. When they do, it will be free software and stay free software, no matter who changes or distributes the program. We call this copyleft: the software is copyrighted, but instead of using those rights to restrict users like proprietary software does, we use them to ensure that every user has freedom" (Free Software Foundation 2008, 1). Using GNU, this means that the assistant professor, who develops a statistical analyses computer program on her own time and using her own computer and software, can choose to assign the newly developed program—instead of following copyright law—a GNU General Public License. Such a license would thereby guarantee future users the ability to use the statistical software any way they want, change it, and share the software and changes with others. (For your information, "the name "GNU" is a recursive acronym for "GNU's Not Unix!"; it is pronounced g-noo, as one syllable with no vowel sound between the g and the n") (GNU Operating System 2010, 1).

## OPEN-ACCESS SCHOLARLY LITERATURE

A concept similar to creating one's own licenses (see above), but involving written academic publications, is that of open access. While still debatable to many academics concerned that open-access journals are not respected, open access scholarly literature "is digital, online, free of charge, and free of most copyright and licensing restrictions ... removes *price barriers* (subscriptions, licensing fees, pay-per-view fees) and *permission barriers* (most copyright and licensing restrictions)" (Suber 2012, 1). In addition, some supporting this notion argue that open access increases citation frequency (Copyright Education and Consultation Program). (One example of a peer-reviewed open-access scholarly journal is the *International Journal of Zizek Studies* (http://zizekstudies.org/index.php/ijzs/index).) Because of varying views of scholarly communication/open access/alternative publishing models, while university library systems often see benefits to such online journals (Northern Illinois University 2013a), professors working towards tenure, promotion, and recognition may reject publishing in them.

## AUTHORS' RIGHTS

Scholarly authors sometimes question what rights they have to their works and what rights they may be asked (by a publisher) to sign away. Usually, contracts agreed to between these two groups address who will own what copyrights (all or partial) to a particular work. One way for an author to keep some of his or her rights is to add a codicil, such as the SPARC Author Addendum, to the original contract. This addendum "is a legal instrument that modifies the publisher's agreement and allows you to keep key rights to your articles. The Author Addendum is a free resource developed by SPARC in partnership with Creative Commons (http://www.creativecommons.org) and Science Commons (http://science .creativecommons.org), established non-profit organizations that offer a range of copyright options for many difference creative endeavors" (SPARC 2006, 1).

## INTERLIBRARY LOAN

Like much of copyright law, those parts of the law that deal with interlibrary loan (ILL) can be very confusing. ILL, the borrowing of an item for use by another library, school, system, or individual who does not own that item, is a common occurrence in academic libraries. Essentially, ILL is an important way to obtain information not easily acquired by purchase. Usually ILL materials are those that a particular institution cannot afford or does not often need.

In our swiftly evolving technological world, ILL has hit a new high—no longer do libraries need to send original items to their requestors via delivery service, snail mail, or paper copy. Now—with the help of scanners and the Internet—a copy of a requested material can be sent digitally. (Interlibrary loan, in the original sense, was about distributing material, not copying. Digital ILL is concerned with both.) Herein lies the rub. Using the Internet, you obtain speed, easy access, and . . . possibly more copies than copyright law allows: the original paper copy (at the owner's library); the scanned copy (on the hard drive of a computer in the owner's library); the copy on the receiving library's hard drive; the digitized copy, which the requestor receives via the Internet; the copy that the requestor prints out for ease of use; and possibly more. Now, instead of two copies, there is a minimum of four or five. When a library purchases an item, it usually purchases only that item, not the ability to copy it indiscriminately. Thus, while it is possible for the library to lend out its own copy, the creation of other copies may violate the agreement of the original item's purchase.

How do you get around this thorny issue and still have access to information and materials in a quick and easy manner? Take an article out of an obscure medical journal as an example. Instead of borrowing the item via ILL, you could purchase the issue in which the article is found, get a subscription to that journal, or pay a fee to the copyright owner to have it copied. However, ILL is often the best alternative and borrowing it in a digital form (electronic full text) the most feasible option. Therefore, unless you have a license or permission to keep a number of copies of the item on your hard drive, your patron's hard drive, and so on, you could encourage the lending library to immediately erase the scanned copy from its computer once the article has been sent, and upon receipt of the item, immediately print out a copy—or send it electronically to your patron along with a statement that he or she only can use that one item and not share it with others. Then, erase the digitally received version from your hard drive. Your library may also have licenses to post articles on the Web or use specific databases. Sometimes, ILL can occur by accessing these sites through URLs. (Please also see "Copying Guidelines" [below] for discussion of ILL and the "Rule of Five.")

## STATUTORY EXEMPTIONS

If you search the U.S. Copyright Office website for statutory exemptions, you will find over two thousand of them. Not all of them, however, directly affect higher education. Nonetheless, there are some very important exemptions that do affect those directly (and indirectly) involved in all types of education. First, though, it is helpful to define exactly what a statutory exemption is.

## Definition

Statutory exemptions are written into the copyright law to provide some ways to use others' works without infringing on an owner's copyright and without needing to obtain permission to use a work. For example, fair use (see chapter 2) is a very important statutory exemption, one that educators should definitely apply. Basically, with fair use, Congress tells us that there are certain ways that protected (copyrighted) works can be used for educational or research purposes while still protecting the owner's rights. There are other exemptions as well that are important to those in colleges and universities, for example, exemption of certain performances and displays and reproduction by libraries and archives. (Please note that statutory exemptions most often apply to public institutions. For-profit and private institutions will need to study each exemption to see if it applies to them or not.)

## The Library Exemption: Limitations on Exclusive Rights: Reproduction by Libraries and Archives

An important statutory exemption for librarians and educators is found in section 108 of the 1976 Copyright Law: "Limitations on exclusive rights: Reproduction by libraries and archives." Section 108 talks about exemptions that are afforded libraries to copy works without violating copyright law. Section 108 provides that libraries may, within certain limits, make copies for preservation purposes, for private study, and for ILL. In order to do so, however, they must meet several requirements (all apply). These include:

- being open to the public or outside researchers;
- making copies that have no direct or indirect commercial advantage; and
- including a copyright notice on each copy made (or a statement that the work may be copyright protected, if there is no copyright notice on the original). In most cases, the library can make only single copies. However, up to three copies can be made for purposes of:
- preservation and security;
- replacement of a lost, stolen, deteriorating, or damaged item; and
- changing the format of an obsolete work to one that can be used in the library (including, if the machine on which the format is played is obsolete) or an "unused replacement" is unavailable at a fair price (U.S. Copyright Law 1976). (See appendix A for the complete text of section 108.)

In addition, there are some limits under this exemption as to what libraries may and may not copy. While almost anything may be copied for preservation purposes, for purposes of ILL, or a researcher's needs, libraries may not copy the following types of works: audiovisual works, including motion pictures; musical works; and works such as pictures, graphs, and sculptures (U.S. Copyright Law, 1976, sec. 108). This means that libraries may copy for researchers or ILL "other types of works that are not specifically excluded (see list above) . . . audiovisual works 'dealing with news' . . . pictures and graphics 'published as illustrations, diagrams, or similar adjuncts' to works that may otherwise be copied. In other words, if you can copy the article, you can also copy the picture or chart that is in the article" (Crews 2006, 76). These statutory exemptions are discussed in more detail in other parts of this book, where they affect copyright use of a certain work.

### The Classroom Exemption: Limitations on Exclusive Rights: Exemption of Certain Performances and Displays

Another example of a statutory exemption of significance to university faculty and librarians is the classroom exemption: section 110 of the 1976 U.S. Code (U.S. Copyright Law), "Limitations on exclusive rights: Exemption of certain performances and displays." This section of copyright law covers exemptions in educational classroom settings and provides for the use of lawfully obtained copyrighted works in face-to-face instruction as well as in transmissions, under certain parameters. Use of the copyrighted works (all points below apply) must be

- in a nonprofit educational institution;
- in a classroom or similar place of instruction;
- a performance or display that is a regular part of systematic instruction;
- a performance or display directly related to the teaching content; and/or
- for persons who are disabled or in special circumstances which otherwise prevent them from attending class. (U.S. Copyright Law, 1976, sect. 110).

Thus, under this exemption, an assistant professor of general science may play a recording of wolf howls to his class before the class goes on a field trip to a captive wolf park, so that the students can recognize sounds of wolf communication.

### The Handicap Exemption

The handicap exemption is actually part of the "The Classroom Exemption: Limitations on Exclusive Rights: Exemption of Certain Performances and Displays" (see above, last bullet point). The Technology, Education, and Copyright Harmonization (TEACH) Act of 2002 amends Section 110(2) by adding films and other dramatic works to the exemption, and also by redefining the terms of use by nonprofit educational institutions of copyrighted materials in distance education, including web courses (Crews 2006). However, you and your school must abide by all of the TEACH Act's requirements in order to use this additional exemption. (See more on the TEACH Act in chapter 13: "Distance Learning and Copyright Law.")

## COPYING GUIDELINES

There are any number of guidelines available for university librarians and faculty who need information on copyright. Usually created by various interest groups, these guidelines are not legal precedent, but they can be helpful when trying to abide by copyright law. Classroom and library guidelines include those for

- books and periodicals;
- music;
- off-air recordings;
- digital imaging;
- distance learning; and
- multimedia (see chapter 2).

Copyright guidelines are flexible; they provide a conservative definition for the use of works, not the maximum that the law permits. You actually could, in good faith, use more of a work than those moderate amounts suggested without infringing on the owners' copyright. Unfortunately, the maximum use is not clearly defined in copyright law. Therefore, be aware, the further beyond the guidelines that you borrow from a work, the greater your chance of copyright infringement. If higher education professionals follow the guidelines, they are considered to have acted in good faith (Guidelines).

Institutions of higher learning may choose to place a set of classroom and library copyright guidelines in their copyright and ethics policies, usually because they are more understandable and definite than the law itself. Confusion arises when librarians, professors, instructors, technology coordinators, administrators, students, and others in the college/university setting apply the guidelines as if they were the maximum amounts allowable, rather than representing the more conservative approach. While using minimal amounts of works will guarantee that there will be no copyright infringements, it is also limiting to those who use, borrow, or copy materials for instructional purposes. Keep this in mind when the guidelines are referred to, for example, the "Multimedia Fair Use Guidelines" (chapter 2), the "Guidelines for Classroom Copying in Not-for-Profit Educational Institutions with Respect to Books and Periodicals" (chapter 12), and the appendixes.

One such set of guidelines—in this case dealing with periodical articles—are the National Commission on New Technological Uses of Copyright Works (CONTU) Guidelines (often called the "Rule of Five" [Tully 2008]). Under Section 108(g)(2) of the copyright law of 1976, that part of the law covering "reproduction by libraries and archives" (U.S. Copyright Law 1976), the lender is not allowed to send more than one copy of one article from a periodical issue. If more are sent, then the borrower must pay copyright fees. The CONTU Guidelines interpret Section 108(g)(2), and help librarians, copyright owners, and other interested parties in "understanding the amount of photocopying for use in interlibrary loan arrangements permitted under the copyright law" (CONTU 1978). Under the CONTU Guidelines, borrowers may not receive more than five copies in one year from a single journal title published within the last five years. While the guidelines do not address non-journal publications or material that is older than five years, they do give both the lenders (libraries and archives) and the borrowers some direction. An intended purpose of these guidelines is to discourage the use of ILL as a substitute for magazine subscriptions. In addition, when material is requested from a digital medium, licensing (see "Licenses" above) may be involved. (Copyright Clearance Center 2005)

Once again, please note that guidelines *do not have the force of law*; instead they are directives that, if followed, will probably never result in litigation or anger by copyright owners, since guidelines are much more stringent than most interpretations of copyright law.

## STATE LAWS

Copyright law may exist within state codes, but "states cannot enact their own laws to protect the same rights as the rights provided by the Copyright Act . . . State 'copyright' laws . . . are limited to works that cannot be protected under federal copyright law" (Radcliffe and Brinson 2014, 1). However, mention of copyright can be found within state laws that focus on related subjects. Thus, while state copyright legislation may exist, the main place to look for copyright laws, acts, and bills would be with the federal government.

## INTERNATIONAL COPYRIGHT LAW AND UNITED STATES COPYRIGHT LAW WITH INTERNATIONAL PROVISIONS

"There is no such thing as an 'international copyright' that will automatically protect an author's writings throughout the world" (U.S. Copyright Office, Circular 38A 2009, 1).

As if U.S. copyright law is not complicated enough, there is also international copyright law for you to be concerned with. While every country has its own laws in this area, which may or may not conform to our federal laws, there are some organizations to which we—and many other countries—belong. These organizations' treaties principally state that we will abide by the copyright laws of the other countries that have signed each treaty, and they will abide by ours. Several treaties, organizations, and acts that exist in this area, and of which the United States is a part, are discussed in this section. Two pieces of U.S. copyright law (the Digital Millennium Copyright Act and the Sonny Bono Copyright Extension Act) and database protection, another area of interest to educators, are also covered. The following treaties and agreements are arranged by international, then U.S. law, and in order of importance, as determined by this author.

### Berne Convention for the Protection of Literary and Artistic Works
International

U.S. membership in the Berne Convention dates from March 1, 1989 (Besenjak 1997). This international copyright treaty, signed by ninety-six countries, is the benchmark of all copyright agreements worldwide. "This convention posits the notion that member nations will treat works from another country as they do those published in their own country, except if the protection term in the country of origin has run out. Then that particular work is also no longer protected in the member countries regardless of their particular copyright laws . . .

Berne member countries ... do not need to have a copyright notice attached to be protected by law" (Butler 2007, 74). More international agreements that focus on intellectual properties include the General Agreement on Tariffs and Trade (GATT) and the Trade-Related Aspects of Intellectual Property Rights (TRIPS) agreement (see below).

An example of the use of the Berne Convention might be when a jazz band conductor who wished to use a musical score that he purchased in Sweden discovers that he does not have enough saxophone parts for all the saxophonists in his band. If the score were found to be in the public domain in Sweden, then the U.S. conductor might copy extra sax parts without the need for obtaining permission or a license to do so from the Swedish copyright holder of the work.

## Universal Copyright Convention (UCC)
International

Along with the Berne Convention, this remains one of the two most pivotal copyright organizations to which the U.S. belongs (U.S. Copyright Office 2010). The United States joined the Universal Copyright Convention (UCC) on September 16, 1955. This group does not enforce copyright. Instead, it relies on its member nations to enforce its agreements (Besenjak 1997). This convention was created to ensure that international copyright protection is available to countries that might not be a member of the Berne Convention. A premise of the UCC is that its members must offer works from other participating countries the same copyright protection as those works created in their own country.

An example of a case of use of the Universal Copyright Convention in a U.S. college could be when a student brought in a DVD that she had purchased in New Zealand. Without knowledge of New Zealand copyright laws, the faculty member could apply U.S. copyright law to the use of that particular DVD in the classroom.

## World Intellectual Property Organization (WIPO)
International

The World Intellectual Property Organization (WIPO) is a United Nations agency that "is dedicated to developing a balanced and accessible international intellectual property (IP) system, which rewards creativity, stimulates innovation and contributes to economic development while safeguarding the public interest" (World Intellectual Property Organization, 1). One area of its IP focus is "on the development of international norms and standards in the area of copyright and related rights (World Intellectual Property Organization, 1). For example, this organization is the group that ruled that Time Warner would have sole ownership to Harry Potter–related Internet (domain) names (Neal 2002; Torrans 2003).

## Trade-Related Aspects of Intellectual Property Rights (TRIPS)
International

Part of the WIPO, TRIPS focuses on copyright protection of such items as computer codes and programs, international broadcasting, and sound recordings (Butler 2007). A case in point for TRIPS might be if the campus instructional technology department leaned on this international intellectual property treaty when considering the copyright implications of computer code that they had purchased online from a non-U.S. site.

## European Union Database Directive
International

This directive speaks to both the creation and content of databases and has possible sway with research worldwide in that "the potential is that public domain databases could by virtue of having their content copyrighted come back under copyright protection in particular countries" (Butler 2007, 75). With this in mind, many compilations currently in the public domain in the United States would become protected under copyright law. This issue is of special interest to the academic community. The way students and researchers access information could be affected, if they were at some point required to obtain permission to use, or pay for the use of, databases that until now have been in the public domain. Research could become more difficult—information harder to obtain and more expensive. Database protection is an area of interest to academics that bears watching in the future.

## Digital Millennium Copyright Act (DMCA)
United States

The DMCA, signed into law in October 1998 by President Clinton, made changes to U.S. copyright law in a number of areas, including online service provider liability, distance education, exemptions for libraries and archives, computer maintenance and copying of software, and digital performances of sound recordings. In addition, the DMCA implements the World Intellectual Property Organization treaties, thus bringing U.S. copyright law into compliance with the WIPO. In actuality, while the DMCA realizes the World Intellectual Property Organization treaties, it also "creates two new prohibitions in Title 17 of the U.S. Code (1976 Copyright Law)—one on circumvention of technological measures used by copyright owners to protect their works and one on tampering with copyright management information—and adds civil remedies and criminal penalties for violating the prohibitions" (U.S. Copyright Office, Library of Congress 1998, 2). This means, for example, that a community college computer science instructor could not legally create a way to unlock a piece of software for a computer-aided drafting class.

## Sonny Bono Copyright Extension Act (CTEA)
United States

In an effort to maintain consistency between the United States and other members of the Berne Convention, in 1998 Congress passed the Sonny Bono Copyright Term Extension Act (CTEA). So named because Congressman Bono was working on this at the time of his death, CTEA extends the duration of copyright in the United States retroactively from the life of the author plus 50 years to the life of the author plus 70 years and, in the case of works for hire to 120 years (Butler 2007). With this act in mind, unless permission were granted by the owner(s) or a license obtained, a public health professor would not be able to legally copy (without permission from the owner) a website on childhood obesity for an undergraduate health class, that had been personally created by a dietician, until 70 years after the dietician's death. (The professor could, however, have students link to the site legally.) The purpose here is not to discuss the above issues in depth. Instead, it is to give an impression of selected items of importance occurring in these areas. More specific information related to international copyright law, national legislation, and various works is covered in chapters 6 through 14. For additional information on which countries are members of various conventions and treaties with the United States, see U.S. Copyright Office, Circular 38A: International Copyright Relations of the United States.

## ORPHAN WORKS

Orphan works are works where finding the owner(s) is problematic or next to impossible. When educators wish to borrow or copy from such a work, they have difficult choices to make. Should they (1) continue searching for an owner, in order to obtain permission to use the work? (2) use only that part of the work which might fit under fair use or another copyright exemption? (3) "give up" and use something else? (4) argue, after searching for a "reasonable amount of time," that in good faith, they have tried, and risk using the work anyway? With orphan works, like many copyright issues, there is no one answer. For several years, library organizations, publishers, the U.S. Copyright Office, and other users with a vested interest in orphan works have pushed to have federal legislation passed that would simplify borrowing from these items. Other suggested solutions have included creating online databases to locate missing owners, placing all works considered orphan in the public domain, revising tax and bankruptcy laws (which might reduce the number of works becoming orphans), and establishing a capped fee that could be paid an owner, if he or she was found (Public Knowledge 2009; Samuelson 2012; Sigall 2006). As of 2012, there are no definite solutions on the horizon; thus the educator faced with such a dilemma might choose, for example, to find another work to use or document what he or she considers a "reasonable amount of time" for a search, and then use as little of the work as possible. At this point in time, the choice of use of an orphaned work is a decision of the borrower.

## FUTURE COPYRIGHT LEGISLATION

At any one point in time, there may be bills and acts dealing with copyright issues somewhere in the U.S. House or Senate. One 2012 example, the Online Protection and Enforcement of Digital Trade Act (OPEN Act; H.R. 3782) would make it a federal violation to manage or support websites if the site is "accessed through a nondomestic domain name, conducts business directed to U.S. residents, has only limited purpose or use other than engaging in infringing activity, and whose owner or operator primarily uses the site to: (1) willfully commit specified criminal copyright offenses or circumvent technological measures controlling access to protected work, or (2) use counterfeit trademarks in a manner punishable under specified provisions of the Lanham Act" (Library of Congress 2012, 1). (The Lanham Act covers federal trademark law [Tysver 2010].) Whether acts such as this will eventually become law depends on the U.S. federal legislative bodies.

Lastly, on March 20, 2013, Maria A. Pallante, the register of copyrights of the United States, presented a statement she had written to the Subcommittee on Courts, Intellectual Property and the Internet, Committee on the Judiciary, U.S. House of Representatives. In this statement, she called for updates to the U.S. copyright law, saying that the law has been unable to keep up with the digital age and that "Congress also may need to apply fresh eyes to the next great copyright act to ensure that the copyright law remains relevant and functional" (Pallante 2013, 2). As this book goes to press, no revisions to the law have been made public.

For the purposes of those of us who work in higher education, it is best to note that future legislation may change copyright law, including how it is interpreted and enforced. Thus we need to remain up-to-date in this area through current print, nonprint, and Internet sources; attendance at professional presentations; attending workshops and classes in copyright law and related issues; and more.

## INFRINGEMENTS AND PENALTIES

Imagine that at a departmental meeting, your department chair asks you and your colleagues to stand if you think you have violated copyright law. If the group is truthful—and even halfway knowledgeable about copyright—it is likely that the whole room will stand. At this point, it is a common occurrence that at least one individual will point out, "I copy all the time, and I've never been caught." Then a conversation might ensue about how institutions of higher learning have more freedom because "no one wants to press a university" or "We're educators; we aren't going to earn any money off what we copy anyway." At this point librarians, technology coordinators, administration, and interested others may also speak up, asking, "Are we in trouble if we provide the equipment and software by which our faculty copies?" There are several misconceptions going on at this point that are worth looking into.

### "Everyone in the Room Has Violated Copyright Law"

Because of the ambiguity in U.S. copyright law, with its duality of representing both borrowers and owners of works, infringing on copyright law is easy to do. It may be a conscious or unconscious act.

Imagine that you facilitate a language lab at your university. You find a great piece of software that you are just positive will make learning Russian an enjoyable student experience. Before you ask the Slavic Languages Department to purchase a license for it, you want to try it out on a class. So, you copy it to all computers in your lab—even though you know that the documentation on the software says that this cannot be done without a license. Are you in violation of copyright law? Most definitely! (You are probably also in violation of contract law—see "Documentation and Licenses" in this chapter.) This is an example of conscious violation.

Assume that you are a young adult (YA) literature instructor. Because of the popularity of the *Twilight* series, you decide to develop a unit on vampire literature for your YA class. As part of this unit, you copy a pamphlet on vampire legends that you purchased at a local bookstore. In your excitement to create this new assignment, you totally forget that such copying may be in violation of copyright law: the pamphlet is not in the public domain, it doesn't fit under the fair use factors, and permission has not been granted. Have you violated copyright law? Most probably! This is an example of an unconscious act of violation.

### "I'll Never Get Caught"

Well, you might not, but . . . Envisage yourself as a music performance professor at a midsized public university. In preparation for a graduate student recital, you have promised the student that you will find a clarinet piece he can add to his repertoire. You find the perfect piece in a little-known musical you borrowed from the music library. Unfortunately, the music was originally written for an oboe, and you recognize that it will need to be rewritten for the clarinet in order for your student to use it. The recital is in a week, and there is little time. The score needs to be revised quickly, so that the student can practice it and get it memorized for his performance. You make the "executive decision" that the piece is so little known that to waste time trying to obtain copyright permission is ridiculous. No one will know the difference anyway. So, you proceed to rewrite the score for the student's recital. Chances are that you are safe—no one will be the wiser and no harm will be done. But. . . . now assume that a member of the audience, by happenstance, recognizes the piece as one that was performed in a musical she attended a few years ago in another state—a musical written by a friend of hers. Will you get caught? If the audience member contacts her friend, and this person decides to pursue the matter, you definitely could be found to have infringed on the composer's copyright. (More on copyright and music is found in Chapter 10: "Music and Copyright Law: Who Will Know If You Copy It?" More on how to deal with those who violate, how and why to respect copyright law, and related topics is found in Chapter 14.)

Now, we turn to additional examples.

### "We Don't Have Enough Money to Buy Everything That We Need, So It's OK to Copy; After All, We're in Education"

Some educators feel that they should be able to copy or borrow from sources indiscriminately; that because they are in education, all materials are "fair game." In particular cases, the educators will even purchase things themselves that they feel they would not be able to get otherwise. For instance, an adjunct math professor finds a sample textbook in the bookstore with an exercise that is perfect for a specific learning module. The adjunct purchases the textbook, with full knowledge that the book's verso (back side of the title page) states that the material therein cannot be copied for classroom use. The adjunct, however, feels that since this is for an educational purpose, it is okay to copy the exercise for every student in the class. Unfortunately, the textbook's publisher feels that every student in the class should own the book instead of the adjunct copying the exercise over and over from one purchased copy. The publisher may have the right, under copyright law, to specify how the work is used. However, there are ways to obtain use of an owner's works by means of fair use, public domain, and permissions and licenses (see chapters 2 through 4), or possibly by statutory exceptions (see this chapter) or the "Guidelines for Classroom Copying" (also in this chapter). Therefore, the adjunct is infringing, unless the copying falls under one of the above. Just being an educator or working with students in an educational setting does not mean that you can legally disregard copyright law.

## "I Don't Violate Copyright Law;
## I Am in Charge of Equipment and Software That Is Used to Copy, However"

Assume that you are a technical college librarian. It is a small school, so you function as a technology specialist as well. All equipment, such as computers, DVD players, televisions, audio recorders, and the like, is under your jurisdiction. The same holds true for all software. An industrial arts faculty member comes in and sits down to use one of the lab computers. You pay no attention to him—he knows what he is doing, and you are busy with other things. Only later do you realize that he was burning a mix of songs from purchased CDs and Internet sources onto a CD for personal use. You recognize it is highly likely that this is a copyright infringement. Should the faculty member be caught for this act, would you also be held in violation for providing the instruments used for the copying? Unfortunately, you could be. This is an example of contributory or indirect infringement. "Anyone who knows or should have known that he or she is assisting, inducing or materially contributing to infringement of any of the exclusive rights by another person is liable for contributory infringement" (Simpson and Weiser 2008, 87). There are three kinds of infringement: (1) direct, in which a user violates the rights of the owner or author by making illegal copies or derivatives of copyrighted works, distributing these copies/derivations, or publicly performing or displaying the works; (2) contributory, in which an individual or group is aware that what they are doing assists another in copyright infringement; and (3) vicarious, where those with authority over an infringer gain benefits from the infringement (Simpson and Weiser 2008).

## Penalties

Penalties for copyright infringements vary from fines to prison sentences. While I am unaware of any cases in which higher education professionals have been imprisoned for copyright violation, the penalties do exist in the U.S. Code (Title 17, sec. 506(a); Title 18, sec.

2319). For example, a DVD warning from *Harry Potter and the Half-Blood Prince* (2009) lists both a fine and jail time: the warning reads as follows:

> The unauthorized reproduction or distribution of this copyrighted work is illegal. Criminal copyright infringement, including infringement without monetary gain, is investigated by the FBI and punishable by up to 5 years in federal prison and a fine of $250,000.
> (*Harry Potter and the Half-Blood Prince* 2009)

While this DVD warning is just an example of the kinds of warnings that are often placed on works, be aware that fines, sentences, and other penalties do exist, although they may vary from that of the Harry Potter DVD. Why? The copyright law of the United States affords damages. As a consequence, there are ramifications for infringing on copyright law! Given some individuals' propensity towards using works indiscriminately, this is an issue to examine carefully.

Also remember that at any given time, while there are a number of bills and acts in the federal legislature concerned with copyright, many of them are focused on increasing the fines or other penalties for disobeying the law.

## PLAGIARISM

Plagiarism is when you borrow from another source without crediting the source or person from whom it was borrowed. Some examples of plagiarism include buying a term paper from an online paper mill, borrowing part of a paper from another student and turning it in as your own, and copying or paraphrasing from an original work without citing the source. Plagiarism can be intentional or unintentional. Intentional plagiarism occurs when someone purposely steals from another. For example, if you are English faculty and one of your students knowingly copies a poem from a poetry anthology and turns it in to you as his or her own, that student has intentionally plagiarized. Unintentional plagiarism occurs when someone does not cite (or does not properly cite) his or her sources. One instance of this might be if you, as a professor, write an article for a professional journal. Because of sloppy note taking, you forget to cite one of the book chapters from which you obtained some of your information. The simplest ways to avoid plagiarizing are to not borrow indiscriminately and to cite your sources (Office of Graduate Studies 2010). In addition, a National Bureau of Economic Research study shows that being educated in what plagiarism is and learning how to follow the rules can reduce plagiarism in students (Inside Higher Education 2010).

There are a number of online plagiarism detection sites (which range from charging per paper to free use) where a teacher or student can plug in a written assignment and find out what parts, if any, are plagiarized. Included in this list of sources are such services as Turnitin, SafeAssign (part of the Blackboard online course package), and DupliChecker. Additionally, it is possible to check phrases and sentences for plagiarism just by plugging them into the search box in Google. Moreover, to obtain information on how "not to plagiarize," there are a wide variety of Internet articles on this subject as well as print periodical articles and books. A quick glance at two books on avoiding plagiarism suggests such activities as making sure that students do their own work, using their own words; all sources are cited correctly; students remember not to mix different quotations together; students be taught how to narrow online search options; and students be encouraged to create original bibliographies (Gilmore 2009; Menager and Paulos 2009).

## How to Cite

It is better to cite something that you have borrowed, rather than risk plagiarizing. How to cite what you borrow is another issue, one that is not within the scope of this book. However, there are any number of citation styles, some of the most common coming from the American Psychological Association (APA), the *Chicago Manual of Style (CMS),* and the Modern Language Association (MLA). Web pages, including blogs and wikis, as well as other items posted online, are especially confusing to cite and citing procedures may vary from style manual to style manual. Below are citation style examples used by APA, *CMS,* and MLA to cite an Internet site/article from an online periodical.

---

**American Psychological Association**
Author, A. A., & Author, B. B. (Date of publication). Title of article. Title of Online Periodical,
    volume number (issue number if available). Retrieved from www.someaddress.com/full/url/.
    (Purdue Online Writing Lab 2010a, 1)

---

*Chicago Manual of Style*
Last name, First name. "Title." Publisher or name of website. Publication date. URL. (Purdue Online
Writing Lab 2010b, 1)

---

**Modern Language Association**
Author. "Article title." Web magazine. Publisher name. Publication date. Medium of publication.
    Date of access. (Purdue Online Writing Lab 2010c, 1)

---

Manuals of style can be found in a number of places: online on college and university sites and for sale in commercial bookstores. There are also other websites that provide information on citation, such as NoodleTools, an Internet site that "provides innovative software that teaches students and supports teachers and librarians throughout the entire research process" (NoodleTools, 1) and EasyBib, "The Free Automatic Bibliography and Citation Maker" (EasyBib 2010, 1).

Thus, while correctly citing material borrowed is an important skill to have when authoring any intellectual work, its relationship to copyright is only peripheral.

## Plagiarism and Copyright

Copyright is not directly related to plagiarism. However, the two are often associated with one another. For example, courts may recognize cases of plagiarism as copyright infringement

(LawBrain 2010). Perhaps this is because both involve copying materials. Historically copyright and plagiarism are also linked. In England, the eighteenth century is noted for the first copyright statutes as well as a strong concern about plagiarism (Mallon 1989). Additionally, it may be possible to both break copyright law and plagiarize. A case in point would be if Mr. Brown, a computer science instructor, decides to take a chapter from a book detailing presentation software and claim it as his own on a personal website. Assuming that the book is not in the public domain, if he does not ask for permission to use the chapter and borrows more than fair use allows, he violates copyright law. Putting the name "Brown" on something he did not write is an example of plagiarism. Thus, Mr. Brown manages to both violate copyright law and plagiarize. Plagiarization might be avoided simply by citing where the software information came from; however, such citing would not mean that it is permissible to violate copyright law.

In 2008 Turnitin, one of the Internet detection services discussed earlier in this chapter, won a court case they had been battling involving the use of student papers. Several high school students had sued Turnitin, saying that copyright ownership to their papers was violated, since the company stored "digital copies of their essays to check future submissions for academic dishonesty" (Oleck 2008, 1). The court found in favor of Turnitin, stating that "fair use was not violated because under federal law, the unauthorized use of copyrighted work for purposes such as teaching, scholarship, and research 'is not an infringement of copyright.' Fair use allows limited use of copyrighted material without requiring permission from the rights holders" (Oleck 2008, 1). In this particular case, at least, copyright and plagiarism parted ways. Now let us return to the main focus of this book, copyright and higher education.

### Sample Flow Chart

Figure 5-1 is an example of the flow charts used in part 2 of this book to respond to copyright questions that have more than one answer. Read through each diagram in part 2 from top to bottom to obtain the answers to the question posted above a particular flow chart. Remember that you are trying to find any criterion under which you may borrow a work. Therefore, you need only to follow each flow chart until you come to that point where you satisfy one of the criteria. Once you reach that point, there is no need to go further.

## CONCLUSION

This chapter examines a number of copyright-related items, including documentation and licenses, interlibrary loan, statutory exemptions for librarians and other higher education professionals, and classroom copying guidelines. It also addresses international copyright law and ways the United States has chosen to add to its own laws in order to comply with international copyright treaties, orphan works, copyright infringements in higher education, educators' attitudes towards such infringements, and the penalties for copyright violations. All of these are things with which you need to be familiar. Although not directly related to copyright law, plagiarism, and correct citing styles are also part of this chapter.

# FIGURE 5-1

**Sample Flow Chart:** The flow chart below is indicative of the flow charts that will be found in the rest of this book.

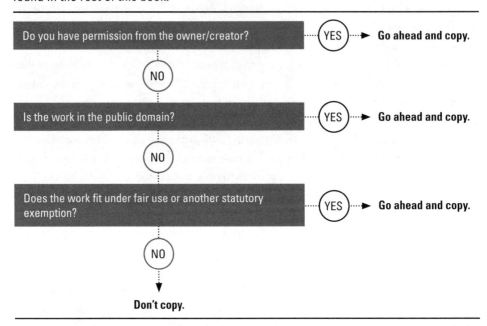

This is because many educators associate these topics with copyright. Finally, there is a sample of the flow charts used in part 2 (see figure 5-1) and an explanation.

Now that you have an idea about a variety of issues that come into play when you are applying copyright law to works in a variety of formats, it is time to turn to the practical application of copyright in college and university settings.

## REFERENCES

Besenjak, Cheryl. 1997. *Copyright Plain & Simple*. Franklin Lakes, NJ: Career.

Bissonette, J. D., and M. Aimee. 2009. *Cyber Law: Maximizing Safety and Minimizing Risk in Classrooms*. Thousand Oaks, CA: Corwin.

Butler, Rebecca P. 2007. "Borrowing Media from Around the World: School Libraries and Copyright Law." *School Libraries Worldwide* 13, no. 2 (July): 73–81.

Charters of Freedom. 1789. Bill of Rights: Amendment IV. www.archives.gov/exhibits/charters/bill_of_rights_transcript.html.

*Chicago Manual of Style*. 2010. 16th ed. Chicago: University of Chicago Press.

Chilling Effects Clearinghouse. "Question: What Are Shrink-Wrap, Click-Wrap, and Browse-Wrap Licenses?" www.chillingeffects.org/question.cgi?QuestionID=207.

CONTU. 1978. "CONTU Guidelines on Photocopying under Interlibrary Loan Arrangements."
www.cni.org/docs/infopols/CONTU.html.

Copyright Clearance Center. 2005. "Using Content: ILL." www.copyright.com/Services/
copyrightoncampus/content/ill_contu.html.

Copyright Education and Consultation Program. "Open Access." https://blogs.cites.illinois.edu/
library-copyright/open-access/#cc.

Creative Commons. "About: What Is CC?" http://creativecommons.org/about/what-is-cc.

———. b. "Creative Commons: Attribution-Noncommercial-Share Alike 2.5 Generic."
http://creativecommons.org/licenses/by-nc-sa/2.5.

Crews, Kenneth D. 2006. *Copyright Law for Librarians and Educators: Creative Strategies and
Practical Solutions*. Chicago: American Library Association.

EasyBib. 2010. "The Free Automatic Bibliography and Citation Maker." www.easybib.com.

Free Software Foundation (FSF). 2008. "GNU Operating System: A Quick Guide to GPLv3."
www.gnu.org/licenses/quick-guide-gplv3.html.

Gilmore, Barry. 2009. *Plagiarism: A How-Not-to Guide for Students*. Portsmouth, NH: Heinemann.

GNU Operating System. 2010. www.gnu.org.

Guidelines—Copyright & Fair Use. http://library.sdsmt.edu/copy/CopyrightGuidelines.htm.

*Harry Potter and the Half-Blood Prince*. 2009. Produced by Heyday Films. 153 min. Warner Bros.
Pictures. DVD.

Inside Higher Education. 2010. "Plagiarism Prevention without Fear." www.insidehighered.com/
news/2010/01/26/plagiarize.

*International Journal of Zizek Studies*. 2007. http://zizekstudies.org/index.php/ijzs/index.

Kunkel, Richard G., JD. 2002. "Recent Developments in Shrinkwrap, Clickwrap and Browsewrap
Licenses in the United States." www.murdoch.edu.au/elaw/issues/v9n3/kunkel93.html.

LawBrain. 2010. "Plagiarism." http://lawbrain.com/wiki/Plagiarism.

Library of Congress: Thomas. (2011). *Bill Summary & Status, 112th Congress
(2011–2012), H.R.3261, CRS summary.* http://thomas.loc.gov/cgi-bin/bdquery/
z?d112:HR03261:@@@D&summ2=m&.

———. (2012). *Bill Summary & Status, 112th Congress (2011–2012), H.R.3782, CRS summary.*
http://thomas.loc.gov/cgi-bin/bdquery/z?d112:HR03782:@@@D&summ2=m&.

Mallon, Thomas, 1989. *Stolen Words: The Classic Book on Plagiarism*. New York: Harcourt.

Menager, Rosemarie, and Lyn Paulos. 2009. *Quick Coach Guide to Avoiding Plagiarism*. Boston:
Wadsworth.

Neal, James G. 2002. "Copyright Is Dead . . . Long Live Copyright." *American Libraries* 33, no. 11
(December): 48–51.

NoodleTools: Smart Tools. www.noodletools.com.

Northern Illinois University. 2013a. "Alternative Models of Publishing." http://niu.edu/
scholarlycomm/alternative_models/index.shtml.

———. 2013b. "Copyright Management for Authors." http://niu.edu/scholarlycomm/copyright
_management/index.shtml.

Office of Graduate Studies. 2010. "Plagiarism: What It Is and How to Avoid It." www.unl.edu/
gradstudies/current/plagiarism.shtml.

Oleck, Joan. 2008. "Judge Rules That Turnitin Does Not Violate Students' Copyrights."
www.schoollibraryjournal.com/article/CA6546427.html.

Open Source Initiative. "The Open Source Definition." www.opensource.org/docs/osd.

Pallante, Maria A. 2013. Statement of Maria A. Pallante, Register of Copyrights of the United
States, Subcommittee on Courts, Intellectual Property and the Internet, Committee on the
Judiciary, U.S. House of Representatives, 113th Congress, 1st session, March 20, 2013.

Public Knowledge. 2009. "Orphan Works." www.publicknowledge.org/issues/ow.

Purdue Online Writing Lab. 2010. "APA Style: Reference List: Electronic Sources
(Web publications)." http://owl.english.purdue.edu/owl/resource/560/10.

———. 2010b. "*Chicago Manual of Style:* Web Sources." http://owl.english.purdue.edu/owl/
resource/717/04.

———. 2010c. "MLA Works Cited: Electronic Sources (Web Publications)." http://owl.english
.purdue.edu/owl/resource/747/08.

Radcliffe, Mark F., and Diane Brinson. 2014. "Copyright Law." http://corporate.findlaw.com/
intellectual-property/copyright-law.html.

Rowling, J. K. 2003. *Harry Potter and the Order of the Phoenix.* New York: Scholastic.

Rupp-Serrano, Karen, ed. 2005. *Licensing in Libraries: Practical and Ethical Aspects.* New York:
Haworth Information.

Samuelson, Pamela. 2012. "Reforming Copyright Is Possible: And It's the Only Way to Create a
National Digital Library." http://chronicle.com/article/Reforming-Copyright
-Is/132751/?cid=cr&utm_source=cr&utm_medium=en.

"School District Pays Copyright Penalty." 2001. *Chicago Tribune,* October 12, sec. 2, 3.

Sigall, Jule L. 2006. Statement of Jule L. Sigall, Associate Register for Policy and International
Affairs before the Subcommittee on Courts, the Internet, and Intellectual Property,
Committee on the Judiciary. www.copyright.gov/docs/regstst030806.html.

Simpson, Carol, and Christine Weiser. 2008. *Copyright for Administrators.* Columbus, OH:
Linworth.

SPARC. 2006. "Author Rights: Using the SPARC Author Addendum to Secure Your Rights as the
Author of a Journal Article." http://www.sparc.arl.org/author/addendum~print.shtml.

Suber, Peter, 2012. "Open Access Overview." http://www.earlham.edu/~peters/fos/overview.htm.

Torrans, Lee Ann. 2003. *Law for K-12 Libraries and Librarians.* Westport, CT: Libraries Unlimited.

Tully, Elisabeth. 2008. "Bibliocycle: The CONTU Rule of Five." http://www.noblenet.org/owhl/
bibliocycle/copyright/the-contu-rule-of-five.

Tysver, Daniel A. 2010. "Lanham (Trademark) Act (15 U.S.C.) Index." http://www.bitlaw.com/
source/15usc.

U.S. Constitution. 1787. www.usconstitution.net/const.html.

U.S. Copyright Law. 1976. Public Law 94-553, sec. 108, 110.

U.S. Copyright Office, Library of Congress. 2010. Washington, D.C.: U.S. Copyright Office.

———. 2009. "Circular 38A: International copyright Relations of the United States." Washington, D.C.: U.S. Copyright Office.

———. 1998. "The Digital Millennium Copyright Act of 1998: U.S. Copyright Office Summary." Washington, DC: U.S. Copyright Office.

Williams, Corey. 2012. "ALA Applauds Internet Blackout in Opposition to PIPA, SOPA." http://www.districtdispatch.org/tag/sopa.

World Intellectual Property Organization (WIPO). "Copyright and Related Rights." www.wipo.int/copyright/en.

———. b. "What Is WIPO?" www.wipo.int/about-wipo/en/what_is_wipo.html.

# PART II

## Specific Applications of Copyright Law

# 6

# The Internet and Copyright Law
## Everything on the Web Is Considered Implied Public Access, Right?

The items in figure 6-1 represent some of the media choices available to today's students: social networking tools; objects that can access the Web, including cell phones; online software; websites that sell music, e-books, and online applications; access points for information; and more. Items such as these open up the possibility of violating copyright law, through the ease of borrowing, copying, and sharing of online resources. Because the Internet is a relatively new phenomenon in terms of copyright—early copyright law was interpreted solely in terms of print ownership (Bettig 1996)—how to protect yourself and your students considering copyright law and media can pose a conundrum.

## FIGURE 6-1

### Web Items

Wikis, blogs, podcasts, video streaming, Second Life, Facebook, Shelfari, Flickr, cloud computing, wordless, Moodle, iPads, BYOD, BrainPOP, myYearbook, Free Online Games, Mousebreaker, Chatroulette, Nings, MP3 players, iPods, Playaways, Animoto, e-readers, Kindles, Nooks, MySpace, Diggo, Twitter, GoodReads, Skype, Delicious, Web syndication, Google Wave, ScreenToaster, Prezi, Slideshare, file sharing, electronic toolboxes, RSS feeds, hyperlinks, AdobeConnect, video streaming, OverDrive, computational knowledge engines, Limewire, LibriVox, social media, YouTube, TeacherTube, Web 2.0, MediaCast, iTunes, pageflakes, Netvibes, Protopage, social gaming networks, LinkedIn, Scribd, concept-mapping tools, Plurk, DRM, Xanga, Web Feeds, QR Codes, content aggregators, Pinterest, online video games.

**For definitions of all terms above, please see appendix B.**

This chapter addresses questions that cover the Internet, higher education, and a wide variety of copyright issues. Questions with more than one answer are presented in flow chart form. Remember, when you use the flow charts in this chapter, you are trying to find any criterion under which you may borrow a work. Therefore, you need only follow each flow chart until you come to that point where you satisfy one of the criteria. Once you reach that point, there is no need to go any further. Additionally, for more information on each area discussed, please refer to the chapter (chapters 1 through 5) that covers that particular subject, as well as appendix B, which defines the terms located in the sidebar. Also, use the index and table of contents for more material on topics that interest you.

## FAIR USE

**Q**   Is there fair use on the Internet?

**A**   While U.S. copyright laws are still catching up when it comes to Internet usage, it is best to apply fair use to all websites, e-mails, and other electronic communications.

**Q**   Can website creators use images (book covers, photos, etc.) from online booksellers or other vendor sources to promote books and other media on their websites?

**A**   Since vendors are in the business of making money, it is likely they will not mind their images existing on your site to promote those things that they sell. However, since images on vendor sites can be copyrighted, please consult the flow chart in figure 6-2 when considering borrowing images for your website.

## FIGURE 6-2

**Web Images**

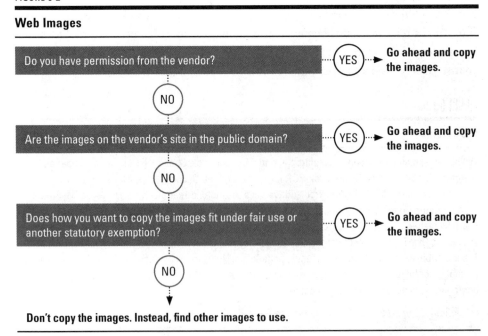

Don't copy the images. Instead, find other images to use.

Q   A friend e-mailed me a copy of a joke. Can I send it on to others or post it on a blog or another website without repercussions?

A   To have a copy does not mean you have a copyright. If the joke was sent to you and there is no documentation attached, assume it is under copyright and do not send it on without permission of the original owner. However, you may discuss it or send parts of it under the fair use factors.

Q   Can I print off a web page and make a copy of it for every student in my class?

A   Use the flow chart in figure 6-3 to determine what is allowed. Remember that sending a URL for the students to access will always be safer than printing something off. (Also, be aware that some sites use technology to prevent any printing of their web pages [About.com 2013].)

## FIGURE 6-3

**Printing Web Pages**

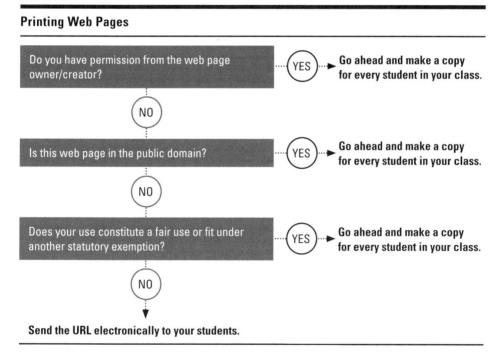

**Send the URL electronically to your students.**

Q   I want to copy several paragraphs from a site on Hurricane Sandy. How much may I borrow from someone's web page under fair use?

A   The amount you may copy is based on the total amount of material on the site, how much you want to borrow, whether or not it is the heart of the work, whether it is fact or fiction, published or unpublished, whether such borrowing will affect the marketplace, and how you are going to use what you borrow (see chapter 2). "When you claim fair use, you take a risk. The wording of fair use language in the Copyright Act is vague and subject to interpretation by the courts!" (Besenjak 1997, 58).

Q   I found a great photograph of Martin Luther King Jr. on another college's website. I want to use it for my sophomore advanced history Internet site. However, said college does not answer my queries. Is it all right to use the photograph anyway?

A   Use the flow chart in figure 6-4 to decide if it is all right to use the photograph.

## FIGURE 6-4

**Photographs on the Web**

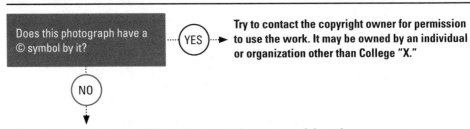

Do not use the photograph. Without documentation or a copyright notice, you cannot assume a work is in the public domain or under fair use. It is also impossible to obtain permission if you are unable to identify the work's creator/owner or if unable to contact the owner of the website.

Q   A doctoral student came into the library with the following question: "Part of my dissertation research includes studying a number of young adult media awards. As such, I thought that I would put small photos of the books that won the awards (available on several commercial bookstore websites) in my dissertation. This comes under fair use, right?"

A   Well, maybe . . . it depends on who the doctoral student borrowed the photos from, if those particular commercial entities are the owners of the photos or not, and if the owners of the photos care that they are copied. Whew! Could be that all such groups would be happy to see their media in a dissertation, since in essence the doctoral student would be advertising their materials (assuming that his or her dissertation would be available to the public upon completion). That said, the photo of said items could be owned by the commercial bookstore sites, by the publishers of the original books, by the creator of the original media, by someone who purchased the rights to that item, and so on. In addition, a book cover can be copyright-protected by itself (in which case it would not come under fair use) or as part of a whole (in which case it might come under fair use). This is a long way of saying that it would be best to encourage the doctoral student to ask for permission to use each and every photo from the owner/s of the work/s. He or she could start by e-mailing the commercial bookstore websites and asking.

## PUBLIC DOMAIN

Q  Is the Internet in the public domain?

A  The Internet is a "single worldwide computer network that interconnects other computer networks, on which end-user services, such as World Wide Web sites or data archives, are located, enabling data and other information to be exchanged" (Internet 2013, 1). Web pages' content and electronic communications that make up the Internet can be and often are copyright-protected. If the content of any web page is in the public domain, it should say so somewhere on the site. (Should is an operative word here—the site owner or administrator does not have to state whether Internet content is copyright-protected.) However, if there is no statement either way, one should assume that the web page content is copyrighted.

Q  Student X needs an image for a report he is doing. He finds a website with images and chooses one to use. Is the image in the public domain?

A  It is possible for anyone who can create a web page to put it in the public domain, simply by adding a statement to that effect to the page. It is also possible for someone creating a web page filled with images to borrow some from copyright-protected sites. Thus, you are safest if you borrow public domain images from a reputable site, one where you can trust that the images really are in the public domain. Study the flow chart in figure 6-5 for more help.

## FIGURE 6-5

### How to Decide If an Image Is in the Public Domain

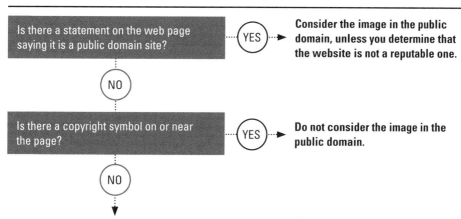

Is there a statement on the web page saying it is a public domain site? — YES → Consider the image in the public domain, unless you determine that the website is not a reputable one.

NO

Is there a copyright symbol on or near the page? — YES → Do not consider the image in the public domain.

NO

**Do not consider the image in the public domain.**
(Works do not have to state that they are public domain, even if they are. If you cannot tell if an item is public domain, assume that it is copyright-protected and treat it as such.)

Q   In our library, we have a photograph archive, consisting of a large collection of photographs gifted to our institution. Many of these photographs are old, as can be seen
by their subject matter and the quality of the original. Of that group, many also have
no copyright statement on them as well as no contact name or date as to when they
were originally photographed. We wish to save this history by digitizing all of these
photographs and placing them on the Web for public use. Can we assume that these
are in the public domain and thus do with them as we wish?

A   Not necessarily. Some of them may be in the public domain. However, it sounds like
at least some of these photographs might be considered orphan works (see chapter 5).
As such, whether or not to digitize them for placement on the Web becomes a library
decision. For *each* photograph, the library could search for a "reasonable amount of
time" (to be determined by the library) and if no information was found, choose to digitize and place said photograph on the Internet. If the library chooses to do this, then
document what has been done and why and save it in a folder or another safe place, in
case an owner should show up at a later date. Then, if an owner does appear, the library
would either need to (1) obtain permission from the owner for the digitization and
placement on the Web, (2) pay a royalty to do so, or (3) take the photograph off the
Web and destroy the digitized version.

## DOCUMENTATION AND LICENSES

Q   Where is the documentation located on a web page?

A   Documentation (that information in most works which states the work's identifying
data, such as author, copyright date, publisher, place of publication, etc.) on a web page
is usually at the bottom of each web page, the beginning or end of the site, or on a special "About" page. It may be as simple as listing the webmaster or moderator of the site
and when the site was last updated. Documentation can also include permissions or
restrictions to which the user of the site must agree, copyright information, and other
criteria that the moderator or owner of the site has determined must be met for site
usage (see chapter 5). Please remember to read all documentation before agreeing to or
checking off on a site. It is to your advantage to know that to which you have agreed.

Q   Do college faculty need to be concerned with licenses for web access?

A   In many higher education institutions, licenses are the responsibility of the main library
or a technology arm of the institution and apply to the number of computers that use a
particular software at one time or in a particular manner, or they are the responsibility
of the library and apply to online databases (Hoffmann 2001) or access to other online
information sources, such as online encyclopedias. However, while college faculty may
not hold primary responsibility for computer licenses (software) and web access (online
databases and online encyclopedias) in that such responsibilities are someone else's job,

the faculty member needs to know and abide by the licensing terms, and ensure that his or her students do the same. (It would be the responsibility of the main library or technology arm of the institution to ensure that faculty had this information.)

**Q**  **Do social and professional websites such as Facebook, Twitter, Shelfari, Pinterest, and LinkedIn have copyright policies and infringement reporting procedures? Does YouTube?**

**A**  Yes. While these vary from site to site, a link to copyright policies and procedures is normally found somewhere on the main page, usually at the bottom. The content of these policies and procedures ranges from providing complaint forms to statements that infringers will be removed from the participating network site to disabling access to infringers to deleting infringing posts or content (Facebook 2013; LinkedIn 2013; Pinterest 2013; Shelfari 2013; Twitter 2013; YouTube n.d.).

**Q**  **How do database licenses work?**

**A**  The license (usually) located at the beginning of the database will tell the user what he or she can copy, print off, and what he or she can't. Some databases let you print out whole articles. Others allow you to search but not print, unless your institution has purchased a site license. Since database rights vary one to another, the main library, or whatever group within the university is responsible for database access, must make sure that users are aware of exactly what rights they have with each one. There are certain things higher education institutions should remember about databases, licenses, and copyright:

- Licenses may be more restrictive than fair use; however, when one agrees to the license, it is a legal contract and must be abided by.
- Database material may or may not be from copyrighted publications.
- "Click-on" licenses on the Internet are nonnegotiated contracts. Because of this, there is currently dissent as to whether or not "clicking away certain copyrights" is actually legal.
- Database collections are not protected by U.S. copyright law (Torrans 2003).

## PERMISSIONS

**Q**  **I am an archivist in our institution's anthropology museum. I am in the process of creating a web page for the museum, and my administration has requested that I also provide links to similar information at other universities. Do I need permission to link the page I am creating to a general anthropology page at another institution?**

**A**  Not at this time. Such linking is usually considered a public domain concept. (This is true for most links. One exception is if the format of the link itself could be copyrighted, such as that of a copyrighted image.) However, it is good "Netiquette" (Internet etiquette) to ask the owner institution/webmaster if you may link your page to the other website.

Q   May I make a deep link to a specific chemistry site without permission? ("Deep linking is . . . used by websites to point a visitor directly to a page within the website instead of the landing page or front page of the site. Deep linking allows visitors to go directly to the information they require, which may be available on a certain page of the website, but not on the web page to which the basic link leads" [Brick Marketing 2013, 1].)

A   Some copyright experts and users argue that linking is an address, similar to cross-references in a library catalog. As such, linking (including deep linking) cannot be copyright-protected. Others disagree, saying that linking (especially deep linking, which can bypass advertising and other pages) may infringe on a copyright owner's rights (American Library Association 2013). While at present there is no legal precedent to claim that deep linking infringes on copyright, to avoid the risk of lawsuits and "cease and desist" letters, it may be easier not to deep link. Use the flow chart in figure 6-6 to make your decision.

## FIGURE 6-6

**Deep Linking**

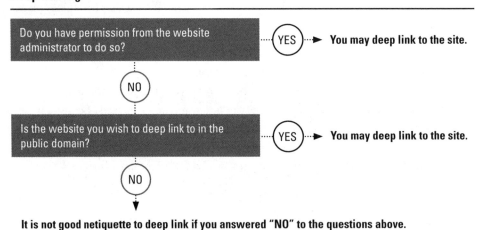

It is not good netiquette to deep link if you answered "NO" to the questions above.

Q   May I copy a list of links about the Oklahoma tornadoes of 2013 that I found on the Web to my meteorology page?

A   Use the flow chart in figure 6-7 to decide if you may copy the list.

## FIGURE 6-7

**Copying Lists**

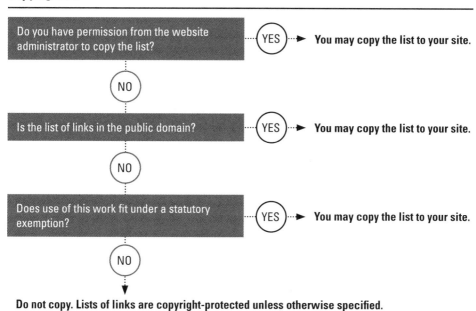

**Do not copy. Lists of links are copyright-protected unless otherwise specified.**

Q  Do I need special permission from Internet authors to borrow or copy parts or all of their web pages?

A  Use the flow chart in figure 6-8 to make your decision.

## FIGURE 6-8

**Borrowing All or Parts of Web Pages**

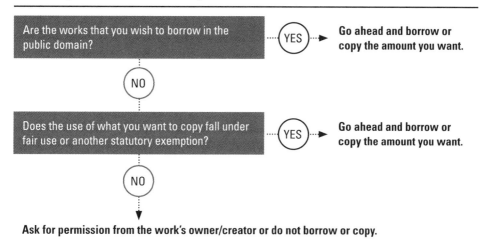

**Ask for permission from the work's owner/creator or do not borrow or copy.**

Q    I found a great picture of a wolf on the Wolf Park (www.wolfpark.net/) website. There
     is a copyright symbol and a person's name at the bottom of the picture. Because our
     school mascot is the wolf, I would like to use this photograph as a screen saver for the
     computer lab computers. Is this possible?

A    While the photograph is copyright-protected, it may be possible with permission.
     Please see figure 6-9 for more information.

# FIGURE 6-9

## Using a Photograph off the Web as a Screen Saver

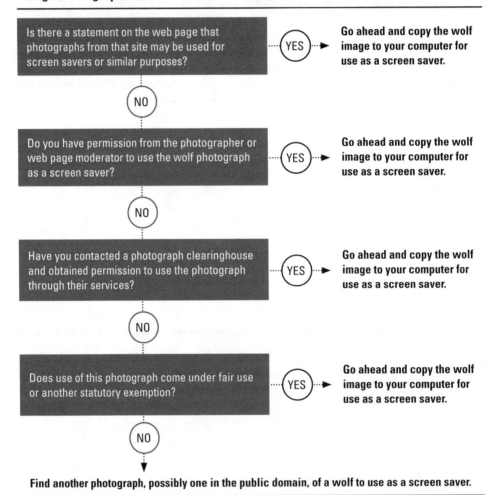

Is there a statement on the web page that photographs from that site may be used for screen savers or similar purposes? — YES ► Go ahead and copy the wolf image to your computer for use as a screen saver.

NO

Do you have permission from the photographer or web page moderator to use the wolf photograph as a screen saver? — YES ► Go ahead and copy the wolf image to your computer for use as a screen saver.

NO

Have you contacted a photograph clearinghouse and obtained permission to use the photograph through their services? — YES ► Go ahead and copy the wolf image to your computer for use as a screen saver.

NO

Does use of this photograph come under fair use or another statutory exemption? — YES ► Go ahead and copy the wolf image to your computer for use as a screen saver.

NO

Find another photograph, possibly one in the public domain, of a wolf to use as a screen saver.

## YOU CREATE IT, YOU OWN IT

Q   Is it a copyright infringement if someone takes an e-mail attachment you sent and posts it on a blog? Imagine that you sent an e-mail to a group of students. You have information vital to a mathematics assignment that you wish them to read before the next class. The information is a piece that you created yourself, just for this class. You attach it to the e-mail and send it out. Weeks later, an instructor at another college tells you that he found a copy of your work on a student's blog. You are incensed; you did not give permission for this piece to be shared beyond your class. A copy posted to a blogging site means that people you do not know could now have your work.

A   The answer to this question is a resounding "yes." Anything you create—and this includes other formats of works as well—is immediately copyright-protected, whether you officially register it with the U.S. Copyright Office or not (U.S. Copyright Office 2006). Thus, whoever originally posted it on the blog (since you did not give your permission) is in violation of copyright law. In addition, those on the blogging site who keep and use your work may also be in violation.

Q   **Who owns the copyright to a web page you created for your English class, if you worked on it at home in the evenings and used your own computer and software?**

A   If you worked on this web page, using your own equipment and software, and all on your own time, then it should be yours, provided you did not sign an agreement with your institution that said otherwise. If you worked on it at your college or university, using only institutional equipment and software, and on school time, then chances are that it could come under "work for hire." Section 201(b) of the Copyright Law of the United States talks about work made for hire. It states, "In the case of a work made for hire, the employer or other person for whom the work was prepared is considered the author for purposes of this title, and, unless the parties have expressly agreed otherwise in a written instrument signed by them, owns all of the rights comprised in the copyright" (U.S. Copyright Law 1976). What this means is that "the hiring party steps into the shoes of the creator and becomes the author of the work for copyright purposes" (Jassin 2012, 1). If you created it partly at home and partly at work, then ownership becomes more complicated. Some institutions of higher education have contractual agreements with their employees or policies that cover this issue. These policies vary in identifying the owner of the work. In this case, check with your institution's regulations. It is important to remember here that like so much else dealing with copyright, there are a number of factors to consider when determining who owns what, such as where, when, and how the work was created. For example, the U.S. Supreme Court ruling in 1989 on the *Community for Creative Non-Violence (CCNV) v. Reid* is such a case (U.S. Supreme Court Media, 2013). In brief, this case considers who owns the copyright to a statue: the artist (Reid) who created the statue in his studio after a verbal agreement with the CCNV, or the CCNV, which commissioned it. First, a district court ruled in favor of CCNV, holding that it was "work made for hire." However, a court of appeals reversed that decision, stating that it was not within the scope of employment for Reid given that he was an independent contractor under agency law, and that the agreement for the statue as a "work made for hire" had not been in writing. The opinion of the U.S. Supreme Court, delivered by Justice Marshall on June 5, 1989, was that it was not "work for hire," since Reid was an independent contractor rather than an employee of the CCNV. In delivering this decision, multiple factors were considered by the court. (Other courts determining who owns the copyright to material on a website could apply these same issues.) The factors to be considered are determining (1) whether a work is created by an employee (work made for hire) within the definition of the 1976 copyright law, Section 101(1) or (2) by an independent contractor within the definition of the 1976 copyright law, Section 101(2); or that of (3) joint authorship, thus copyright co-ownership under Section 201(a) of the Copyright Law of 1976 (U.S. Copyright Law, sec. 101(1), 101(2), 201(a); U.S. Supreme Court Media 2013).

Q    Who owns e-mails?
A    The sender/creator owns the e-mail, no matter what computer receives it.


## INFRINGEMENTS AND PENALTIES

Q    Is file swapping/downloading of material to your classroom computer an infringement of copyright law?
A    File swapping is an issue that probably happens more in our personal lives than in the educational environment. However, because it is so popular, it is addressed briefly here. File swapping can be an infringement of copyright law, since it involves the sharing of files from one computer to another, usually (1) without obtaining permission from the work's original owners/producers and (2) without following the fair use factors. What makes the concept of file swapping (and other borrowing of materials) even more confusing is that the software and equipment used to make the copies are often created and obtained legally. Thus, you may be able to purchase file-swapping software, but if you use it in the way it is intended to be used, then you have violated copyright law! (This is similar to the copying of movies, computer software, and other works that we will discuss in future chapters. While the equipment and software needed to copy works are usually legal, the actual act of copying such works without permission may not be legal.)

Q Is downloading an educational video game off the Internet, to your iPad, an infringement of copyright law?

A Use the flow chart in figure 6-10 to decide if the copying you want to do is legal according to copyright law. Use the same three criteria in figure 6-9 to decide if you can legally send material to another source electronically.

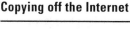

**Copying off the Internet**

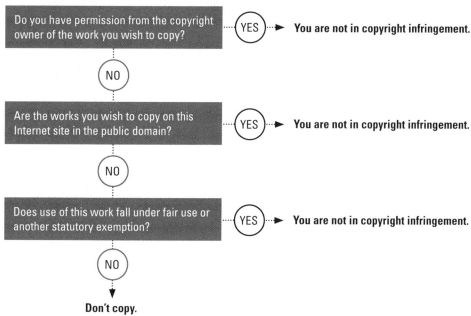

Q Can colleges and universities discipline students who illegally download items off the Internet using the institution's network?

A It is possible. Here is a policy example from one Midwestern university: "Northern Illinois University respects copyrights and it is the policy of NIU to comply with copyright law. Using NIU's network to download or share copyrighted music, movies, television shows, games or any other copyrighted works without the permission of the copyright owner is a violation of NIU policies and may result in legal sanctions, judicial office penalties, and/or network termination, among other results" (Northern Illinois University 2013, 1).

Q   Is it a copyright infringement to attach a one-page chart from an online professional periodical to a wiki on library information skills that the education librarian is creating?

A   Use the flow chart, figure 6-11, to determine how to add a chart to a wiki.

# FIGURE 6-11

**Attaching an Online Chart to a Wiki**

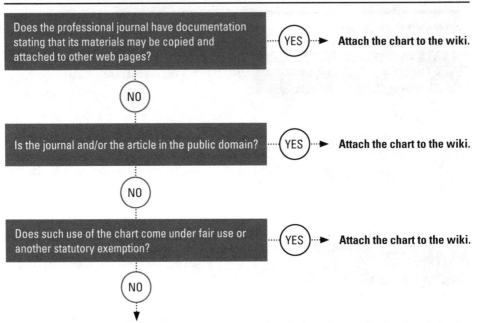

Does the professional journal have documentation stating that its materials may be copied and attached to other web pages? ····( YES )···▶ **Attach the chart to the wiki.**

( NO )

Is the journal and/or the article in the public domain? ····( YES )···▶ **Attach the chart to the wiki.**

( NO )

Does such use of the chart come under fair use or another statutory exemption? ····( YES )···▶ **Attach the chart to the wiki.**

( NO )

**Instead of attaching the chart to the wiki, link to the chart in the online professional periodical.**

Q   Let's suppose that "Helen Avatar" built a building on her own island in Second Life, "a 3-D virtual world entirely created by residents" (Botterbusch and Talab 2009, 9). "Helen," an architect in real life, spent a considerable amount of time creating a unique design with which many other Second Life users were very impressed. Later, as "Helen" traveled through the virtual world, visiting friends, she observed an edifice much like hers on another island. The only difference was the color. She believed that another avatar (computer user's "alter ego" in a web environment) had stolen her design. Can this be considered a virtual world copyright infringement?

A   Because avatars in Second Life can create, as well as buy and sell goods with their Linden Dollars, it could be possible for copyright infringement to occur. Indeed, Second Life has a Digital Millennium Copyright Act site which states in part, "The DMCA provides a process for a copyright owner to give notification to an online service provider concerning alleged copyright infringement. When a valid DMCA notification is received, the service provider responds under this process by taking down the offending content ... these notifications and counter-notifications are real-world legal notices provided outside of the Second Life environment ... Please note: The DMCA provides that you may be liable for damages (including costs and attorneys fees) if you falsely claim that an in-world item is infringing your copyrights. We recommend contacting an attorney if you are unsure whether an in-world object is protected by copyright laws" (Second Life, 1).

**Q**   **Is it a copyright violation to take a screen shot of a particular website?**

**A**   It is possible that it could be. Basically, the person taking a screen shot would be creating a derivative work (a copy of part of a website). Without the proper permissions or licenses and if the website were not in the public domain, such a use could be considered an infringement of the owner of the website's rights.

## INTERNATIONAL COPYRIGHT LAW

**Q**   **Let's assume your class is studying religions around the world. One of your students finds an excellent site on Druids. However, the site comes from another country. Do we need to be concerned with international copyright law when we use the Internet?**

**A**   While the United States belongs to a number of conventions and treaties designed to bring copyright laws worldwide into line (see chapter 5), in fact, there is no one copyright law in the world. Each country has its own laws. However, under the Berne Convention, the idea is that the member nations must treat the works of non-citizens the same as they would protect the works of their own citizens. This means that laws that apply to works created in the United States should also apply to works created in other countries—no matter the format (Yu 2001). Thus, when you use web pages from other countries, you are safest—from a copyright standpoint—if you treat the web pages as if they had been created in the United States. (Your other option—often more complicated—is to research the copyright laws of the country in which the website was created and abide by them.)

**Q**   **Let's assume that you are a librarian in the College of Education's Learning Center. You and a Spanish professor decide to collaborate on a literature unit where the students will read books from Mexico via VoiceThread ("VoiceThread is a powerful web 2.0 technology that allows language learners the opportunity to interact in an online discussion, while practicing good speaking and writing skills" [Barbara 2009].) This activity is "in the Cloud," that is, on the Web and accessible to the public. Is this legal?**

**A**   If such an activity is essential for learning, then it is legal. However, if putting it on the Web is not a crucial part of the assignment, then this public performance could be a copyright infringement. Use the flow chart in figure 6-12 to determine if you can read these books in a VoiceThread.

## FIGURE 6-12

**Reading a Book in the Cloud**

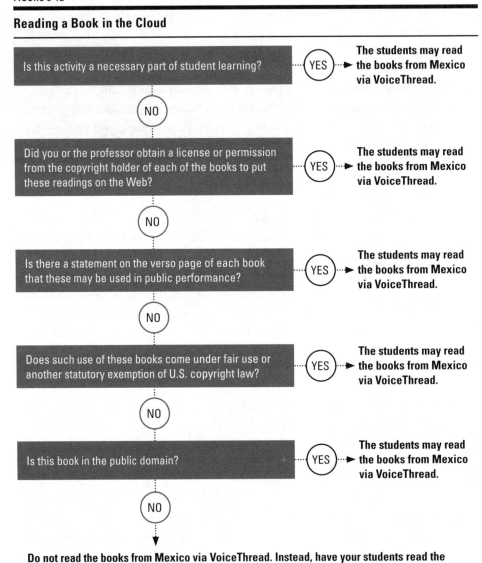

| | |
|---|---|
| Is this activity a necessary part of student learning? | ⋯ YES ⋯▶ **The students may read the books from Mexico via VoiceThread.** |

NO

| | |
|---|---|
| Did you or the professor obtain a license or permission from the copyright holder of each of the books to put these readings on the Web? | ⋯ YES ⋯▶ **The students may read the books from Mexico via VoiceThread.** |

NO

| | |
|---|---|
| Is there a statement on the verso page of each book that these may be used in public performance? | ⋯ YES ⋯▶ **The students may read the books from Mexico via VoiceThread.** |

NO

| | |
|---|---|
| Does such use of these books come under fair use or another statutory exemption of U.S. copyright law? | ⋯ YES ⋯▶ **The students may read the books from Mexico via VoiceThread.** |

NO

| | |
|---|---|
| Is this book in the public domain? | ⋯ YES ⋯▶ **The students may read the books from Mexico via VoiceThread.** |

NO
▼

**Do not read the books from Mexico via VoiceThread. Instead, have your students read the books in the Spanish classroom.**

## AVOIDING COPYRIGHT PROBLEMS

Q   May I borrow material from a nature website to place on an environment site I am creating for my class? Do I need to cite the owner/creator of the work from which I want to borrow?

A   Sometimes the owner of a borrowed work just wants credit for the work. This means that if you are creating a web page or posting to the Web, and you want to borrow from a site (or another work) to do so, you should ask the owner/creator of the material for permission to use his or her work (unless your borrowing comes under the fair use factors, another statutory exemption, or public domain). Then, on your web page, put in a reference crediting the owner/creator of the work from which you borrowed. This reference can be at either the beginning or the end of your web page or at the point of the citation itself. Failure to cite a work, besides possibly making an owner/creator angry, is also plagiarism. So when you borrow anything, cite! (Remember: plagiarism is different from copyright infringement. You can cite the owners for something you have copied and still be infringing on their copyright.)

Q   Is downloading an online dictionary to my iPad the same as downloading it to my laptop, that is, do I need to be aware of copyright law when using newer Internet access tools such as iPads and iPods, Kindles, Nooks, and similar handheld devices?

A   Yes! It does not matter the device; given the same action—copyright law is interpreted the same.

Q   Given the fact that BYOD (Bring Your Own Device) is very common in colleges and universities, especially for students, do higher education librarians and other professionals need to be concerned about new copyright infringements?

A   While the devices that students bring with them to school are evolving (e.g., from laptops to a wide variety of handhelds) and will undoubtedly continue to evolve, higher education personnel do not need to be any more concerned than they already are. Just be aware that new devices and applications may mean new ways of decoding copyright law.

Q   Will cloud computing change how we work with copyright law?

A   Apply copyright law to cloud computing, "a set of pooled computing resources and services delivered over the web . . . resembles a cloud" (Insemot 2012, 1) the same way you would apply the law to anything else that you use on the Web.

Q   Our technology department wants to make an electronic toolbox for the faculty and place it on the college Intranet. In it, they will place educational materials that they think we may need, such as book chapters, lists of Internet links, magazine articles, and even books, if they can be scanned. Since no one will be able to access the electronic toolbox without a password, is there a copyright issue here?

A   Any or all of the items mentioned above may be copyright-protected; whether or not there is a password to get into the site makes no difference. In addition, some of the items may originally be in print and some in a digital format. Since the electronic toolbox means that all works must be digital, this venture can become very confusing. Basically, each work will have to be considered separately in terms of copyright law. See figure 6-13 for more information.

## FIGURE 6-13

**Is an Electronic Toolbox Legal?**

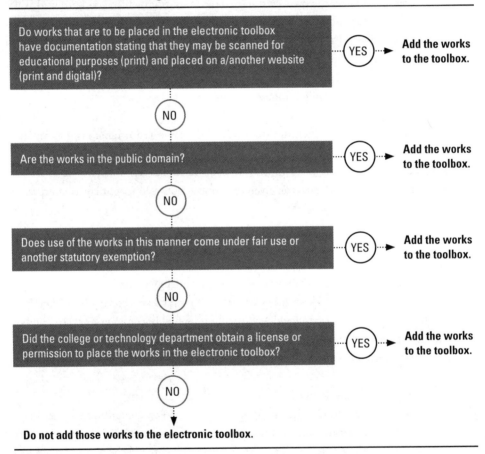

Do works that are to be placed in the electronic toolbox have documentation stating that they may be scanned for educational purposes (print) and placed on a/another website (print and digital)? — YES → **Add the works to the toolbox.**

NO

Are the works in the public domain? — YES → **Add the works to the toolbox.**

NO

Does use of the works in this manner come under fair use or another statutory exemption? — YES → **Add the works to the toolbox.**

NO

Did the college or technology department obtain a license or permission to place the works in the electronic toolbox? — YES → **Add the works to the toolbox.**

NO

**Do not add those works to the electronic toolbox.**

Q   Do we need a copyright officer (or online service provider agent) and what does this person do?

A   Yes, you need one! As of 1998 and the establishment of the Digital Millennium Copyright Act (DMCA), colleges and universities should designate a person to collect all copyright violation reports that occur in your institution. "The online service provider agent is to (1) be listed in the 'Directory of Service Provider Agents for Notification of Claims of Infringement,' found on the U.S. Copyright Office Web site; (2) report all online copyright infringements via the identified school/district (or institution of higher education) to the U.S. Copyright Office; and (3) post all reported infringements on a school web page available to the public. If the school/district (or institution of higher education) does so, then their liability concerning copyright violations that occur via their online service is lessened from what it would be without such a designated agent" (Butler 2009, 34–35).

## CONCLUSION

The twenty-first century is a challenging period to be a college or university librarian or educator, with digital communication devices becoming the norm, while budgets remain the same or decrease. Add to that the confusion over copyright law, which in the best of times can be difficult to interpret. As an educator often trying to do more with less, consider the following questions when borrowing or using another's digital works: Does what I want to borrow fit under the fair use factors? Is what I want to borrow in the public domain? Can I obtain permission to use all or part of this work from the owner/author? If the answer to none of these questions is "yes," then find another work to use or another way to teach the class. Remember that there are ways to work within the law and still have the materials essential for teaching your students. It may be that you just need to be a little creative, read the works' documentations (sometimes the license or documentation actually lets you do more than you think possible), or learn a few grant-writing skills in order to legally obtain the necessary works. In addition, when using the material in this chapter, if you do not find your exact question, choose a similar one to use or follow the generic flow chart in figure 5.1. Technology is evolving rapidly, and it is possible that the one you are using was not available at the publication time of this book.

## REFERENCES

About.com. 2013. "Block Web Page Printing." http://webdesign.about.com/od/advancedcss/qt/block_print.htm.

American Library Association. 2013. "Hypertext Linking and Copyright Issues." www.ala.org/ala/issuesadvocacy/copyright/copyrightarticle/hypertextlinking.cfm.

Barbara. 2009. "Using VoiceThread as a Tool for Language Learning." http://tccl.rit.albany.edu/knilt/index.php/Using_VoiceThread_as_a_Tool_for_Language_Learning.

Besenjak, Cheryl. 1997. *Copyright Plain and Simple*. Franklin Lakes, NJ: Career.

Bettig, Ronald V. 1996. *Copyrighting Culture: The Political Economy of Intellectual Property*. Boulder, CO: Westview.

Borland, John. 2003. "Judge: File-Swapping Tools Are Legal." http://news.com.com/2100-1027
         -998363.html.
———. b. 2003. "Why File Swapping Tide Is Turning." http://news.com.com/2008-1082
         -5078418.html.
Botterbusch, Hope R., and R. S. Talab. 2009. "Copyright and You: Ethical issues in Second Life."
         *TechTrends* 53, no. 1 (January/February): 9.
Brick Marketing. 2013. "What Is Deep Linking?" www.brickmarketing.com/define-deep-linking.htm.
Butler, Rebecca P. 2009. *Smart Copyright Compliance for Schools*. New York: Neal-Schuman.
Facebook. 2013. "Facebook Copyright Policy." www.facebook.com/legal/copyright.php.
Hoffmann, Gretchen McCord. 2001. *Copyright in Cyberspace: Questions and Answers for Librarians*.
         New York: Neal-Schuman.
Insemot. 2012. "5.6 What Is Cloud Computing?" http://www.insemot.eu/en/good-to-know/
         52-what-is-cloud-computing.
"Internet." 2013. *Collins English Dictionary, Complete & Unabridged 10th Edition*. http://dictionary
         .reference.com/browse/Internet.
Jassin, Lloyd J. 2012. "Working with Freelancers: What Every Publisher Should Know about the
         'Work for Hire' Doctrine." www.copylaw.com/new_articles/wfh.html.
LinkedIn. 2013. "Copyright Policy." www.linkedin.com/static?key=copyright_policy.
Northern Illinois University. 2013. "Copyright and File Sharing Facts." http://www.its.niu.edu/its/
         security/copyright.shtml.
Pinterest. 2013. "Copyright." http://about.pinterest.com/copyright.
Rubin, Bonnie Miller. 2010. "Teen, Tween Media Use Rising." *Chicago Tribune*, January 20, 2010,
         section 1: 4.
Second Life. "DMCA: Digital Millennium Copyright Act." http://secondlife.com/corporate/dmca.php.
Shelfari. 2013. "Copyright Policy." www.shelfari.com/CopyrightPolicy.aspx.
Torrans, Lee Ann. 2003. *Law for K–12 Libraries and Librarians*. Westport, CT: Libraries Unlimited.
Twitter. 2013. "Terms of Service." http://twitter.com/tos.
U.S. Copyright Law. 1976. Public Law 94-553, sec. 101, 201.
U.S. Copyright Office. 2006. "Copyright in General." www.copyright.gov/help/faq/faq-general.html.
U.S. Supreme Court Media. 2013. *Community for Creative Non-Violence v. Reid*.
         http://www.oyez.org/cases/1980-1989/1988/1988_88_293.
YouTube. "What Is Copyright?" http://www.youtube.com/yt/copyright/what-is-copyright.html.
Yu, Peter K. 2001. "Conflicts of Laws Issues in International Copyright Cases."
         www.google.com/search?q=Conflicts+of+Laws+Issues+in+International+Copyright+Cases
         &ie=utf-8&oe=utf-8&aq=t&rls=org.mozilla:en-US:official&client=firefox-a.

7

# DVDs, Video Streaming, On Demand, and Copyright Law

## Are the Use of These and Other Movie Formats Legal in College and University Classrooms?

**H**igher education faculty sometimes use fiction and nonfiction DVDs, CDs, videos, and/or video streaming in their classrooms—this is a given. This often-commonplace activity of showing movies in an educational setting has been under fire for years, however, usually due to misunderstandings on the legal use of such items. As we study how to work within copyright law and show movies in education, please keep in mind that most questions and answers in this chapter can apply to any of the formats listed above.

In this chapter, we examine the lawful uses of movies in academia. Questions with more than one answer are presented in flow chart form. Remember, as you review the flow charts in this chapter, you are trying to find any criterion under which you may borrow a work. Therefore, you need only follow each flow chart until you come to that point where you satisfy one of the criteria. Once you reach that point, there is no need to go any further. Additionally, for more information on each area discussed, please refer to the chapter (chapters 1 through 5) in which that particular subject is covered.

## FAIR USE

Q   You discover that the video that you always use to support the unit on sexuality in your introductory health class is falling apart. You ask the Health Sciences librarian if he will transfer it to a DVD along with two other deteriorating sex-education tapes that you use all the time. That way you will have the three readily available when you need them, in a format that should not wear out easily. The original videos can be stored as backup. He suggests that it would be better for your department or the university library system to purchase them on DVD or in another format, if available. You feel that such a purchase would be wasted money. What should be done here?

A   Use the flow chart in figure 7-1 to decide if you should burn a DVD or purchase a copy of the videos in another format. It is important to note here that if you find that you are allowed to copy the videos to DVD that you only show them to your class in the library. Section 108 of the 1976 Copyright Act, and later expanded upon for digital works in section 404 of the Digital Millennium Copyright Act (DMCA) of 1998, permits libraries and archives to make up to three copies (including digital) of unique or deteriorating works, provided the newly digitized copies are only used in the library or archive premises (DMCA 1998). The DMCA also permits libraries and archives "to copy a work into a new format if the original format becomes obsolete—that is, the machine or device used to render the work perceptible is no longer manufactured or is no longer reasonably available in the commercial marketplace" (DMCA 1998, 15). Such a copy is also to be shown only in the library.

## FIGURE 7-1

**Burning Videos to DVDs**

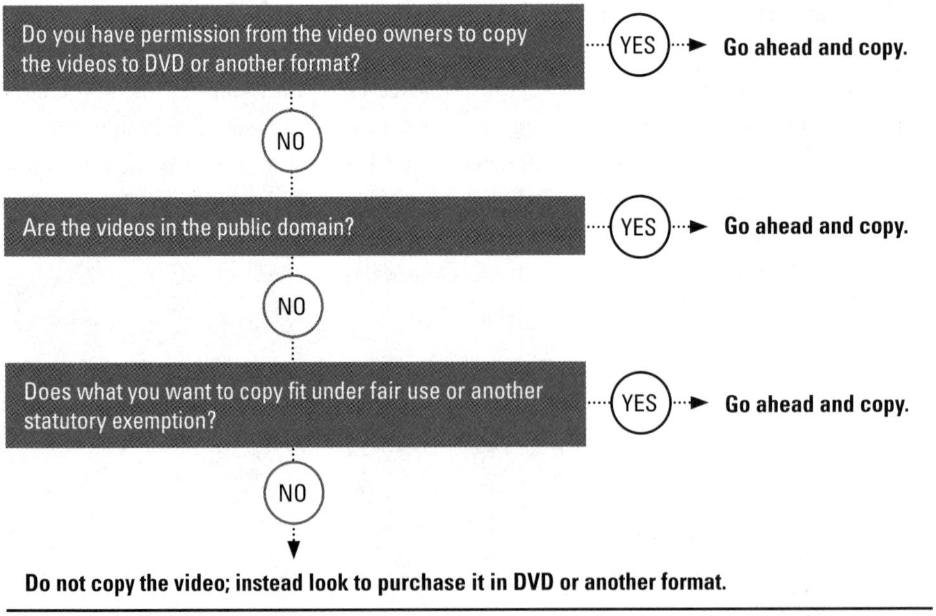

Q   Is a film professor allowed to copy a bunch of movie clips, string them together onto a DVD or CD (or videotape), and use it in a film appreciation class?

A   Use the flow chart in figure 7-2 to decide if this is allowable under copyright law.

## FIGURE 7-2

**Copying Movie Clips**

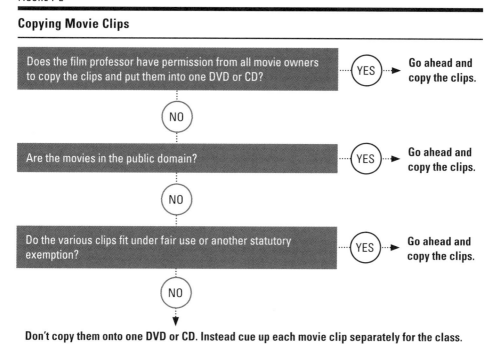

Does the film professor have permission from all movie owners to copy the clips and put them into one DVD or CD? — **YES** ▸ **Go ahead and copy the clips.**

**NO**

Are the movies in the public domain? — **YES** ▸ **Go ahead and copy the clips.**

**NO**

Do the various clips fit under fair use or another statutory exemption? — **YES** ▸ **Go ahead and copy the clips.**

**NO**

**Don't copy them onto one DVD or CD. Instead cue up each movie clip separately for the class.**

Q   May I show a popular movie clip in my anthropology class?

A   Unless the clip is the heart of the work (see chapter 2), showing it should fit under the fair use factors.

Q   I would like to know if there are any alternatives to copyright law when it comes to using movies in the classroom and for research.

A   There are a number of groups that support a broader view of copyright. Among them are Creative Commons, the Free Software Foundation (see chapter 5), and Critical Commons. Such organizations provide information for owners of works to create their own licenses (Creative Commons; GNU Operating System 2013), as well as material on the law, showcases for creative productions, and, in some cases, possible alternatives to copyright guidelines (Critical Commons).

Q   The law librarian has been approached by three professors collaborating on a research project. As part of their research, they are viewing and collecting data from several old films. Can they use pieces of these films when they present their research at a professional conference?

A   Yes, they can. They should always use the least amount they need, cite all films borrowed from, and earn no money from their presentations.

Q   I am a librarian at a private liberal arts college. Can I apply fair use or another statutory exemption to the movies (no matter their format) in my library?

A   Perhaps. All parts of the law still exist, whether you are in a public or private institution. The difference is that while the law remains the same, most statutory exemptions address nonprofit educational venues, in which case they would not apply to your school. Thus, it is best to obtain public performance rights, a license, or permission from the copyright owners to use the movies in your library.

Q   A professor has approached the Reserve Services Department of the university library system and asked if someone there might copy a CD of hers and put the copy on reserve. She says that she needs the original for her work, while her students also need the information for a class she is teaching. What should we do?

A   Chances are that making a copy of the original is a copyright infringement. Please see figure 7-3 for more information.

## FIGURE 7-3

**Making a Second Copy of a CD to Put on Reserve**

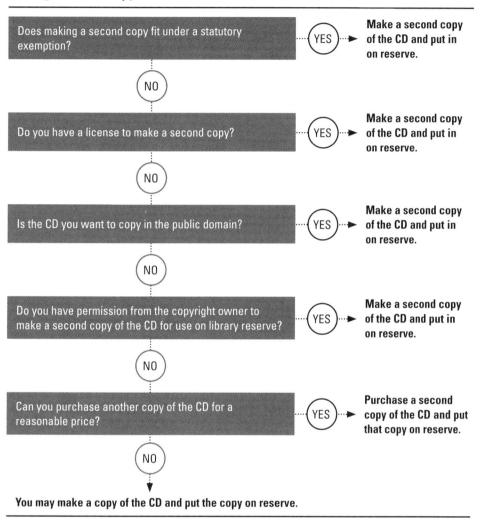

Does making a second copy fit under a statutory exemption? — YES → Make a second copy of the CD and put in on reserve.

NO

Do you have a license to make a second copy? — YES → Make a second copy of the CD and put in on reserve.

NO

Is the CD you want to copy in the public domain? — YES → Make a second copy of the CD and put in on reserve.

NO

Do you have permission from the copyright owner to make a second copy of the CD for use on library reserve? — YES → Make a second copy of the CD and put in on reserve.

NO

Can you purchase another copy of the CD for a reasonable price? — YES → Purchase a second copy of the CD and put that copy on reserve.

NO

You may make a copy of the CD and put the copy on reserve.

## PUBLIC DOMAIN

Q   How do I find out if a movie is in the public domain?

A   Follow the steps in the flow chart in figure 7-4. In addition, the U.S. Copyright Office does not maintain lists of works in the public domain. However for a fee—$165.00 per hour (two-hour minimum) (U.S. Copyright Office 2012)—they will search their records to see if the work you are interested in is part of the public domain. You may also do your own search, either in person or online (www.copyright.gov/help/faq/faq -services.html#whoowns) for free. (Online records are available only for works registered in 1978 and after.) (U.S. Copyright Office 2012).

## FIGURE 7-4

**Public Domain Movies**

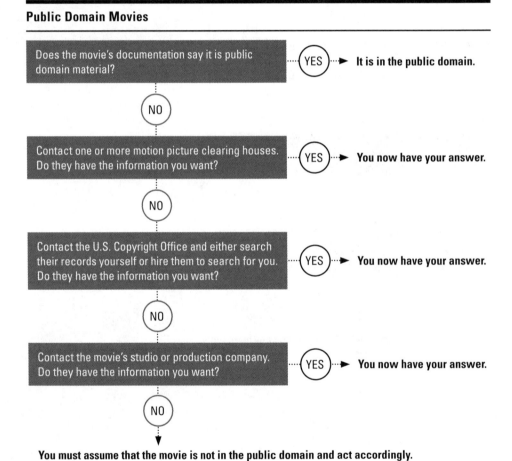

You must assume that the movie is not in the public domain and act accordingly.

Q  My cartography class is studying the history of our geographic area. I understand that there is a governmental film showing old military sites, which I would like to share with my students. However, I cannot get a hold of it. Since government documents are in the public domain, what gives?

A  While most government documents are in the public domain, it does not mean that all are available for public consumption. There are many classified government documents, often denoted as such for security or privacy reasons. In some cases, you may be able to obtain a government document through the Freedom of Information Act, which "requires federal agencies to make certain types of records publicly available" (Fishman 2010, 47).

Q  Are YouTube videos in the public domain?

A  It depends on the video in question. YouTube specifies that it complies with copyright law, and reserves the right to remove offending videos, block use of the site by offenders, and terminate users' accounts (YouTube, 1).

Q  Can I create a parody of a movie that is in the public domain?

A  Yes! (See chapter 3 for more information on public domain.)

Q  How do I place a video that the class has made in the public domain?

A  Put a statement on the video that it is in the public domain; that is all that you need to do.

## DOCUMENTATION AND LICENSES

Q  May I rent an entertainment DVD from a video store or online vendor and use it in my class?

A  Section 110(1) of the copyright law states that it is not an infringement for instructors or students to use videos (including those labeled "for home use only") in the classroom, as long as they are legally obtained, and the use is for face-to-face instruction in a nonprofit educational institution (U.S. Copyright Law 1976). (In today's world, this section of the law can also be applied to DVDs, CDs, and other movie formats.) Use the flow chart in figure 7-5 to decide when you can show a video/CD/DVD or other movie format to your class.

## FIGURE 7-5

**Using Entertainment DVDs in Class**

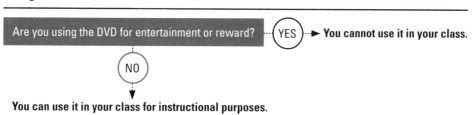

Q   An art instructor encourages her class, based on their memories, to paint characters from favorite movies for an in-class activity. Is this an infringement?

A   If it supports the students' learning, then, no, this is not an infringement.


Q   You are the student-teaching coordinator at your university. A teacher-education student comes to you with a question during your site visit. Here is the question: "The parent–teacher organization in this school is having a 'movie' night in the learning center, showing *Harry Potter and the Sorcerer's Stone*. They are charging $3.00 per person, proceeds to go towards purchasing more learning-center materials. They tell me that they have purchased 'public performance rights,' so it is okay. What are public performance rights?"

A   When users purchase public performance rights, they have purchased the rights to display the work in a public forum (in this case for a movie night at the school). Public performance rights for a movie might be purchased from a vendor, a clearinghouse, or the owner/creator of the work. (See also chapter 4.)


Q   I am the assistant basketball coach at our college. The team spent most of the day working with the local high school team. I would like to reward them with a movie on Friday afternoon. I plan to show it in a classroom on campus. Can I legally do this?

A   Use the flow chart in figure 7-6 to decide if such a showing of the movie is legal. You may find that you have to purchase performance rights. There are also companies that specialize in acquiring permissions from motion picture studios. These companies then sell a license to use all or some (usually listed) of the movies produced by each studio. One example of this type of company is Movie Licensing USA. This organization offers licenses for such studios as Walt Disney, Columbia, DreamWorks, Warner Brothers, and others (Movie Licensing USA).


Please note, in the flow chart in figure 7-6 (as well as in several other flow charts throughout this book), that there is more than one way for the borrower to ask for permission to use a work. You can ask the owner(s) of the work directly for permission, contact a clearinghouse, or purchase a license to borrow the work. If you satisfy the conditions of one of the permission questions, there is no need to follow the flow chart any further.

# FIGURE 7-6

**Using Movies for Rewards**

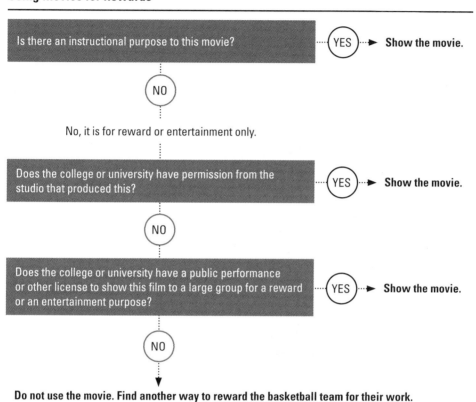

Is there an instructional purpose to this movie? — YES → **Show the movie.**

NO

No, it is for reward or entertainment only.

Does the college or university have permission from the studio that produced this? — YES → **Show the movie.**

NO

Does the college or university have a public performance or other license to show this film to a large group for a reward or an entertainment purpose? — YES → **Show the movie.**

NO

**Do not use the movie. Find another way to reward the basketball team for their work.**

Q    Can the film librarian make a copy of a DVD for a part-time instructor to use if the
     university owns the original, and another instructor wants to use the identical DVD
     at the same time?

A    Probably not. However, there are some instances where this might work. See figure
     7-7.

## FIGURE 7-7

**Copying a DVD**

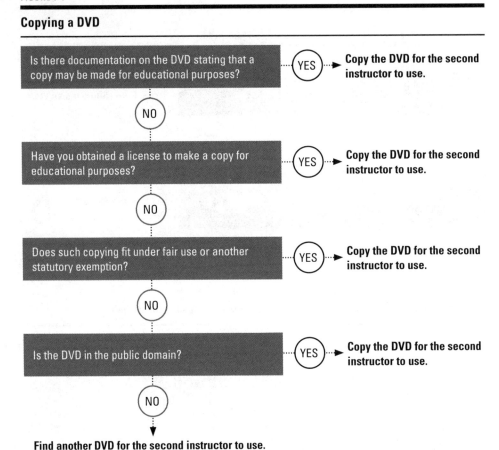

Is there documentation on the DVD stating that a copy may be made for educational purposes? — YES → **Copy the DVD for the second instructor to use.**

NO

Have you obtained a license to make a copy for educational purposes? — YES → **Copy the DVD for the second instructor to use.**

NO

Does such copying fit under fair use or another statutory exemption? — YES → **Copy the DVD for the second instructor to use.**

NO

Is the DVD in the public domain? — YES → **Copy the DVD for the second instructor to use.**

NO

**Find another DVD for the second instructor to use.**

Q   Do schools need to purchase public performance rights for videos if they are educational?

A   If the videos support the class curriculum, they do not need public performance rights. Such rights are needed, however, if the video is used for entertainment or reward purposes.

Q   A colleague wishes to order a DVD of a classic movie to use in an English class. The vendor says that she must purchase a specific licensing agreement. What is going on—shouldn't such use be legal under the classroom exemption?

A   The owner of the DVD's copyright can determine how it is used. If that individual or group wishes to state specific uses via a license, then the educator (or the educator's institution) needs to obtain the license in order to use the movie. If no license is required, then the classroom exemption (Section 110 of the copyright law) will apply.

## PERMISSIONS

Q   I am teaching a technology standards course this spring. Part of the course covers ethics. I plan to have the students read case studies that are on a professional organization's website. Once they have studied a case, I am asking them to create a video vignette based on the case, which they will then present to the class. I would also like to use their vignettes for future classes that I teach on this subject. Can I do so?

A   As long as the use of case studies and the subsequent video creation are for a curricular purpose and stay in the original classroom (or are used by the students for a portfolio), then such use is OK. Showing these videos to other classes, for educational reasons, also works under the classroom exemption (17 USC 110). (However, one could argue that getting permission from the students, whose videos you plan to use, is the cautious thing to do. It certainly could create goodwill with former students.)

Q   As a new mathematical sciences assistant professor, you conceive the idea of having your undergraduate students create a website dealing with basic algebraic equations. To catch the viewer's eye, you want to add clips from popular movies that have a math or numerical theme. How do you obtain clearance to use videos and DVDs that you plan to place on an official university website?

A   Use the flow chart in figure 7-8 to decide which clips— if any—you can use legally.

## FIGURE 7-8

**Borrowing Movie Clips**

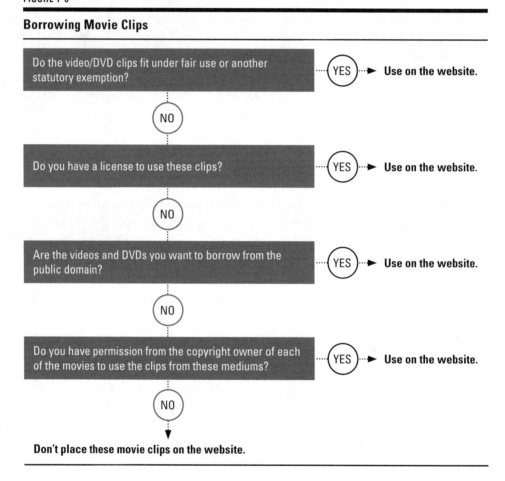

Do the video/DVD clips fit under fair use or another statutory exemption?  — YES ► **Use on the website.**

NO

Do you have a license to use these clips?  — YES ► **Use on the website.**

NO

Are the videos and DVDs you want to borrow from the public domain?  — YES ► **Use on the website.**

NO

Do you have permission from the copyright owner of each of the movies to use the clips from these mediums?  — YES ► **Use on the website.**

NO

**Don't place these movie clips on the website.**

Q    Am I allowed to show a DVD over a closed-circuit system to several classrooms at the same time?

A    Possibly. Use the flow chart in figure 7-9 to decide.

## FIGURE 7-9

**Closed-Circuit Systems and DVDs**

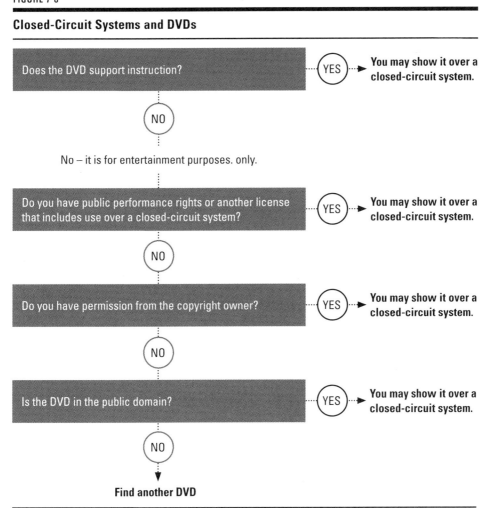

**Q**   What is "video-on-demand," and can I ask the campus technology coordinator to obtain a movie for me to use in my classroom this way?

**A**   "Video-on-demand. . . . make(s) it possible . . . to select . . . motion pictures . . . and order them and receive them instantly . . . over the Internet . . . or satellite broadcast" (Donaldson 2008, 431). For example, it may be possible for your campus technology coordinator to find an Internet source—such as Movielink, Blockbuster, or iTunes—and obtain a movie (free, for rent, or for sale) for you to show in your classroom via a computer and projection device. In such a case, he and you need to be aware of any specific licenses or copyright policies on these sites that might determine how the film can be used. For more information, see figure 7-10.

**Q**   Can a student copy Google images off the Internet for use in a film he is creating without getting permission to use the works?

**A**   If such use is for a learning purpose, such as a class assignment, and the images will be used only in the classroom or for the student's personal portfolio, then yes, such use is possible.

**Q**   I'm teaching a literature class, and I would like to show book trailers off YouTube to my students as part of a class lesson. Do I need to obtain permission from YouTube or the owner of each book trailer to do so?

**A**   No, you do not, as long as the use is for an educational purpose.

**Q**   Can instructors use personal video-streaming accounts in the classroom?

**A**   That is actually a contractual issue and depends on the type of license you agreed to when you obtained your personal account. Check with your provider.

## YOU CREATE IT, YOU OWN IT

**Q**   Imagine that you are an associate professor at a large midwestern university. You have just finished a unit on copyright law, so your students are focused on borrowing legally. You assign the students, in groups of four, to make a short movie. All groups elect to use original materials in their movies. They figure that this way they will own the whole work, and thus no copyright violations will occur. One group chooses to film its movie outside city hall in front of a new statue the city purchased a year ago. While the sculpture, an unusual piece by a new female artist, is very prominently displayed in their film, it is not the subject of said film. Is there a copyright violation here?

**A**   If the artist has chosen to retain her copyright of the sculpture, even though she sold the sculpture to the city, it is possible there is a violation here, since "it is a fundamental tenet of copyright that certain pieces of art, including sculpture, are eligible for copyright protection. . . . Consequently, permission must be obtained from the copyright

## FIGURE 7-10

**Using Video on Demand**

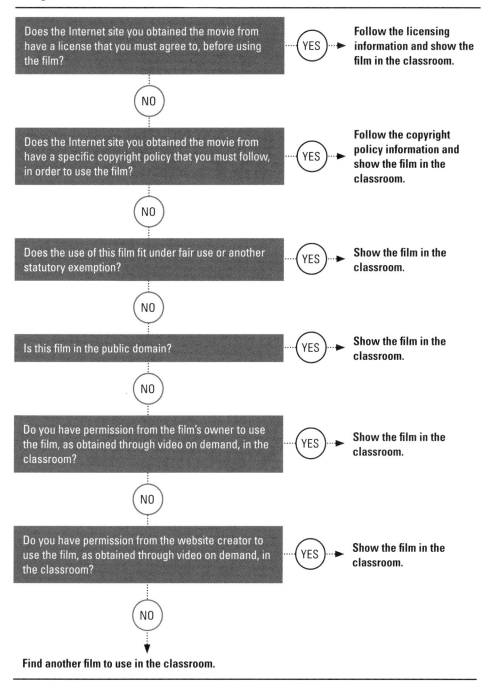

Does the Internet site you obtained the movie from have a license that you must agree to, before using the film? — **YES** → Follow the licensing information and show the film in the classroom.

NO

Does the Internet site you obtained the movie from have a specific copyright policy that you must follow, in order to use the film? — **YES** → Follow the copyright policy information and show the film in the classroom.

NO

Does the use of this film fit under fair use or another statutory exemption? — **YES** → Show the film in the classroom.

NO

Is this film in the public domain? — **YES** → Show the film in the classroom.

NO

Do you have permission from the film's owner to use the film, as obtained through video on demand, in the classroom? — **YES** → Show the film in the classroom.

NO

Do you have permission from the website creator to use the film, as obtained through video on demand, in the classroom? — **YES** → Show the film in the classroom.

NO

**Find another film to use in the classroom.**

holder in order to reproduce images of the sculpture" (Copyright Website 2011). (A possible exception might be if the sculpture were the subject of the movie. In such a case, it might constitute fair use. See chapter 2 for a discussion of fair use.) Students often "get away" with copyright violations that occur as part of a school assignment. However, it is best to follow copyright law in all instances. Figure 7-11 shows a flow chart that provides more direction.

## FIGURE 7-11

**Statues, Filming, and Copyright**

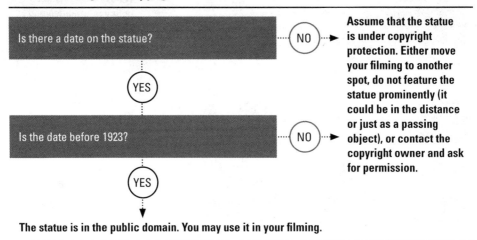

| | |
|---|---|
| Is there a date on the statue? | NO → Assume that the statue is under copyright protection. Either move your filming to another spot, do not feature the statue prominently (it could be in the distance or just as a passing object), or contact the copyright owner and ask for permission. |
| YES | |
| Is the date before 1923? | NO → |
| YES | |

The statue is in the public domain. You may use it in your filming.

Q   Assume that you are a graduate student in elementary education. You plan to teach a unit on folk and fairy tales, as part of an internship you are taking at a local elementary school. You decide to have the students you are working with (second graders) put on a program for the rest of the school. The idea is for your students to act out the stories of "Cinderella," "Aladdin," and "The Three Little Pigs" after they have read and interpreted the stories. There will be no written script. You resolve to tape this program and donate it to the school library. You also have the idea of interspersing your students' story interpretations with excerpts from commercial movies of "Cinderella," "Aladdin," and "The Three Little Pigs." Is it a copyright infringement to read and interpret the original stories on a DVD or video? To add the commercial excerpts?

A   Classical stories and characters, including the three discussed above, are in the public domain and are frequently borrowed by motion picture companies, book publishers, musicians, and others. So, no, it is not an infringement to tape your students' interpretations of public-domain folk and fairy tales. However, derivative pieces of public-domain works can once again attain copyright protection when the borrower puts his or her "stamp" on those revised parts of the work. For example, when an illustrator chooses to draw Snow White as an African American and the seven dwarfs as Asian, this "new" interpretation of old work places this interpretation under copyright protection for the illustrator or owner of the work. Thus, while the classroom exemption may apply for the use of the excerpts, it is still in your best interest to make sure that the excerpts of commercial movies you borrow are fair use, under public domain, or that you have the needed permissions or licenses. The flow chart in figure 7-12 will help you decide if you can legally add excerpts from commercial movies to a class DVD or video.

## FIGURE 7-12

**Adding Commercial Film Excerpts to Class-Created DVDs and Videos**

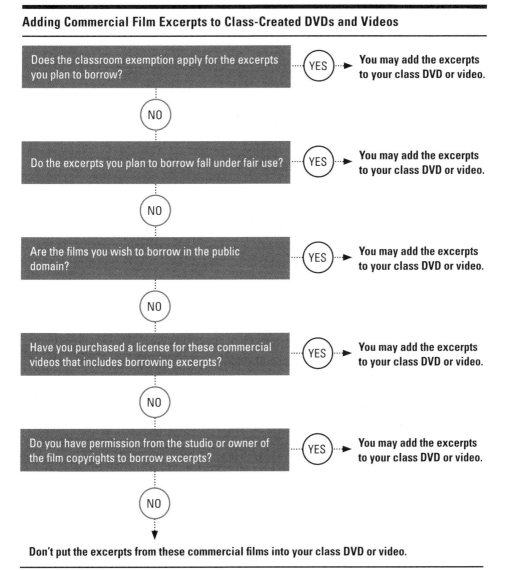

Don't put the excerpts from these commercial films into your class DVD or video.

Q    The university instructional technology (IT) group has just purchased a VHS to
     DVD converter. They are advertising that they will take any and all campus videos
     and transfer them to DVD, saying that since such conversions are for education, this
     use is OK. Is this true?

A    Absolutely not! There is no such thing as a legal blanket policy that allows the transfer-
     ring of a work from one format to another—even for educational purposes. Essentially,
     by using the converter in this manner, the university instructional technology group
     is creating any number of derivative works. However, if not available for purchase or
     rent—on a case-by-case basis—the IT group may be able to determine which videos
     can be copied and which cannot. See figure 7-13 for additional directions.

## FIGURE 7-13

**Transferring Videos to DVDs**

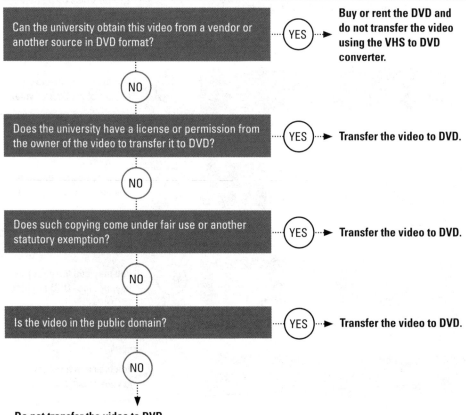

Do not transfer the video to DVD.
Instead encourage university personnel to use it "as is" or find a similar DVD to use.

## INFRINGEMENTS AND PENALTIES

Q  Suppose your biology class is studying bird beaks. You find a great CD on birding in South America, which you check out from the public library. Can you use it in class without violating copyright law?

A  Yes, you can use this CD in class without it being considered a copyright infringement. This is because you are using it for an instructional purpose.

Q  Imagine you teach science for a small college. You know of a great movie that supports your unit on planets. However, you are afraid to purchase it because it talks about evolution (of the planets), and mention of evolution is not encouraged at your particular institution. You decide to purchase a special DVD player that can mute or skip over objectionable parts of DVDs as they are played. Your administrator refuses to fund your purchase, stating that such a player is in violation of copyright law. Is it?

A  There are filtering DVD players available, such as ClearPlay and TV Guardian, which can block or skip unacceptable DVD content as it is viewed (Clearplay 2012; Family Safe Media 2013). Use of such equipment is legal, since you have retained the original item and are just not using selected parts of it.

Q  Within the last year, the administration at your technical college has obtained (1) several recordable DVD drives and copying software; (2) CD burners for all instructor computers and half of the lab computers; (3) more DVD and CD players; and (4) more audio-recording devices. The idea behind all this is that with these recording devices, the school will be able to take more material off popular television, movies, CDs, and the Internet, copy them for use, and eventually save money by purchasing less. At the moment, the focus at your technical college is on burning films to DVDs. Overall your administration feels that they will save money. Do such actions infringe on copyrights?

A  Yes! While the past few years have seen a flood of hardware and software that can be used for copying become available on the market, this does not mean that the copies made from such media are legal. Under copyright law, in this case, fair use, public domain, permissions, and licensing of materials still apply. Therefore, do not use the items purchased for your technical college for illegal copying. It is in violation of copyright law and subject to penalty.

Q  How does a library replace a DVD that has been "lost or stolen"?

A  This is a confusing piece of the law. For this question, look to part (d) of Section 108 of the copyright law: Limitations on Exclusive Rights: Reproduction by Libraries and Archives: "The rights of reproduction and distribution under this section apply to a copy, made from the collection of a library or archives where the user makes his or her request or from that of another library or archives of no more than one article or other contribution to a copyrighted collection" (U.S. Copyright Law 1976: Section 108 (d)). In layman's terms, you can borrow the item in question from another library and make a copy.

## INTERNATIONAL COPYRIGHT LAW

Q   One of your foreign students has returned to campus from his home in Southeast Asia. While there, he purchased a DVD copy of a movie, one that has recently come out in the theaters in the United States. The DVD's jewel case has no movie photograph on the cover, there is no copyright information anywhere on the case or DVD, and only the name of the movie is on the DVD. Furthermore, your student tells you that the quality of the DVD is not good. To make things more complex, you search the Internet and find the same movie there as well. What's going on?

A   Chances are that the DVD and Internet copies of the movie are pirated. Piracy, the unauthorized replication or use of media, is not part of copyright law, but it is often associated with it, since pirated items are frequently found to be in copyright violation. Film piracy occurs when an individual or group (1) obtains a copy of a movie on disk or tape from someone in the film distribution area before the authorized release date or (2) actually sneaks into a theater and tapes the movie as it is shown. The stolen copy is then brought to a clandestine production area, where it is mass-produced on disk or digitally broken into file pieces easy enough to put on the Internet. At that point it is then distributed. Some such organizations pirate for monetary purposes; others (especially those who place such films on the Web) do it because they feel such media should be free for all consumers (Munoz and Healey 2003). Since the movie is still in the theaters in the United States, it is highly likely that use of your student's movie would violate United States copyright law. In addition, the United States belongs to several international organizations with treaty agreements in the area of copyright (see chapter 5). Depending on who produced the pirated film and where, this means that such pirating could also be in violation of copyright in other countries. Bottom line: don't use the DVD that your student brought from overseas or the movie you found on the Web.

Q   I teach at an American university overseas. I recently found a fantastic video clip on the Web that I would like to use in my class. It appears to have a Creative Commons license. Exactly what does that mean for my use of the clip?

A   It does not matter where you teach; the same Creative Commons license will apply. What does matter is what rights the original owner of the video specified under the license. In order to use the video, you will need to follow the exact stipulations that the original owner placed on the work through the Creative Commons agreement.

Q   Can we stream a video on a Japanese website to our language lab for use with students?

A   Japan belongs to several of the same copyright conventions as does the United States. Thus, treat a video from a Japanese website the same as you would treat one from a U.S. website.

Q   I teach in a private international college with an American curriculum. Can we apply fair use and the classroom exemption in our use of DVDs and videos?

A   No, just because you have an American curriculum does not mean that you can apply U.S. laws to the works you use in your schools. Instead, apply the copyright laws for the country in which the school resides.

## AVOIDING COPYRIGHT PROBLEMS

Q  I am the band director at a major East Coast university. Our football team is playing in a conference game in another state, and we are taking the band along. This is a university-sanctioned outing. The bus ride each way is seven hours long. The band members would like to bring personal DVDs (commercial entertainment films) along to watch on the buses. (The buses we are chartering have TVs and DVD players.) Can we do so legally?

A  Use the flow chart in figure 7-14 to decide if you can legally show personal DVDs on the band buses.

## FIGURE 7-14

**Using Personal DVDs on University-Sanctioned Outings**

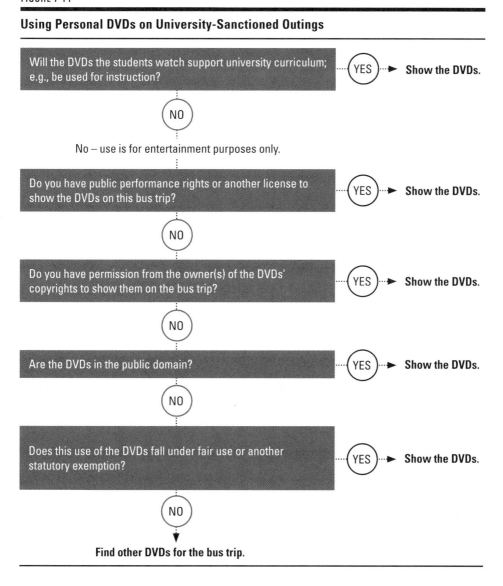

Q    I purchased this DVD from a local store—may I use it in class?

A    As has been shown throughout this chapter, that depends on how you want to use it. See figure 7-15 for more information.

## FIGURE 7-15

### Using Locally Purchased DVDs in Class

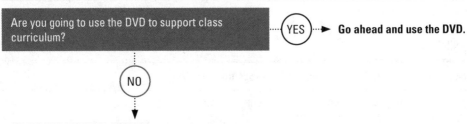

**DON'T USE THE DVD, UNLESS:**
- you have purchased public performance rights;
- you have a license to use for class entertainment purposes; or
- you have permission from the copyright owner to use it for other than curricular purposes.

Q    Can the president of the student Boogie Board Association (yes, our campus is close to the beach!) show several film clips on body-boarding in Hawaii to the group, if we are meeting on campus in the student union?

A    Probably/maybe/it depends. Look to figure 7-16, "Using Film Clips Outside of the Classroom for a University Organization," for more on this issue.

## FIGURE 7-16

### Using Film Clips Outside of the Classroom for a University Organization

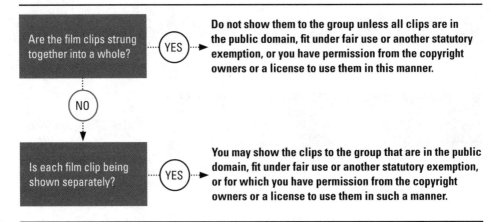

Q I am a film librarian in a small university library system. I am so tired of being the "copyright police." Is there anything online that I can just send people to, so they might be reminded—in a nonconfrontational way—that copyright is an issue that they need to address?

A There are many "cute but informative" things on the Web that may help you: cartoons, a graphic novel, and a YouTube clip are some examples (Aoki et al. 2006; National Institute for the Defense of Competition. . . 2001; Teaching Copyright).

Q I am a part-time instructor at a small college in my hometown. When I teach a beginning kinesiology class, I have a favorite movie that I like to show. Some of the full-time instructors have seen this, and they would like to use it also. As a favor to the department, can I burn the movie to a CD and donate it to the learning center? Is there a copyright problem here?

A In all probability, you would be creating an unauthorized copy. Don't do it! (For your information, libraries can sometimes make copies of works that are deteriorating, damaged, or missing, if no replacements can be found, or replacements are not at a fair price. This exemption can be found in Section 108 of the Copyright Law of the United States.)

Q Your dean informs all full-time and adjunct faculty in the college that they may not use any DVDs unless they have been purchased by the college learning center. You argue that there are many places DVDs can come from and still be used. Who is right?

A You are. As long as the film is being shown for an instructional purpose, you can rent it from a video store, check it out from the university or public library, borrow it from a student, purchase it from a discount store, or get it from other sources.

Q What is copyright preregistration and how can it affect the students and faculty that we work with in library settings?

A "Preregistration is a service intended for works that have had a history of prerelease infringement. It focuses on the infringement of movies, recorded music, and other copyrighted materials before copyright owners have had the opportunity to market fully their products . . . You *may benefit* by preregistering your work if:

- you think it's likely someone may infringe your work *before* it is released; and
- you have started your work but have not finished it" (U.S. Copyright Office 2011, 1).

Q Can the technology specialist legally stream an educational film he found on the Web to more than one science classroom at the same time?

A Video-streaming, which "allows for Internet access to entire copies of motion pictures . . . subject to whatever constraints the streaming source places on access" (Lutzker 2010, 1), must follow copyright law the same as the use of any other movie. In addition, the streaming source, as Lutzker (2010) says above, may have a license or grant specific permissions to the users of the film in question. Follow the Internet sources' license/ specific permissions first, if these are available. See also figure 7-17.

## FIGURE 7-17

**Video Streaming and Copyright**

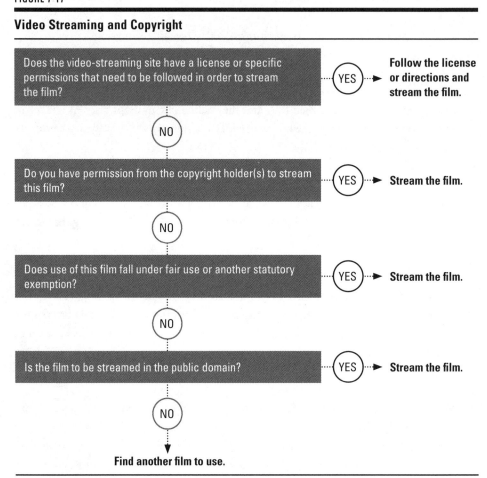

## CONCLUSION

In colleges and universities today, many copyright questions deal with the use of DVDs, CDs, videos, and/or video streaming. Because copyright law is so gray, although there are general rules, the critical answers to DVD/CD/video/video streaming use are often missing. The questions, answers, and flow charts in this chapter are designed to help you as you use both instructional and entertainment media in the library and college classrooms. For your information, while we are more likely in the twenty-first century to be using DVDs and films obtained via the Web, examples using videos and movie CDs have been kept in this chapter for those institutions where the technology may be less current. Please remember that, for the purposes of this chapter, all the mentioned media can be used interchangeably for any movie/film format.

## REFERENCES

Aoki, Keith, et al. 2006. "Tales from the Public Domain: Bound by Law?" http://web.law.duke.edu/cspd/comics.

Clearplay. 2012. Homewww.clearplay.com.

Copyright Website. 2011. "Copyright Casebook: Batman Forever and the Water Vampire." www.benedict.com/Visual/Batman/Batman.aspx.

Creative Commons. "About: What Is CC?" http://creativecommons.org/about/what-is-cc.

Critical Commons. "About." http://www.criticalcommons.org/about-us.

The Digital Millennium Copyright Act of 1998 [DMCA]. 1998. "U.S. Copyright Office Summary." Washington, DC: U.S. Copyright Office.

Donaldson, Michael C. 2008. *Clearance & Copyright: Everything You Need to Know for Film and Television*. Los Angeles: Silman-James.

Family Safe Media. 2013. www.familysafemedia.com/tv_guardian_summary.html.

Fishman, Stephen. 2010. *The Public Domain: How to Find & Use Copyright-Free Writings, Music, Art & More*. Berkeley, CA: Nolo.

GNU Operating System. 2013. www.gnu.org.

Lutzker, Arnold P. 2010. "Educational Video Streaming: A Short Primer." *AIME News* 24, no. 1 (Spring): 1–4.

Movie Licensing USA. "Studios We Represent." www.movlic.com/studios.html.

Munoz, Lorenza, and Jon Healey. 2003. "Studio Waging Uphill Fight Against Bootlegging." *Chicago Tribune*, December 7, Arts & Entertainment, 16.

National Institute for the Defense of Competition and Protection of Intellectual Property (INDECOPI) and the World Intellectual Property Organization (WIPO). 2001. "Copyright." http://www.wipo.int/freepublications/en/copyright/484/wipo_pub_484.pdf.

Plumi. 2009. "Critical Commons: About Us." http://criticalcommons.org/about-us.

Teaching Copyright. "A Fair(y) Use Tale." http://www.teachingcopyright.org/handouts/a-fair%28y%29-use-tale.

U.S. Copyright Law. 1976. Public Law 94-553.

U.S. Copyright Office. 2013. www.copyright.gov.

U.S. Copyright Office. 2012. "Copyright: Can I Use Someone Else's Work? Can Someone Else Use Mine?" www.copyright.gov/help/faq/faq-fairuse.html.

———. 2012b. "Copyright: Fees." www.copyright.gov/docs/fees.html.

U.S. Copyright Office. 2011. "Preregister Your Work." http://www.copyright.gov/prereg.

YouTube. "Frequently Asked Copyright Questions." http://www.youtube.com/yt/copyright/faq.html.

# 8

# Television and Copyright Law

## What Are the Legalities of Using Television in the Higher Education Environment?

Recordable DVDs and digital video recorders, cable channels, satellite TV, streaming video, place-shifting technologies, TV recording/computer software, and television viewing and taping have come a long way from the three channels and black-and-white vision of a half century ago. As such new technologies evolve, so too, do the questions surrounding them, especially as they pertain to use by faculty, librarians, and others who work in higher education.

Activities such as using streaming video in the classroom, making a copy of a program from a cable network for class, stringing together television advertisements for an assignment, or saving and using a copy of a popular television broadcast year after year create the possibility of copyright infringement, whether you realize it or not. However, there are ways to borrow from television without infringing on copyright law. How do you recognize legal from illegal use of television programs in higher education? The discussion in this chapter will help with this endeavor.

The questions that follow cover television programs, educators, and copyright. Questions with more than one answer are presented in flow chart form. Remember, when you use the flow charts in this chapter, you are trying to find any criterion under which you may borrow a work. Therefore, you need only to follow each flow chart until you come to that point where you satisfy one of the criteria. Once you reach that point, there is no need to go any further. For more information on each area discussed, please refer to the chapter (chapters 1 through 5) in which that particular subject is covered.

## FAIR USE

Q    When you tape a television show for curricular use, what rules apply?

A    Well, that depends. Let's assume that you are taping off a major broadcast network (i.e., a network that can be received via cable or not). Called "off-air" taping, there are several guidelines that apply to this type of instructional taping. These are publicly recognized as the "Guidelines for Off-Air Recording of Broadcast Programming for Educational Purposes" (Guidelines for Off-Air Recording. . . 1981). Be aware that these guidelines (below) are only in effect "in the course of relevant teaching activities" (U.S. Congress 1984). For your information, most copyright guidelines are meant to interpret the fair use factors found in the 1976 Copyright Act, sec. 107. One of the ways to access this is through the U.S. Copyright Offices' website (www.copyright.gov).

- During the first 10 days after taping, the programs may be viewed by the class for instruction once and repeated once for reinforcement.
- Off-air taped programs may be retained for 45 days. The last 35 days, the teacher may view the tape for evaluation purposes only.
- Programs may be taped at individual teachers' requests, but not for anticipated requests.
- After 45 days, the tape should be erased.
- Location for performance of the off-air taped program should be either in classrooms or other areas used for instructional purposes; in one building, cluster of buildings or a campus; or in the residences of those students who receive formal home instruction.
- The taped program may not be edited. However, you do not have to use the whole thing in class.
- This is a one-time only opportunity. Teachers may not ask for the same program to be taped more than once.
- Taped program must be used for educational use only.
- In some cases, more than one copy may be made of a tape if it is necessary to meet teachers' needs. In such a case, rules for the extra copies are the same as those for the original.
- All off-air copying must include the copyright notice found on the broadcasted program.
- Ask the copyright holder if you need more rights than those normally assigned to educators. Copyright holders often say "yes" to educational purposes.
- Some channels, such as PBS, give more rights (than those above) to educators. Check with the individual networks for this information (Torrans 2003).

Q    Now let's assume that the television program you wish to tape for curricular purposes is from either a cable or satellite network. What rules apply in these cases?

A    In both cases, you now need to follow the specific educational copying criteria as determined by the cable or satellite channel. (Such criteria are often found on websites for particular networks or in network publications.) With these types of broadcasts, there is no one set of copying rights available—all rights are determined by the individual copyright owners.

Q   **Last Monday night one of the major networks aired a special on social networking. You tape it to use in your class. Before showing it to the students, you delete the commercials from the tape. Can you legally cut the commercials out of a taped network broadcast without obtaining permission from the network?**

A   No, you cannot. By cutting out the commercials, you have created a derivative work. This does not constitute a fair use (see chapter 2). However, you can show the social networking special basically as you wish by using the remote to run through each commercial. You may also show a fair-use portion of the tape, which does not include a commercial. In other words, while you may not alter a program, you do not have to use all parts of it.

Q   **Let's imagine that you are teaching a freshman psychology class. There are several popular daytime talk shows that feature people chatting about their problems. You decide to copy short segments, aired during a single week, from these programs and compile them into one tape for class discussion the following week. Is this legal?**

A   No. Once again, you have prepared a derivative work. Under copyright law, you may not do this without permission. What you can do—although it is more cumbersome— is tape each segment (assuming each use fits under the fair use factors) on a different tape or DVR. Then pop each taped segment into the appropriate player as you need it. (For information on permissions and obtaining licenses for such use, please see chapter 4, "Obtaining Permission," as well as the sections "Documentation and Licenses" and "Permissions" in this chapter.)

Q   **Can I copy the visual track off of a TV program for use with my students?**

A   No. By taking the sound off the show, you have created a new work. However, you can overcome this by turning down the sound on the TV/monitor when showing the students the program.

Q   **I understand that after forty-five days, I may no longer use a television program I have taped. However, it is a great program. I want to use it every semester. Therefore, I plan to ask several of my students to also tape it. I will then use one of their tapes each semester. That way, I can keep using the program for at least four semesters. Is that OK?**

A   No, it is not OK. Off-air recordings cannot be recorded more than once for use by the same instructor, no matter who records them or how many times the program is broadcast (Guidelines for Off-Air Recording. . . 1981). In this case, it would be best if you purchased the tape from the network.

## PUBLIC DOMAIN

**Q**   A professor in the journalism department has called the library and asked if he can tape a portion of the daily activities of the U.S. House of Representatives off C-SPAN for a class. What should I tell him?

**A**   Tell him "yes." Floor proceedings for both the House and Senate are in the public domain (C-SPAN Video Library).

**Q**   Martin Luther King Jr.'s birthday is coming. I'd like to show my students his "I Have a Dream" speech. One of the major networks has a version. May I use it?

**A**   Use the flow chart in figure 8-1 to decide if you can show the speech you have taped from network television.

## FIGURE 8-1

**Taping Off a Major Network**

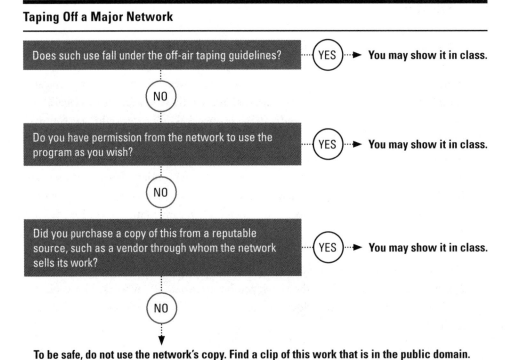

To be safe, do not use the network's copy. Find a clip of this work that is in the public domain.

## DOCUMENTATION AND LICENSES

**Q**   A college professor is teaching a World War II history class, and has found a great special about the Holocaust on a cable channel. Is she allowed to use it in her class?

**A**   Perhaps. The flow chart in figure 8-2 will help with this decision. Many cable networks automatically provide educational rights for a selected period of time (their determination). For example, Cable in the Classroom often grants rights for at least a year from the air date of the program (Cable in the Classroom). Numerous cable networks post copyright guidelines and taping rights on the Internet. It is in an educator's best interest to search the Web before taping, for such procedures.

## FIGURE 8-2

**Using Taped Cable Programs in the Classroom**

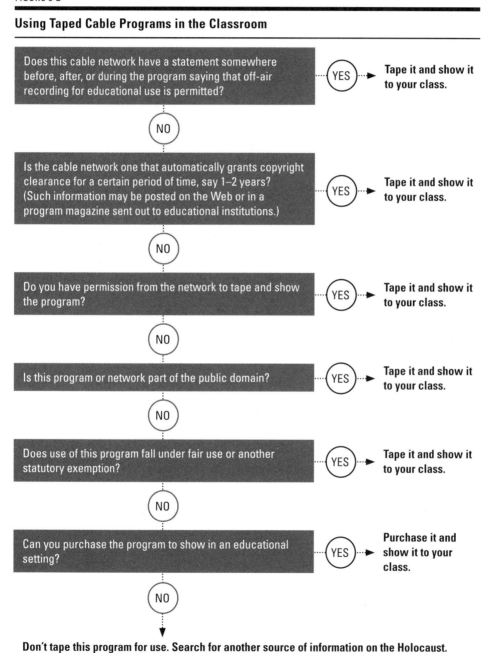

Does this cable network have a statement somewhere before, after, or during the program saying that off-air recording for educational use is permitted? — YES → **Tape it and show it to your class.**

NO

Is the cable network one that automatically grants copyright clearance for a certain period of time, say 1–2 years? (Such information may be posted on the Web or in a program magazine sent out to educational institutions.) — YES → **Tape it and show it to your class.**

NO

Do you have permission from the network to tape and show the program? — YES → **Tape it and show it to your class.**

NO

Is this program or network part of the public domain? — YES → **Tape it and show it to your class.**

NO

Does use of this program fall under fair use or another statutory exemption? — YES → **Tape it and show it to your class.**

NO

Can you purchase the program to show in an educational setting? — YES → **Purchase it and show it to your class.**

NO

**Don't tape this program for use. Search for another source of information on the Holocaust.**

Q   I was reading the educator's guide for a cable network program, and I see a broadcast on Mendel's genetic research that I would like to show to my biology undergraduates. Since we have cable in our building, and this network is on our cable system, I assume that we can show this live to the students. Am I correct?

A   Unless there is a statement to the contrary at the beginning and/or end of the program or in the cable network's educator's guide, then yes, you may show the program live to your biology students.

Q   I am a new librarian in the college of education's learning center. There is a TiVo system in our center, and instructors are requesting that I use it to tape shows for them to use in the classroom. They really like the idea that they can skip the ads with this system, making it easier to teach. I am concerned that they are now working with derivative works, and these are illegal. Am I correct? What should I do?

A   Essentially a TiVo system works as a digital video recorder; that is, the ads are there, whether the teacher runs through them or not. Thus, there is no derivative work involved in using this system. Consider each program taped through TiVo as you would the off-air taping of any show—is it a major broadcast or from cable or satellite? Then act accordingly (see discussions above for major broadcasts and cable and satellite networks).

## PERMISSIONS

Q   Is it okay to tape a television program for instructional use in my classroom?

A   The answer varies with the source of the program. Use the flow chart in figure 8-3 to determine what you may do.

## FIGURE 8-3

**Taping Television Programs for Instructional Use**

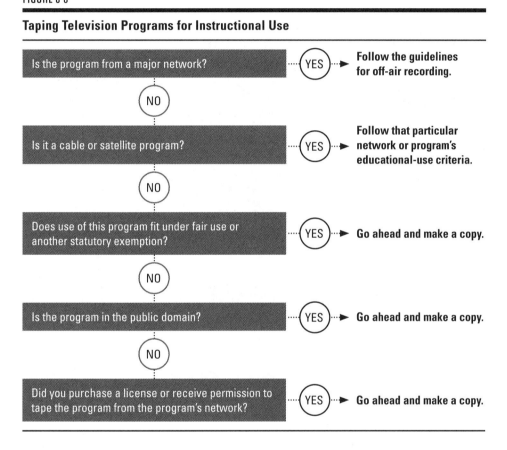

| | |
|---|---|
| Is the program from a major network? —— YES | Follow the guidelines for off-air recording. |
| NO | |
| Is it a cable or satellite program? —— YES | Follow that particular network or program's educational-use criteria. |
| NO | |
| Does use of this program fit under fair use or another statutory exemption? —— YES | Go ahead and make a copy. |
| NO | |
| Is the program in the public domain? —— YES | Go ahead and make a copy. |
| NO | |
| Did you purchase a license or receive permission to tape the program from the program's network? —— YES | Go ahead and make a copy. |

Q   I'm a technology coordinator at a small community college. May I make more than one copy of an off-air recording if two or more of my instructors need it at the same time?

A   Yes. Just follow the "Guidelines for Off-Air Recording" (Guidelines for Off-Air Recording. . . 1981).

Q    Our junior college has a satellite dish. Since the administration pays for this piece of
     equipment and the television access it provides, as a teacher, I feel that taping pro-
     grams off it should be free. Am I allowed to copy programs off-air from satellite trans-
     missions? From cable networks?

A    Satellite and cable have equivalent copyright limitations. See the flow chart in figure 8-4.

## FIGURE 8-4

### Copying Off-Air from Satellite or Cable Transmissions

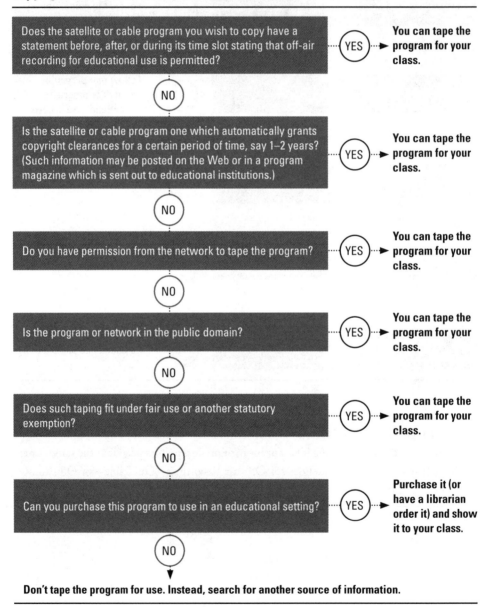

Don't tape the program for use. Instead, search for another source of information.

Q   As a reference librarian, you commonly work with college students and faculty. One faculty member often comes in with questions about information. He has recently told you that he feels, as an educator, he can borrow what he needs when he wants without asking for permission (including when it comes to televised programs). He says that it is "easier to ask for forgiveness," if he is ever caught. How do you respond?

A   Just say, "Not in copyright infringement cases!" (Leone 2012, 2).


## YOU CREATE IT, WHO OWNS IT?

Q   Several students in an educational technology class have prepared short DVDs about their department, with student and faculty interviews and shots of the class building, inside and out. As the technology teacher, you would like to retain their DVDs to show as "best examples" to future classes. May you do so?

A   If students created their own DVDs, whether for your class or not, they own the copyrights to these. As a result, you will need the students' permission to use the DVDs in future classes.

(To this permission request, you might also add how long you plan to use the work and in what capacity. See chapter 4. Reminder: get these permissions in writing and specify each student's name, the particular work, and the class for which the work was originally created.)


Q   I want to digitize a televised version of *Hamlet,* and put it on our English class website. This way my students can access it outside the classroom. Can I legally do this, since I am essentially creating a derivative work?

A   That depends on where you obtained the original version of the work. See the flow chart in figure 8-5 to decide what television programs you can digitize and place on a class website.

## FIGURE 8-5

**Digitizing a Television Program**

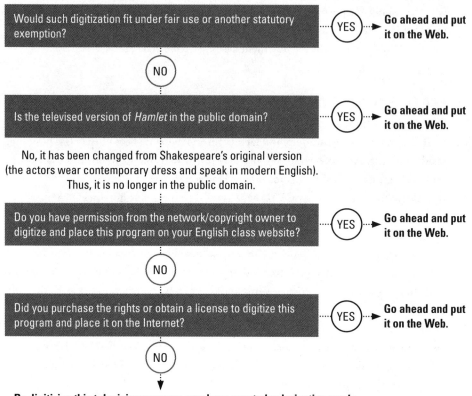

Would such digitization fit under fair use or another statutory exemption? — YES → **Go ahead and put it on the Web.**

NO

Is the televised version of *Hamlet* in the public domain? — YES → **Go ahead and put it on the Web.**

No, it has been changed from Shakespeare's original version (the actors wear contemporary dress and speak in modern English). Thus, it is no longer in the public domain.

Do you have permission from the network/copyright owner to digitize and place this program on your English class website? — YES → **Go ahead and put it on the Web.**

NO

Did you purchase the rights or obtain a license to digitize this program and place it on the Internet? — YES → **Go ahead and put it on the Web.**

NO

**By digitizing this television program, you have created a derivative work.
Instead of placing this on the Web, find another way to get a copy of *Hamlet* to your students.**

## INFRINGEMENTS AND PENALTIES

Q   I'm a college professor, and I'm taping these television shows because my small liberal arts college can't afford to purchase them. I haven't asked for permission, and I know it could be in violation of copyright law, but the students need this information, and this is the only way I know of to get it to them. Will I get caught? Will I get punished? What can happen to me?

A   You may never get caught. However, not getting caught doesn't make copyright infringements legal. For example, a disgruntled fellow employee, a student, or anyone else could report your illegal taping to the network. Penalties for illegal television taping vary, and can include (1) schools' being forced to purchase all illegal tapes; (2) faculty losing their jobs (or other disciplinary actions); (3) colleges and universities paying fines; (4) educators receiving cease-and-desist letters; (5) librarians being required to purchase a license; and/or (6) adverse publicity for your particular college/university. While you may not get caught, be aware that there are institutions and faculty who do, and they are sometimes penalized. Thus, illegal taping is a gamble—how badly do you want to risk it?

Q Your class is discussing how the media influence our culture. To demonstrate this, a colleague brings in a DVD on which he has strung together several television commercials. Is he in copyright infringement?

A Perhaps. The simplest answer is that it is possible he has infringed on copyright law since commercials are protected under this law, and he has made copies of them. In addition, by stringing them together, he may have created a derivative work (see discussion above on derivative works). However, since advertisers want people to see what they are selling, chances are that no company will care that he has copied these and is showing them in class. Additionally, one could argue, since this is for an educational purpose, that fair use or the classroom exemption may apply. See the flow chart, figure 8-6, for more information.

## FIGURE 8-6

**Stringing Commercials Together to Use in Class**

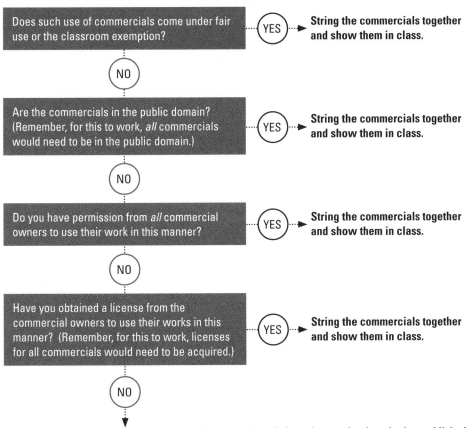

| | | |
|---|---|---|
| Does such use of commercials come under fair use or the classroom exemption? | YES → | **String the commercials together and show them in class.** |
| NO | | |
| Are the commercials in the public domain? (Remember, for this to work, *all* commercials would need to be in the public domain.) | YES → | **String the commercials together and show them in class.** |
| NO | | |
| Do you have permission from *all* commercial owners to use their work in this manner? | YES → | **String the commercials together and show them in class.** |
| NO | | |
| Have you obtained a license from the commercial owners to use their works in this manner? (Remember, for this to work, licenses for all commercials would need to be acquired.) | YES → | **String the commercials together and show them in class.** |
| NO | | |

**It would be safest to tape each commercial separately and show them under the criteria established in "Guidelines for Off-Air Recording of Broadcast Programming for Educational Purposes."**

Q   I hear that there is new technology available that lets us view our televisions remotely. The possibilities for utilization in our university classrooms sound endless! For example, we could access a television broadcast when taking a class on a field trip. Can we use such technologies to support our curriculum? Would using such a technology be considered a copyright violation?

A   You are talking about place-shifting technology or video streaming, which "allows anyone with a broadband Internet connection to have video streams from their home television set, DVR or other video source . . . forwarded for viewing remotely on a computer, netbook or mobile phone at any location where they have a high-speed Internet connection or cellular data network" (Sling Media 2012a: 1; Sling Media 2012b). If you purchased the place-shifting technology with a specific license, then you must abide by that license, "even if the copyright law would allow for a more liberal exploitation in the absence of a license" (Lutzker 2010, 3-4). Use figure 8-7 as you consider such a technology.

## FIGURE 8-7

**Using Place-Shifting Technologies/Video Streaming in Education**

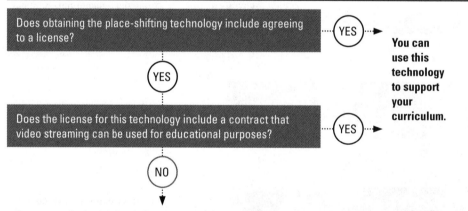

Does obtaining the place-shifting technology include agreeing to a license? — YES → **You can use this technology to support your curriculum.**

YES

Does the license for this technology include a contract that video streaming can be used for educational purposes? — YES →

NO

**Do not use the technology. Abide by the license and find another way to work with students other than video streaming.**

## INTERNATIONAL COPYRIGHT LAW

Q I live near the Canadian border, and we pick up Canadian television stations all the time. Can I tape one of their programs and use it in my college classroom?

A Use the flow chart in figure 8-8 to find out if you can tape a program for class use.

## FIGURE 8-8

**Taping Foreign Television**

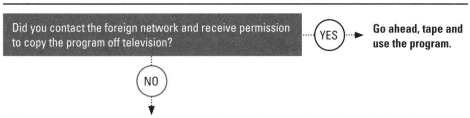

Did you contact the foreign network and receive permission to copy the program off television? ···· YES ···▶ Go ahead, tape and use the program.

NO

The country in question probably belongs to international treaties and organizations that deal with copyright, just as the United States does. Treat your use of the foreign television program in the same manner that you would treat such use of an American television program.

Q Wow—these recordable DVDs are really great! When I attend a professional conference in Ecuador, I am going to tape my favorite South American soap opera to use with my advanced Spanish class! Since it is from a different country, I can ignore copyright laws when using this, right?

A Wrong! Ecuador and the United States belong to several of the same international copyright organizations (United States Copyright Office 2010, 4). Therefore, you are safest if you treat the soap opera as if it were one that you had taped in the United States.

## AVOIDING COPYRIGHT PROBLEMS

Q How can I make sure that we never violate copyright law when working with television programs?

A The only "for sure" way to *always* avoid copyright problems when using television programming is to find something other than this format with which to work.

## CONCLUSION

So, can you copy a television program for use in a higher education environment? Yes, no, maybe, sometimes, it depends. . . . As we have seen when it comes to copyright law, each work must be considered on its own merit. There is often no one answer for any specific medium.

## REFERENCES

Cable in the Classroom. "Copyright & Recording Guidelines." http://www.ciconline.org/Legal/
      CopyrightRecordingGuidelines.

C-SPAN Video Library. "Licensing and Permissions: Policy." http://www.c-spanvideo.org/rights.

Guidelines for Off-Air Recording of Broadcast Programming for Educational Purposes. 1981.
      *Congressional Record* 127, no. 145 (October): unp.

Leone, Joseph T. 2012. "Easier to Ask Forgiveness Than Permission?" http://blogs.missouristate
      .edu/instructionaldesign/2012/06/05/easier-to-ask-forgiveness-than-permission.

Lutzker, Arnold P. 2010. "Educational Video Streaming: A Short Primer." *AIME News* 24, no. 1
      (Spring):1–4.

Sling Media. 2012a. "Legal Information: Web Site Terms of Use." www.slingmedia.com/get/
      terms-of-use.

———. 2012b. "What Is Placeshifting?" http://www.slingmedia.com/go/placeshifting.

Torrans, Lee Ann. 2003. *Law for K–12 Libraries and Librarians*. Westport, CT: Libraries Unlimited.

U.S. Congress. 1984. "Guidelines for Off-Air Taping for Educational Purposes." *Congressional
      Record* (October 14). Washington, DC: United States Congress.

United States Copyright Office. 2010. "International Copyright Relations of the United States."
      Washington, DC: United States Copyright Office.

# 9

# Computer Software, Handheld Applications and Mobile Technologies, and Copyright Law
## What's Free, and What Is Not?

Unauthorized copying of computer software and handheld applications, whether available online or by disk, is illegal. This is supported by the 1976 copyright law, updated and expanded upon in 1980 (Stern 1985), and revised to include piracy in 1992 (Simpson 2005). Most of us realize this and can verbalize it readily. However, what about online and DVD encyclopedias and dictionaries, e-books, computer software codes, Internet-based applications, databases, and digital rights management—is there a connection to all of these and copyright? The answer to all is a resounding "yes." This chapter will take a look at a number of these "computer-based technologies" available to higher education (as well as the general public in many cases) in order to answer questions of copyright law as it applies to various uses. (Please be aware that the term *computer-based technologies* is used here in a very broad sense, to identify a number of things associated with educational technologies that librarians and other higher education professionals and students use and that are in some way associated with handheld or computer use. More on such technologies, including the Internet and multimedia, are addressed in other chapters.)

It is so tempting and often easy to copy software and other digital applications—and, in many cases, who will know? The following questions cover a variety of handheld and computer-based technologies in terms of copyright law and higher education. Questions with more than one answer are presented in flow chart form. Remember, when you use the flow charts in this chapter, you are trying to find any criterion under which you may borrow a work. Therefore, you need only follow each flow chart until you come to that point where you satisfy one of the criteria. Once you reach that point, there is no need to go any further. For more information on each area discussed, refer to the chapter (chapters 1–5) that covers that particular subject.

## FAIR USE

Q    May I print off an article from a web-based encyclopedia and copy it for each member of my class?

A    Use the flow chart in figure 9-1 to determine whether to copy an article off a web-based encyclopedia. The section in chapter 5 entitled "Copying Guidelines" may also be applied to this question.

## FIGURE 9-1

**Printing Off a Web-Based Encyclopedia**

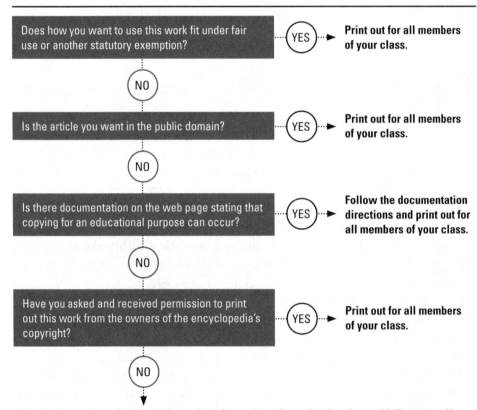

Don't print out the article for each member of your class. Assuming that the work's license and/ or documentation does not prohibit such use, you may, however, show your students the article in class – by printing out one copy and passing it around, displaying it on a computer monitor, or projecting the article to a screen via a projection device for the whole class to see at the same time.

Q    May I "borrow" material from commercial software on plant regeneration and put it on a web page? We are studying this subject in biology, and I want the students to access it from home.

A    Use the flow chart in figure 9-2 to decide if you can put the material on a web page.

## FIGURE 9-2

**Borrowing from Software**

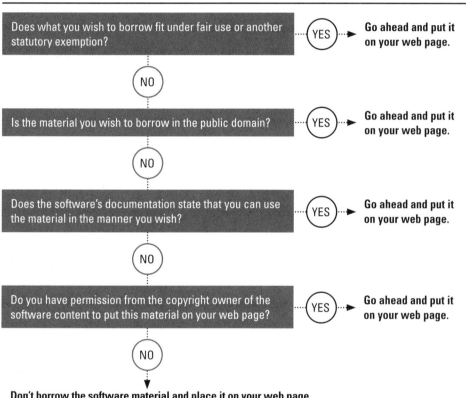

Does what you wish to borrow fit under fair use or another statutory exemption? — YES → **Go ahead and put it on your web page.**

NO

Is the material you wish to borrow in the public domain? — YES → **Go ahead and put it on your web page.**

NO

Does the software's documentation state that you can use the material in the manner you wish? — YES → **Go ahead and put it on your web page.**

NO

Do you have permission from the copyright owner of the software content to put this material on your web page? — YES → **Go ahead and put it on your web page.**

NO

**Don't borrow the software material and place it on your web page.
You can, however, use the software in class to show your students the subject.**

Q    Is computer software code copyright-protected?

A    Unless the copyright owners say otherwise, it is safest to assume that borrowing or cracking computer software code is an infringement of copyright law.

## PUBLIC DOMAIN

Q   If the application you purchased on the Web does not have a copyright notice on it, does that mean it is in the public domain?

A   No, it does not. It just means that the application's creators did not put a copyright notice on it. While Internet works are often viewed as if they were in the public domain, in reality they should be treated the same as any other work. If it doesn't state that it is in the public domain, you should presume that it is not. Thus, assume it is copyrighted, unless the documentation says otherwise.

Q   While searching the Web for iPad applications to support a class you are teaching, you come across a site with a statement that all applications provided on that site are in the public domain. How can you use these applications?

A   Any way you want! You can make copies for students to take home, print out parts of it for in-class activities, or use sections on a web page you are designing. It is yours to use as you see fit.

Q   Are QR Codes in the public domain?

A   QR Codes or "Quick Response Codes" are "two-dimensional barcodes that can be read by many cell phones and smartphones . . . small squares with black and white patterns, appear in a variety of places, such as magazine and newspaper ads . . . (and are) used to encode some sort of information, such as text or a URL" (About.com: Cell Phones 2013, 1). While QR Codes seem readily available in public places, they are created by individuals or companies—usually to provide information or to sell something—and without a statement to the contrary, need to be considered as copyright-protected.

## DOCUMENTATION AND LICENSES

When using handheld or computer software and applications, it is extremely important to read all documentation first. The documentation may include a contract or license, and if that is the case, it is your responsibility to follow the contract in your use of the digital item. Reading documentation is a step that many users skip. Their reasoning includes that it takes too long; the words are in too fine a print; it's boring, and so on. What such users often do not recognize is that by not reading the documentation, they may eventually break the law without realizing it. (Or, they may actually be able to do more with the application or software than they think!) Ignorance is no excuse. For example if the law has been broken, you are liable, whether you realized there was an infringement or not. With this in mind, consider the following questions about documentation and handheld applications and computer software.

Q   Can I copy a favorite computer program that I own to my classroom computer for use with students?

A   Use the flow chart in figure 9-3 to determine if you can copy personal software.

## FIGURE 9-3

**Copying Personal Software to a Classroom Computer**

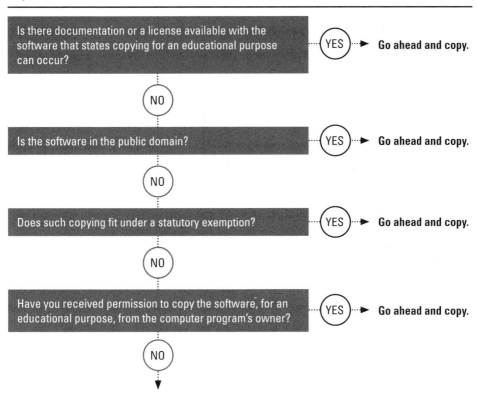

Is there documentation or a license available with the software that states copying for an educational purpose can occur? ···· YES ····► **Go ahead and copy.**

NO

Is the software in the public domain? ···· YES ····► **Go ahead and copy.**

NO

Does such copying fit under a statutory exemption? ···· YES ····► **Go ahead and copy.**

NO

Have you received permission to copy the software, for an educational purpose, from the computer program's owner? ···· YES ····► **Go ahead and copy.**

NO

**Don't copy your personal software to the classroom computer. By doing so, you have created another copy. Remember, you only own the copy that you purchased.**

Q    Can all 300 of the library's student computers use the same word-processing program
     at the same time?

A    The flow chart in figure 9-4 gives the steps for making this decision.

## FIGURE 9-4

**Placing Software on All Library Computers**

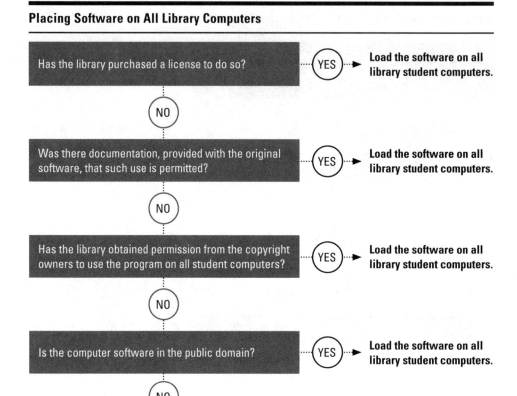

Don't use that particular word-processing software on the library's student computers.
Instead find a program with a license giving you the rights that you need.

Q    How can I tell what copyrights the application I purchased from an online store has?

A    There should be documentation, accessible via the Internet (on the site where the
     application was purchased), that states whether it is under copyright protection or in
     the public domain. In addition, when copyrighted, there is *usually* a copyright notice
     on or near the application. You can also ask your librarian or instructional technology
     specialist for his or her records regarding this application. The application may have
     a license by which you must abide. It, too, is part of the documentation material. If
     there is a license, remember that it is a contract, and when you obtain a license to use
     a copyrighted work, you are essentially contracting to use certain copyrights afforded
     that work. (See chapter 5 for more information on documentation and licenses.)

Q  I just bought a used computer from the university for my home use. There is still a copy of some of the lab software on it. Can I use it?

A  That depends on the license or documentation that the university originally purchased with the software. Ask the university for clarification.

Q  I wrote a grant to purchase five iPads. I want to download several e-books to each for students to use in the library. Am I to consider copyright of the e-book in terms of software or as if it were in print?

A  First of all, protection of copyright is the same for all works, regardless of format. Second, the documentation/license of where you purchased such e-books will tell you how you can use your e-book. For example, iTunes has a "Terms and Conditions" section which states how media it sells, including e-books, may be used (www.apple.com/legal/itunes/us/terms.html#APPS). Remember that you must abide by the license (see chapter 5), even if what it states is different from copyright law. Bear in mind, however, if there is no license, that all rights and exemptions under the copyright law apply, and that what the copyright owner may state on media he or she owns is basically a reiteration of some of these terms.

Q  The Special Collections librarian is working with a new historical database that the library has just contracted to use. She sees that it will pull up full-text articles on Civil War battles. It occurs to her that she could print off some of these articles and put them on in-house reserve (they are not allowed to leave the library) for a large class studying the Confederacy. Is it OK to do so?

A  The answer depends on the license agreement that the library signed with the database owner. Please see figure 9-5 for more information.

## FIGURE 9-5

**Printing Out from a Database**

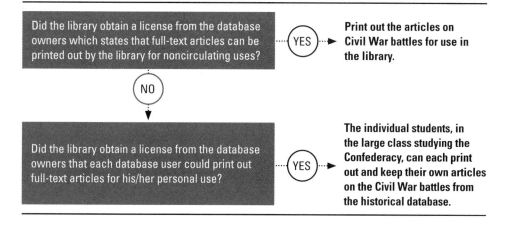

Q    I found some software on the Web that I would like to purchase for use in my class. It
     says that it has a "Creative Commons License." Exactly what does that mean for me?
A    It means that you are to follow the license, the same as you would for any other soft-
     ware license; that is, the owner of that specific software has chosen to identify what
     rights users may have to his or her work and has done so using this particular license.

Q    I have some software, which I used for a few years. Now I want to sell it and get some-
     thing newer. Since I bought the DVD, I have the right to sell it, under the first sale
     doctrine, correct?
A    Well . . . maybe. In 2010, the Ninth Circuit Court of Appeals (federal court) deter-
     mined that "a software user is a licensee, not an owner of a copy, when the copyright
     owner (a) specifies that the user is granted a license, (b) significantly restricts the user's
     right to transfer the software, and (c) imposes 'notable' use restrictions" (DuBoff and
     King 2013, 14). This means that you need to reread the documentation that came with
     this software—does it state that you are a licensee (this means that ownership of the
     software is retained by the software company) or the owner of the software?

Q    What is OverDrive and how can I use it legally?
A    "OverDrive Media Console is free software that allows you to download and enjoy
     audiobooks, music, and video on a computer, or e-books and audiobooks on a mobile
     device. Navigate, play and bookmark titles, plus transfer to a compatible device in just
     a few clicks" (OverDrive Help 2012, 1). OverDrive, like much other software available
     on the Internet, has its own licenses posted (service and digital content) as well as
     copyright and other information under its "Terms & Conditions" (OverDrive 2012).
     When you use any Internet software, it is always best to be aware of what the docu-
     mentation of that software is. Then, just follow all terms and conditions/licenses and
     your use of the item should be legal use.

## PERMISSIONS

Q    Can I burn a CD of software I purchased from a computer store (it is older software,
     but I really like it and want to hang onto it) to a DVD for safekeeping purposes? I will
     then use the copy, and keep the original in a secure place.
A    Use the flow chart in figure 9-6 to decide if this is allowed.

## FIGURE 9-6

**Copying Software to Another Format**

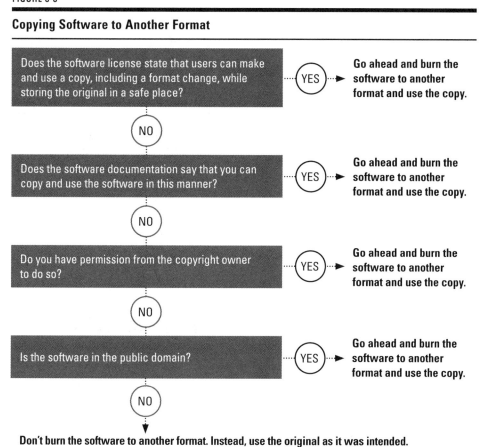

Does the software license state that users can make and use a copy, including a format change, while storing the original in a safe place? — YES → Go ahead and burn the software to another format and use the copy.

NO

Does the software documentation say that you can copy and use the software in this manner? — YES → Go ahead and burn the software to another format and use the copy.

NO

Do you have permission from the copyright owner to do so? — YES → Go ahead and burn the software to another format and use the copy.

NO

Is the software in the public domain? — YES → Go ahead and burn the software to another format and use the copy.

NO

**Don't burn the software to another format. Instead, use the original as it was intended.**

In addition to the above, libraries may make copies of a number of works for preservation, interlibrary loan, and some private study purposes (U.S. Copyright Law 1976). Let's look at preservation copying. Could it apply to the software in figure 9-6?

It could apply if:

- the software is deteriorating, damaged, lost, stolen, or in an obsolete format
- and the user is willing to use the DVD version only on the library premises
- and the library has already conducted an investigation and discovered that a replacement cannot be obtained at a fair price
- then up to three preservation copies of the software may be made (U.S. Copyright Law 1976; DMCA 1998). While this gets complicated, it is possible, if the individual is willing to work with the librarian or college technology specialist, that they could find a way to copy the software.

Q    May I make copies of lab software available via the Internet for my students, so that they can get their assignments done?

A    Use the flow chart in figure 9-7 to guide your decision.

# FIGURE 9-7

**Making Lab Software Available for Students**

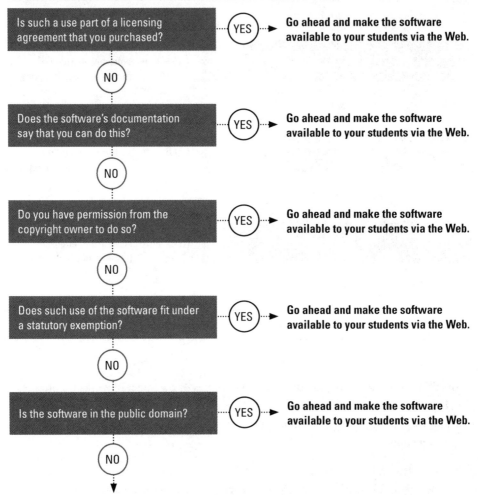

Do not make the software available over the Web for your students. Instead, make sure that they have time in class to complete their assignments or extra lab time outside of class.

Q   My college owns an old version of a software program that we use with our freshman classes. We would like to upgrade to a newer version, but we can't find it. Can we just copy the old one for use in the computer lab?

A   Assuming that this program really can't be found, under the preservation copying exemption (see discussion above about library copying for preservation purposes) your college could make a copy for use in the library or a lab (within the library) and available to the freshman classes. Before doing this, however, search widely for upgraded software and ask permission from the copyright holder.

Q   What is Digital Rights Management (DRM) and how might this affect us as educators?

A   DRM is any technology that can control how we use digital works. As the American Library Association states, "DRM has uses far beyond simply enforcing traditional and long-standing protections extant in current law. By embedding controls within the product, providers can prevent the public from use that is non-infringing under copyright law as well as enforce restrictions that extend far beyond those specific rights enumerated in the Copyright Act (or other laws)" (2014, 1). What this means for us in higher education is that the placing of such technology in any computer-based software that we purchase for use might mean that we could not use the item to its full potential under law. Thus, DRM technologies may well alter such concepts of copyright law as the first sale doctrine and fair use or other statutory exemptions, as well as implement time, preservation, and archival limits and/or dissemination of software needed in colleges and universities (American Library Association 2014). The main thing to be aware of here is that while DRM technologies are not illegal, their placement in educational software could change what we present to our students, as well as how often.

## YOU CREATE IT, YOU OWN IT

Q   Two students in my computer science class are creating a piece of gaming software as extra credit. They wish to give the software "to the world" and hope that gamers everywhere will eventually be able to use their finished work as a basis for developing future action adventure games—as long as the new users also share their derivative works "with the world." Is copyright law a concern here?

A   Well, it sounds like they are trying to create open source software, which "allows . . . input of differing agendas and ideas to the development of software . . . making (the software) . . . stronger and more feature-rich" (Abram 2009, 2). As such, they are offering gamers everywhere certain rights to their software, for example the ability of users to work with the software without asking for permission to use and/or change it, as long as the users do what the creators say. Thus, this is actually a contractual issue. (See chapter 5 of this book for a more detailed explanation of open sourcing and contracts and licenses.)

Q   I just found this really cool software on the Web. It is called Many Eyes (http://www-958.ibm.com/software/data/cognos/manyeyes/), and it creates visuals from data. As a doctoral student, I think that this could be a very helpful way for me to visualize the data I have been collecting. Since I will be doing a digital dissertation, I think I will also compare my visual to another that I will create from data I borrowed from a statistics textbook. Good idea, huh?

A   You own the data you have collected and can put it in your dissertation, digital or otherwise, visually or numerically. However, have you read the "Terms of Use Agreement" for Many Eyes? Part of this agreement states: "You also agree not to submit anyone else's copyrightable material to the Services unless You obtain written permission of the copyright holder to license the copyrightable material to IBM, consistent with the terms of this Agreement" (Many Eyes, 1). This means, before you compare your visual with one you create from a textbook (using Many Eyes), that you need permission from the textbook's copyright owners to do so.

Q   My word processing program has clip art available. Can I use this in a brochure that I am making to advocate for the rare books department in the college library?

A   Read the license and documentation accompanying the word processing program. It will tell you exactly how you can use the program, including the clip art.

Q   A professor, as part of his research, creates a mathematical process using prime numbers. He wishes to give it (copyright ownership) to a charity to help fund that charity's work. Can he do so?

A   If created on his own time, using his own computer and software, then he owns the process and can do with it as he wishes. If created on a university computer, using university-owned software, and during university time, then the university may have whole or part copyright ownership of the process. The professor needs to check his contract as well as university policies to see whether he can gift this process or not.

Q   How do I make sure others realize the PowerPoints that I have created are owned by me?

A   As is stated in chapter 1 of this book, "Under current copyright law, almost anything a person creates is automatically copyright-protected, whether it is officially registered or not." Thus, the PowerPoints you created are owned by you, unless you did them as "works for hire." You do not need to put the © on your PowerPoints to show who they are owned by, but you can.

## INFRINGEMENTS AND PENALTIES

Q   A student in your English class brings in a flash drive with a piece of software copied to it. She recommends it as freeware (software placed by its owner/creator into the public domain) that creates footnotes for term papers. You suspect that it is pirated. How can you tell?

A   Illegal copies of software usually have one or more of the following characteristics:

- no documentation is available
- there are no rebates or guarantees included with the software
- if the software is labeled, the label looks unprofessional
- there is no shrinkwrap license
- if on a disk, the disk it is on is a copy
- the software is already loaded on a used machine you purchased (Butler 2002b)

Q   Who is liable if a student is caught illegally downloading a program in a computer lab: the student who infringed, the instructor who assigned the unit on which the student was working, the librarian or computer lab supervisor who unwittingly provided the equipment used in the infringement, the technology coordinator who provided the software needed for the infringement, the dean of the college, or the university provost?

A   All *could* be held liable under copyright law. This is because liability follows the "pecking order." There are three categories of copyright infringement. They are listed below, using our example of the student illegally downloading software.

- **Direct Infringement**—This is what the student, who knowingly violates the rights of the copyright owner by downloading the software, is doing.
- **Contributory or Indirect Infringement**—This is where we find the instructor, the librarian, the computer lab supervisor, and the technology coordinator. Any or all of these people may have assisted indirectly in the downloading of the software:
  - by providing the hardware or software, and/or
  - by assigning a project that needed that software, and so on. In addition, these people either knew, or should have known, that they were assisting the student in violating copyright law.

- **Vicarious Infringement**—This is where the dean and the provost could fit in, only if they, in some way, derive a financial benefit from downloading the software. This is because these individuals control, directly or indirectly, the direct and contributory infringers (Simpson 2005).

Q   So I've pirated some software. No one will ever know. Besides, they are after the big copier, not "little ol' me."

A   Well, that may be true. Maybe no one will ever find out that you illegally copied software. (Although, don't forget, that by copying software illegally, you may be violating your professional ethics and modeling undesirable behavior to others.) Moreover, software producers and copyright owners usually are after those who violate in a big way, copying many programs many times. Be aware, however, that some computer software watchdog organizations and copyright owners offer confidential Internet sites or phone numbers by which infringements may be reported. An example is the Business Software Alliance which provides an online form, a phone number, and a chance to chat live for those who wish to report an infringement (Business Software Alliance 2014). Another organization that will take your privacy reports is the Software and Information Industry Association (www.siia.net/piracy/report/soft) which states on its website, "Report piracy here and you may be eligible for a reward of up to $1 million" (Software. . . 2014, 1). Remember that no one can guarantee you will not be caught. If you are planning on copying software illegally, make sure that you haven't made any enemies who might report you!

Q    **I don't believe you! Give me an example of someone getting caught copying software. What were the penalties?**

A    In a Chicago suburb, an individual who worked at a particular school downloaded Acrobat software illegally onto several computers used by school administrators. A lawsuit ensued, brought about by a software group that pursues copyright infringements. The penalties can be extreme. For example, in this case, the school district paid $50,000 to the watchdog organization, the offending employee resigned, and the school district's principals were required to purchase their own computers and software (School District Pays 2001). Penalties vary from case to case depending on the infringements, the court overseeing the lawsuit, those involved in the lawsuit, and so on.

Q    **Who is most likely to infringe (concerning copyright) in higher education?**

A    According to a 2002 article published in *Applied Economics*, males, students in the sciences, and computer majors are more likely to violate copyright law, in terms of computer software use, than are older students and those in the fields of business or economics (Chiang and Assane 2002).

Q   I am a graduate student in instructional technology. A fellow student and I have been hired by a local business to create PowerPoints that the business can run in a loop, on a computer screen, at various spots in the store. The PowerPoints will "sell" various store items by demonstrating how they work. We are taking images off the Web for use in the PowerPoints. Do we need to cite these in our products?

A   YES! You do need to cite where the images are from—that could be a plagiarism issue, if you do not. In addition, since you are working for a commercial entity, you may need to obtain permissions or a license to use the images in these PowerPoints. See the flow chart in figure 9-8 for more information on this.

## FIGURE 9-8

**Using Internet Graphics in Commercial PowerPoints**

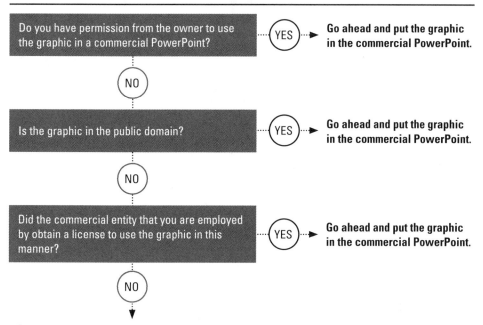

Do you have permission from the owner to use the graphic in a commercial PowerPoint? ···YES···▶ **Go ahead and put the graphic in the commercial PowerPoint.**

NO

Is the graphic in the public domain? ···YES···▶ **Go ahead and put the graphic in the commercial PowerPoint.**

NO

Did the commercial entity that you are employed by obtain a license to use the graphic in this manner? ···YES···▶ **Go ahead and put the graphic in the commercial PowerPoint.**

NO

**Don't use the graphic. Look for one in the public domain or for which you can obtain permission or a license to use.**

## INTERNATIONAL COPYRIGHT LAW

Q   A former student of mine, who is traveling in Hong Kong, has sent me a compilation
    of computer-assisted drafting (CAD) software. It is so much cheaper than buying it
    in the states! Is it pirated?

A   The flow chart in figure 9-9 will help you evaluate the situation. In this case, the flow
    chart steps are not definitive; however, they will guide you in determining whether the
    software is pirated or not.

## FIGURE 9-9

### Pirated Software

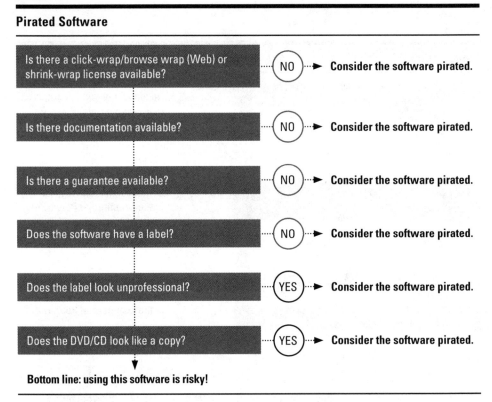

**Bottom line: using this software is risky!**

Q   Can I use it anyway?

A   Since it is so cheap, it is probably pirated. Remember, the United States is a signatory
    to several international copyright treaties (see chapter 5). Your pirated software could
    easily be a copyright infringement in the country of origin as well as in the United
    States. Don't use the CAD software that your student sent you.

Q   My library has purchased a license for a database that provides newspaper articles worldwide. Do I need to make sure that my students follow international copyright law when they use articles from a newspaper published in another country?

A   First of all, there is no such thing as "international copyright law." There are, however, any number of conventions, treaties, and agreements on copyright to which the United States and various other countries belong; for example, the World International Property Organization (WIPO) Treaty, the TRIPs Agreement (dealing with international trade), the Berne Convention, and so on. In addition, a contract law international convention (the E.C. Convention on the Law Applicable to Contractual Obligations) does have a database directive providing that all such compilations are under copyright law (Goldstein and Hugenholtz 2010). Bottom line: the easiest thing for you to do is to follow the licensing agreement for the database, as well as any other documentation posted for database users. This information will tell you exactly what you and your students may do with the database material.

## AVOIDING COPYRIGHT PROBLEMS

Q   We have an older piece of software on CD that a full professor uses faithfully every semester. While it is still in good shape, the library believes it would be prudent to make a backup copy. Can this be done for archival purposes?

A   If the software was legally attained, then yes, one archival copy may be made under Section 117 of the U.S. Copyright Law (Russell 2005).

Q   Can the college library sell used e-books or other digital files (if the originals are deleted from its files) to another entity?

A   According to the March 2013 court case, *Capital Records v. ReDigi Inc.,* the answer is no, since for digital files, even if the original is destroyed, a copy was made first. While ReDigi ("a virtual marketplace for 'pre-owned' digital music" [Minow 2013, 1]) is planning an appeal to this decision, for now, the only way to sell digital media is to also sell "the hardware onto which it was originally downloaded" (Minow 2013, 1).

Q   Can my music students use music notation software such as Notion 4, Finale, or Sibelius to transcribe hip-hop scores and put the computer-generated music up on Blackboard or another course management system for class presentation purposes?

A   Basically that depends on the hip-hop scores in question. See figure 9-10 for help.

FIGURE 9-10

## Using Music Notation Software and Uploading It to a Course Management System

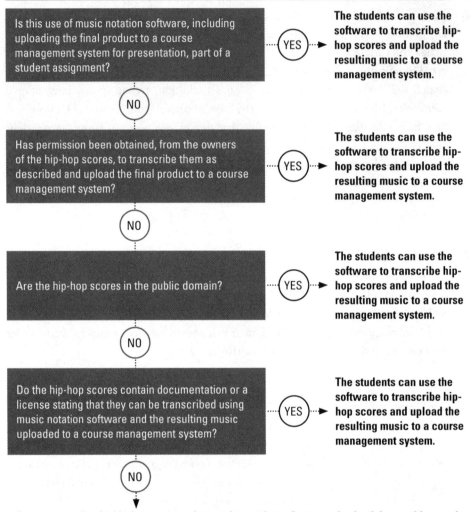

Is this use of music notation software, including uploading the final product to a course management system for presentation, part of a student assignment?

YES → The students can use the software to transcribe hip-hop scores and upload the resulting music to a course management system.

NO

Has permission been obtained, from the owners of the hip-hop scores, to transcribe them as described and upload the final product to a course management system?

YES → The students can use the software to transcribe hip-hop scores and upload the resulting music to a course management system.

NO

Are the hip-hop scores in the public domain?

YES → The students can use the software to transcribe hip-hop scores and upload the resulting music to a course management system.

NO

Do the hip-hop scores contain documentation or a license stating that they can be transcribed using music notation software and the resulting music uploaded to a course management system?

YES → The students can use the software to transcribe hip-hop scores and upload the resulting music to a course management system.

NO

Do not transcribe the hip-hop scores using music notation software and upload the resulting music to a course management system.

Q    One of the instructors at our technical college found several videos on a YouTube site that he would like to use to illustrate various types of welding. Is it legal to convert the files and save them to his desktop using a program such as Zamzar or Vixy (this way, he does not have to depend on the Internet when he needs the videos)?

A    Using an online file conversion program (e.g., Zamzar, Vixy, TillaWire, Freecorder 7, Replay Media Catcher 4) changes videos, music, images, and other media into formats such as AVI, MP3, MPEG4, and WMV. One of the main staples of copyright ownership is the ability to create derivative works, and it could be argued that a file conversion program does just that. Many sites providing videos and other media (for example, YouTube), while often assumed by users to be featuring public domain media, may have policies or copyright statements announcing that illegal use of the media on their sites will result in penalties and/or the infringer being removed from said website. Therefore, it is best to use the videos in their original formats. See figure 9-11 for more information concerning this matter.

# FIGURE 9-11

## Using File Conversion Programs

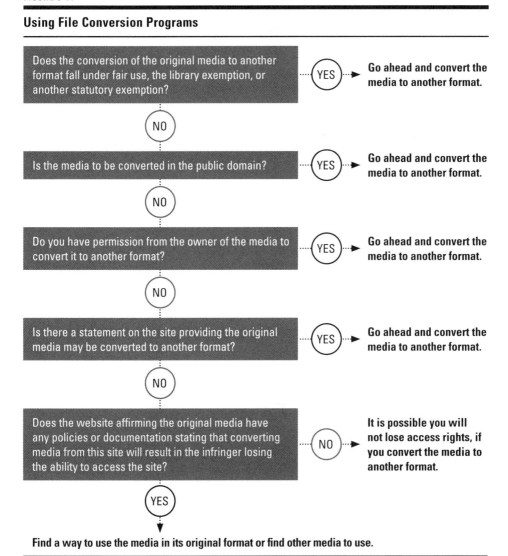

Does the conversion of the original media to another format fall under fair use, the library exemption, or another statutory exemption? **YES** → Go ahead and convert the media to another format.

**NO**

Is the media to be converted in the public domain? **YES** → Go ahead and convert the media to another format.

**NO**

Do you have permission from the owner of the media to convert it to another format? **YES** → Go ahead and convert the media to another format.

**NO**

Is there a statement on the site providing the original media may be converted to another format? **YES** → Go ahead and convert the media to another format.

**NO**

Does the website affirming the original media have any policies or documentation stating that converting media from this site will result in the infringer losing the ability to access the site? **NO** → It is possible you will not lose access rights, if you convert the media to another format.

**YES**

Find a way to use the media in its original format or find other media to use.

Q    As an instructional technology specialist at a small university, you are often called upon to help faculty create multimedia products for use in their teaching. An instructor approaches you to help him create an example of a corporate training module. As part of this product, he requests that you use photo-editing software to alter some old photographs he has, so that each photo represents someone from the past in a present-day corporate environment. He tells you that he has no idea where the photos originally came from; he found them in a desk drawer in a classroom and no one has claimed ownership. There are no labels, stamps from photographers, copyright dates, or any other identifying marks on the photos. Can you alter these photos as he requests?

A    Well, that depends! It *could* be in the public domain, but you do not know. It *could* be that the owner would give you clearance to modify the photos; but since the instructor cannot find the owner/s, who knows? The instructor—as the finder of the photographs—and you—as the possible modifier—do not control the use of these photos. In essence, they could be considered orphan works (see chapter 5). So what to do? Here are some things to do that may help:

- Do an "extensive" search for the owner. (Copyright law does not define such a search for us; it is up to you, the user, to decide what is "extensive." This search is your *good faith effort* at finding the owner.)
- Document the search: where you looked, who you contacted, and so on.
- Record this documentation in an accessible place; for example, a folder on your hard drive.
- Remind the instructor, that while neither of you actually controls use of the photos, it will be up to him as to whether he wants to use them or not—and take the possible risk for using them without permission, licenses, and so on.
- If he says he wants to take the risk (and you are okay with taking the risk as far as modifying them goes):

  — Modify the photos with the photo-editing software for use in the instructor's multimedia project.
  — Document all modifications and place with your search documentation (example: in the hard-drive folder).

- Use the modified photos in the multimedia project.
- Be prepared to stop using the photos and/or pay the owner for the modification and use, should the owner be found or show up asking for compensation.

## CONCLUSION

In addition to the previous information in this chapter, here are some steps toward making copyright compliance easier:

- Make sure that all documentation is available to the users.
- Consult the documentation—yes—you need to actually read it!
- Ensure that any archival copies of software or other computer-based technologies (for which you have a physical format, such as DVD or CD) are kept in a secure place. You may even wish to lock the copies up so that others will not be tempted to borrow them.
- Be sure that your college or university has an applications/software/computer-based technologies policy and ethics code. If not, encourage your librarians, technology specialists, or higher education administrators to create one. Within the code include a written policy for the use of personal software on university computers, whether in a lab, classroom, or on a professor's desk. Do the same for applications that might be found on an employee's university-provided handheld device. Have this policy/ethics code accessible to all who use applications, computer software, and other computer-based technologies. (For example, it might be placed in your university's copyright policy.)
- Be aware of any licenses for the computer-based technologies you use. Some licenses may let you and your students copy and take home programs or parts of them for educational purposes. Your library, technology department, or college should have a log of these.
- Read all warning notices, such as copyright notices, licensing restrictions, and terms of use—software and other computer-based technologies may contain such notices, for example, during start-up. (This may be in addition to the work's documentation.)
- Be diligent in following all licensing restrictions.
- Understand that not all computer-based technologies' documentation and licenses are the same. For example, some computer software may let you install a copy on your home machine as well as on a school machine, while others may not (Butler 2002).

This chapter 9 conclusion is based largely on an article first published in *Knowledge Quest*: Butler, Rebecca P. 2002. "Computer Software and Copyright Law—Read This First." *Knowledge Quest* 31, no. 1 (September/October): 32–33.

## REFERENCES

About.com: Cell Phones. 2013. "QR Codes: A Definition." http://cellphones.about.com/od/
    phoneglossary/g/Qr-Codes.htm.

Abram, Stephen. 2009. "Integrated Library System Platforms on Open Source." White Paper.
    Provo, Utah: SirsiDynix.

American Library Association. 2014. "Digital Rights Management (DRM) & Libraries."
    www.ala.org/ala/issuesadvocacy/copyright/digitalrights/index.cfm.

Business Software Alliance. 2014. "Report Piracy Now! Your Report Is Confidential."
    https://reporting.bsa.org/usa/report/add.aspx.

Butler, Rebecca P. 2002. "Computer Software and Copyright Law—Read This First."
    *Knowledge Quest* 31, no. 1 (September/October): 32–33.

———. 2002b. "Software Piracy: Don't Let It Byte You!" *Knowledge Quest* 31, no. 2 (November/
    December): 41–42.

Chiang, Eric, and Djeto Assane. 2002. "Software Copyright Infringement among College
    Students." *Applied Economics* 34, no. 2 (January): 157–66.

Digital Millennium Copyright Act (DMCA). 1998. Public Law 105-304.

DuBoff, Leonard, and Christy King. 2013. "Recent Changes in Intellectual Property Law—Part I."
    *TechTrends* 57, no. 1 (January/February): 14–15.

Goldstein, Paul, and Bernt Hugenholtz. 2010. *International Copyright.* New York: Oxford University
    Press.

iTunes Store. 2013. "Terms and Conditions." www.apple.com/legal/itunes/us/terms.html#APPS.

Many Eyes. "IBM Many Eyes Terms of Use Agreement (the 'Agreement')." http://www-958.ibm
    .com/software/data/cognos/manyeyes/research_agreement.html.

Minow, Mary . 2013. "Selling Used Digital Files: A Setback, But Not the End of the Story."
    http://lj.libraryjournal.com/2013/04/copyright/selling-used-digital-files-a-setback-but
    -not-the-end-of-the-story.

OverDrive. 2012. "Terms & Conditions." http://www.overdrive.com/terms-conditions.

OverDrive Help. 2012. "Overdrive Media Console." http://help.overdrive.com/overdrive-media
    -console.

Russell, Carrie. 2005. "The Long and Short of It." *School Library Journal* 51, no. 12 (December): 31.

"School District Pays Copyright Penalty." 2001. *Chicago Tribune,* September 12, sec. 2: 3.

Simpson, Carol. 2005. *Copyright for Schools: A Practical Guide,* 4th ed. Worthington, OH: Linworth.

Software and Information Industry Association. 2014. "Report Piracy." www.siia.net/piracy/report/
    soft.

Stern, Richard H. 1985. "Section 117 of the Copyright Act: Charter of the Software Users' Rights
    or an Illusory Promise?" *Western New England Law Review* 7: 459–85.

U.S. Copyright Law. 1976. Public Law 94-553, sec. 108.

# 10

# Music and Copyright Law
## Who Will Know If You Copy It?

The purpose of this chapter is to cover, as simply as possible, information—for academic librarians and professionals—on U.S. copyright law and music/audio in a variety of formats. Copyright information for music can be extremely complex. For example, one recording might have at least three copyright registrations: one for the song's sheet music, one for the lyrics, and one for the performer's version of the song. In the past few years, additions of online stores, such as iTunes, which sell music for downloading to iPads, iPods, computers, cell phones, and so on, have made borrowing and using music legally more obvious. However, obtaining music for educational as well as personal use is still confusing. This chapter attempts to clarify some of the more common questions surrounding music and other sound recordings. References to further information, accessible in other chapters, are also provided.

First, it is important to define, as does the U.S. Copyright Office, the differences between musical compositions and sound recordings. In "Circular 56a," the U.S. Copyright Office does exactly that. According to this definition, a musical composition consists "of music, including any accompanying words. . . . A musical composition may be in the form of a notated copy (for example, sheet music) or in the form of a phonorecord (for example, cassette tape, LP, or CD)." The U.S. Copyright Office further defines the creator/author of the musical composition as "generally the composer, and the lyricist, if any" (U.S. Copyright Office 2009b, 1). "Circular 56a" further defines a sound recording as resulting from "the fixation of a series of musical, spoken, or other sounds," and the sound recording author as "the performer(s) whose performance is fixed, or the record producer who processes the sounds and fixes them in the final recording, or both" (U.S. Copyright Office 2009, 1). Sound recordings do not include the sounds accompanying motion pictures or other audiovisual works (U.S. Copyright Office 2009). It may be worded in more "legalese" than we like to read when we are searching quickly for a simple answer to our copyright questions, and it may be more confusing than we would like it to be; however, what is said in "Circular 56a" is that there are two separate kinds of audio works: musical compositions and sound recordings. They are not the same, they do not necessarily have the same owners or authors (although they can), and their rights under copyright law can be different as well. It is possible, for example, for the score of a musical to be in the public domain, while a recording of the same musical is registered under copyright. It is also possible that the copyright owner(s) of a collection of country and western music your students want to perform for a southwestern night is/are the performer of the work and the recording company who produced the work. With this in mind, who owns what or who to ask for permission to use works can sometimes get quite confusing. (This is one of the places where clearinghouses and other organizations that help users obtain the correct permissions for use of works come in. They may save you a lot of time and exasperation! See chapter 4.) You should also be aware that while the right to copy applies to both musical compositions and sound recordings, the right to perform only applies to musical compositions. However, like most things dealing with copyright, there are exceptions. Thus, if you want to perform a particular song, unless it is in the public domain, you need the permission of the owner(s) of its musical composition. If you want to copy the sheet music of this song (again, unless it is in public domain), you also need the permission of the owner(s) of the musical composition. However, if you want to copy a version of this song, which you own on CD, to a web page, then, assuming the work is not in the public domain, you need permission of the owner(s) of the sound recording. Are you still following? Now, let's talk about rights.

Help! You just said that rights to these works vary? While the best way to find out about rights to musical compositions and sound recordings is to study the U.S. Copyright Law of 1976, especially Sections 106, 114, and 115 (Sections 107–121 also have information on the topic), chances are that this may not be feasible for you in the course of a regular day. Indeed, it is best to be aware that the rights afforded musical compositions and sound recordings under law are not necessarily always the same. For example, if music available legally from an Internet site, and so on (musical compositions) have been distributed to the public, then a compulsory license is required to duplicate these works. (A compulsory license operates in a similar manner to fair use. In the case of music, this means that the owner of a copyrighted song can be compelled to let someone else perform it, as long as the new performer does not change the song in any way. In addition, it is possible that the new performer will have to pay a royalty fee for the use of the song. However, for reproductions of sound recordings no mention is made of a compulsory license; nonetheless, their rights include the right to reproduce the original music or other sounds (Bell 2004; U.S. Copyright Office 2008). To take a more specific example, suppose a steel pan professor writes a song for the bass pan and a vocalist. He created the sheet music (notes and lyrics). He also created a recording in which he sings this song. What he has generated is the musical composition. Now, say that he sells the rights to perform his song to another steel pan performer and a regional music production company. The recording, digital online music files, and so on, that the second steel pan person performs and that the regional music company produces are owned by them—depending on their agreement it may be owned by either one or by both. These are the sound recordings and the owner of the copyright (steel pan player, regional music company, or both) has the right to reproduce the music. Websites to go for helpful information on music/audio copyrights include the U.S. Copyright Office at www.copyright.gov/ and the "Music Copyrights Table" at www.tomwbell.com/teaching/Music(C)s.html.

Another important point that is mentioned often in this chapter is that of licenses (for general information on this subject, see chapter 5). For musical works, there are four types of licenses: mechanical, performance (how the owners of the works can collect royalties for public performances), synchronization (for reproducing and distributing a work via nonprint and movies), and print (for reproducing and distributing print musical compositions) (Frankel 2009). For the purposes of this chapter, unless otherwise directed, we will be talking of mechanical licenses, which "allow for the reproduction and distribution of a musical work as a recording in return for royalties paid to the copyright holder" (Frankel 2009, 23)

You now know that illegally copying music and other audio is not limited to file sharing (see chapter 6) or transferring music from one format to another. The following questions cover musical recordings and sheet music, other audio recordings, academic librarians and other higher education professionals, and copyright. Questions with more than one answer are presented in flow-chart form. Remember, when you use the flow charts in this chapter, you are trying to find any criterion under which you may borrow a work. Therefore, you need only to follow each flow chart until you come to that point where you satisfy one of the criteria. Once you reach that point, there is no need to go any further. For more information on each area discussed, please refer to the chapter (chapters 1 through 5) that covers the particular subject.

## FAIR USE

Q   Students in my journalism class are creating web pages as part of a class assignment. Several want to add audio clips from popular rap songs. How can they do this without it being an infringement of copyright law?

A   Use the flow chart in figure 10-1 to determine what the students can legally do with the rap songs.

## FIGURE 10-1

**Adding Popular Music to Web Pages**

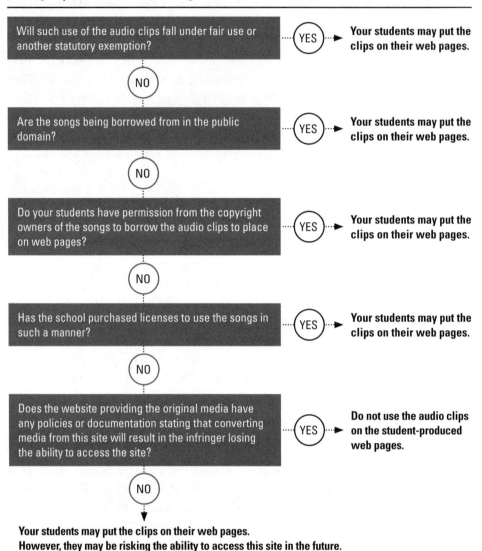

Will such use of the audio clips fall under fair use or another statutory exemption? — YES → **Your students may put the clips on their web pages.**

NO

Are the songs being borrowed from in the public domain? — YES → **Your students may put the clips on their web pages.**

NO

Do your students have permission from the copyright owners of the songs to borrow the audio clips to place on web pages? — YES → **Your students may put the clips on their web pages.**

NO

Has the school purchased licenses to use the songs in such a manner? — YES → **Your students may put the clips on their web pages.**

NO

Does the website providing the original media have any policies or documentation stating that converting media from this site will result in the infringer losing the ability to access the site? — YES → **Do not use the audio clips on the student-produced web pages.**

NO

**Your students may put the clips on their web pages. However, they may be risking the ability to access this site in the future.**

Q    I am the head music librarian at our university. A professor has come to me with a conundrum. He has discovered some sheet music in our archives that appears to be "orphaned," that is, no owner can be found. Is there any way that he can use this music under fair use?

A    It may be possible. "Fair use of orphan works may . . . be appropriate if a library keeps good and accessible records about its diligent search for the owner/author and establishes a waiting period between announcing its belief that the work is an orphan and making the work available" (Samuelson 2012, 3) (Also see chapter 5 for more information on orphaned works.)

Q   I teach students who are blind. As a necessity, all materials I use with them are either oral or in Braille. Can volunteers read books and tape them digitally for my students to use?

A   If the selected books cannot be purchased in an audio format, then, yes, the books may be read and taped for the blind students to use. Such digitization needs a notice identifying the original copyright owner and copyright date as well as a notice that the copies will not be reproduced or distributed in another format (Legislative Branch Appropriations 1997, sec. 121).

Q   I am a vocal music instructor. I like to use popular music in my classes to demonstrate different vocal arrangements. Sometimes I take songs off the Web or CDs and burn them to a class CD or copy them to a thumb drive for curricular use. Am I violating copyright law?

A   Use the flow charts in figures 10-2-1 and 10-2-2 to decide if this is a violation of copyright law. There may be exceptions, so be sure to check the U.S. Copyright Office's website (www.copyright.gov) for further information.

## FIGURE 10-2-1

**Copying Popular Music for Class Use**

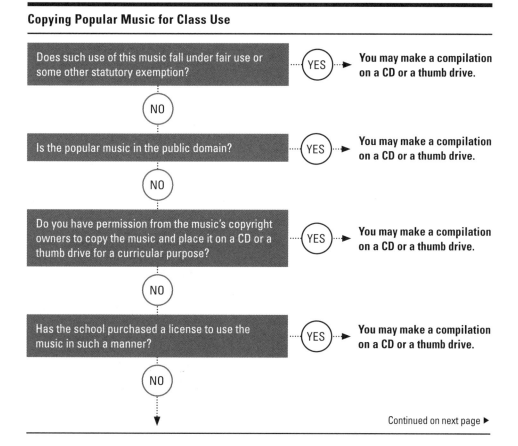

Does such use of this music fall under fair use or some other statutory exemption? — YES → You may make a compilation on a CD or a thumb drive.

NO

Is the popular music in the public domain? — YES → You may make a compilation on a CD or a thumb drive.

NO

Do you have permission from the music's copyright owners to copy the music and place it on a CD or a thumb drive for a curricular purpose? — YES → You may make a compilation on a CD or a thumb drive.

NO

Has the school purchased a license to use the music in such a manner? — YES → You may make a compilation on a CD or a thumb drive.

NO

Continued on next page ▶

# FIGURE 10-2-2

**Copying Popular Music for Class Use**

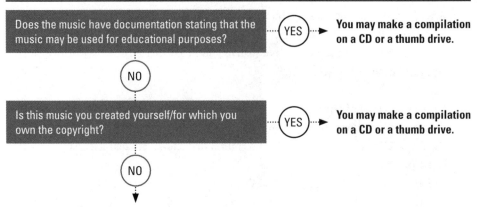

Does the music have documentation stating that the music may be used for educational purposes? ···YES···► **You may make a compilation on a CD or a thumb drive.**

NO

Is this music you created yourself/for which you own the copyright? ···YES···► **You may make a compilation on a CD or a thumb drive.**

NO

**Don't compile the selected popular music onto one CD or a thumb drive. Instead, cue up your selection on each legally purchased recording and play separately to the class.**

Q   I am teaching a unit on diet to my kinesiology students. I want to take a well-known Beyonce tune and change the words to make a song about healthy eating. This is for a teaching purpose, so there should be no problem with copyright, correct?

A   Wrong! You have just created a derivative work, and this may be an infringement of copyright law. Unless you can argue that this is a parody, find another work to use—preferably one you wrote yourself or perhaps from a company that provides public domain and royalty-free music for purchase, such as (RoyaltyFreeMusic.com) or soundzabound (www.soundzabound.com/). In addition, there are some websites, such as GMP Music (/www.gmpmusic.com/about/), which will let you "temporarily (short term) place the music track you selected in a production for the purpose of determining the acceptability of the music for that specific application" (GMP Music, 1).

Q   I want to give my English students a humorous example of a parody. I have found a songbook that attaches lyrics about mustard to the tune "Yellow Submarine." I am assuming they can do this, because it is a parody?

A   In this case, you are correct (see chapter 2 for a definition of parody). That is how these particular songbook authors can use a former Beatles tune like "Yellow Submarine" in their book. Additionally, this particular songbook also has a statement on its last page which defines the rights they are giving a would-be borrower to their parody lyrics: "YELLOW MUSTARD JAR, an original parody of YELLOW SUBMARINE, is a production of the National Mustard Museum, copyright 2012. Sing it as often as you wish but tell your audience who wrote it and we can all be friends. Please do not make any illegal or unauthorized copies" (National Mustard Museum 2012, 4).

## PUBLIC DOMAIN

Q   **If I don't register the fight song I wrote for the sports team, is it automatically in the public domain?**

A   No, it is not in the public domain unless you choose to place it there. Copyright registration is voluntary. Nonetheless, all works become copyrighted the instant they are created. If you wish to file a lawsuit against an infringer, however, it is helpful to have your work officially registered with the U.S. Copyright Office (2006).

Q   **My music class is studying the history of American and European music. I want to model good copyright behavior for my students, and at the same time, provide them with a variety of music genres that they can download to their iPads, iPods and other handheld devices. Where are some websites that I can go to find public domain music?**

A   There are a number of websites offering users "free," that is, public domain, music for download. Classic Cat (www.classiccat.net/) is such an example. Others offer a combination of public domain downloads and sheet music, such as PD Info (http://www .pdinfo.com/Public-Domain-Music-List.php) and Musopen (www.musopen.org). Be aware that these sites normally sell the public domain materials or ask for donations in terms of time, money, or more music (Classic Cat 2011; Musopen; PD Info 2013). Another possible music site of interest is Grooveshark, which offers listeners the ability to hear music online for free (Grooveshark 2013). Check out all music download sites very carefully. Some may not be licensed distributors and while appearing legitimate, offer illegal works (Sohn 2008).

Q   **I have been collecting public domain songs in a variety of audio formats for many years. I would like to take all these songs and transfer them to a digital format, and then create a recording that I can place in the cloud with the collection on it, for use in my music history class. Since I am creating any number of derivative works, with a final derivative work in mind, is this a legal use of these songs?**

A   It sure is! You can transfer these songs to any format you want, and place them in a collection. Since the original songs are in the public domain, you can even sell the final compilation, if you should so desire. Relax and have some fun with this project!

Q   **A colleague of mine has arranged a piece written originally for the piano for the flute. She thinks the original piece is in the public domain. I suggested that she find out for sure, but she says it does not matter, since if it is not in the public domain, then she is protected by "innocent intent." What is that and is she correct?**

A   Innocent intent or innocent infringement basically means that the infringer did not realize that he or she violated someone's copyright. "Innocent infringement can occur when an infringer believes that a copyrighted work is in the public domain. It can also occur when a music publisher, record company, or record distributor relies on a songwriter's promise that an infringing song was written by the songwriter when it was actually copied from someone else's copyrighted work" (Safari Books Online, 1). In truth, innocent intent or infringement is not protection against copyright violation. It could be, however, a reason for a court to award less damages to the owner of a work (Safari Books Online).

Q   If I copy song lyrics from 1908 and put them up on Facebook, are they still in the public domain?

A   As long as you copy the 1908 version of the lyrics and do not revise them in any way, then yes, they remain in the public domain, no matter where you put them.

Q   Can you file share public domain music?

A   Of course. Internet file sharing, the distribution of "digital information . . . by downloading, uploading, or even both at the same time . . . isn't illegal by definition—it depends on the distributed content" (Harris 2014, 1) As long as the music is free to consume any way the user wants, file sharing will be no problem.

## DOCUMENTATION AND LICENSES

Q   The band director is always photocopying sheet music for the marching band. He says he does this to keep the originals nice, and be able to use the sheet music for many years to come. I say he is violating copyright law. Can he do this?

A   Without the proper permissions, he cannot legally copy sheet music for the marching band. Sheet music has been copyright protected since 1831 (Justia). Figure 10-3 walks you through the process of deciding when it is permissible to copy sheet music. In addition, there are guidelines for the copying of classroom materials and music that might apply, given the right parameters. (See chapter 5: "Other Important Copyright Information" for more information on this or the U.S. Copyright Office at www .copyright.gov for possible exceptions.)

## FIGURE 10-3

**Copying Sheet Music**

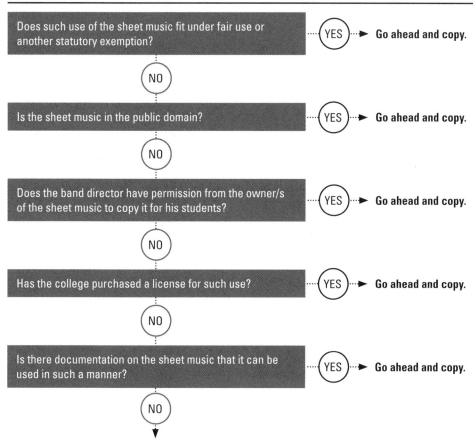

Does such use of the sheet music fit under fair use or another statutory exemption? — **YES** → **Go ahead and copy.**

**NO**

Is the sheet music in the public domain? — **YES** → **Go ahead and copy.**

**NO**

Does the band director have permission from the owner/s of the sheet music to copy it for his students? — **YES** → **Go ahead and copy.**

**NO**

Has the college purchased a license for such use? — **YES** → **Go ahead and copy.**

**NO**

Is there documentation on the sheet music that it can be used in such a manner? — **YES** → **Go ahead and copy.**

**NO**

**Don't copy the originals. Use them as intended, and when they deteriorate or become lost or stolen, purchase new sheet music.**

Q   When the College of Music purchases a license to perform a song in public concert, exactly what rights do they purchase?

A   The College of Music purchases the rights that the copyright owner licenses to them (the rights that the copyright owner agrees that the College of Music can have). These rights vary; they may include the right to charge admission fees for the concert, photocopy the accompanying sheet music, perform the song a specific number of times, tape the performance, and so on. It is important that you make sure you obtain the license or permissions for the specific rights that you need. Fines are often levied to those who infringe on licensing rights and they can be steep (HowStuffWorks 2013).

Q    When is it legal to play recorded music in the library while students and faculty, indi-
     vidually, in small groups, and in classes, are coming in and out throughout the day?

A    There are a number of possible answers to this question. See figures 10-4-1 and 10-4-2
     for information. (Be aware that what is true in this flow chart would also work for
     playing musical recordings in a college or university classroom or lab as well.)

## FIGURE 10-4-1

**Playing Recorded Music in the Library**

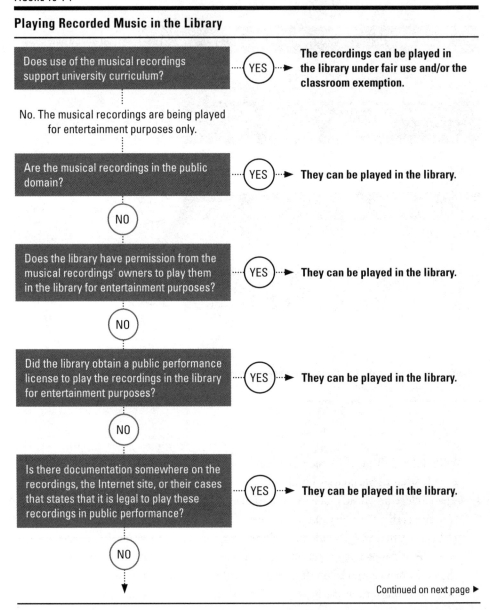

Continued on next page ▶

# FIGURE 10-4-2

## Playing Recorded Music in the Library

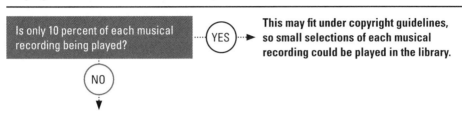

Is only 10 percent of each musical recording being played? — YES → This may fit under copyright guidelines, so small selections of each musical recording could be played in the library.

NO ↓

The library needs to find music, with the proper permissions or licenses, to play in its facility.

Q   We are very proud of the musical that the theater department performed this past year, and would like to post a video of a performance of one of the songs from it on YouTube. Can we do so legally?

A   Perhaps. The first thing you need to do is to access the copyright guidelines for the site on which you would like to post. For example, YouTube copyright information is available at http://www.youtube.com/yt/copyright. In many cases, posting a song from the musical via video on YouTube or another video-sharing website constitutes a public performance, as well as the creation of a derivative work. This means that you need to consider whether the song from the musical (1) is copyright-protected; (2) is in the public domain; or (3) has a license for reproduction attached to its use. In addition, "many colleges and universities have blanket performance licenses from ASCAP, BMI, or SESAC to cover campus music use" (National Association for Music Education 2012, 1). For more information, please follow figures 10-5-1 and 10-5-2.

# FIGURE 10-5-1

## Posting a Song on a Video-Sharing Website

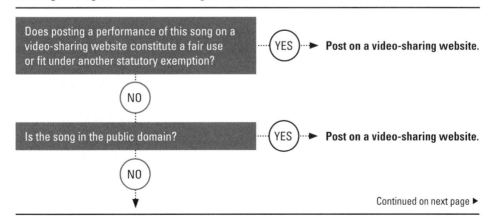

Does posting a performance of this song on a video-sharing website constitute a fair use or fit under another statutory exemption? — YES → Post on a video-sharing website.

NO ↓

Is the song in the public domain? — YES → Post on a video-sharing website.

NO ↓

Continued on next page ▶

FIGURE 10-5-2

**Posting a Song on a Video-Sharing Website**

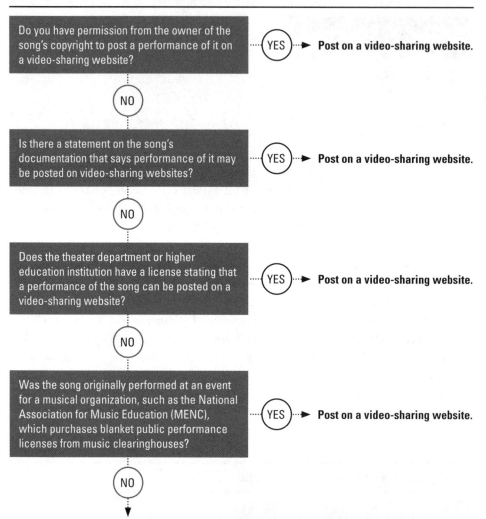

Do you have permission from the owner of the song's copyright to post a performance of it on a video-sharing website? — YES → **Post on a video-sharing website.**

NO

Is there a statement on the song's documentation that says performance of it may be posted on video-sharing websites? — YES → **Post on a video-sharing website.**

NO

Does the theater department or higher education institution have a license stating that a performance of the song can be posted on a video-sharing website? — YES → **Post on a video-sharing website.**

NO

Was the song originally performed at an event for a musical organization, such as the National Association for Music Education (MENC), which purchases blanket public performance licenses from music clearinghouses? — YES → **Post on a video-sharing website.**

NO

**Do not post a video of the song's performance by your theater on a video-sharing website. Instead, find another way to share the performance of the song with others.**

Q  iPads, iPod Shuffles and Nanos, Droids, Nooks, Kindles, MP3 players, Playaways—there are many handheld devices available in today's world—and more are being developed every day. Reading an e-book with one of these devices may impact a physically or learning-disabled student's reading in a positive way. How can we be sure that we are using these items in a legal manner?

A  The best way to legally use these new tools and the audio that can be or is downloaded on them is to follow the documentation of the downloaded item (or of the device, if the download is already available on it; e.g., Playaways). For example, Apple's "Legal Information & Notices" informs users as to how they can and cannot legally use works downloaded from iTunes (Apple 2013). An example of a site offering free text to speech downloads, solely for disabled students, is Bookshare (www .bookshare.org). This site also has a legal area specifying how the works on it may be used (Bookshare 2013).

Q   Our jazz band wishes to perform a Duke Ellington tune and record it for sale. We have been told that we may need a mechanical license for that. What is a mechanical license and where would we go to get one?

A   "A mechanical license grants the rights to reproduce and distribute copyrighted musical compositions (songs) on phonorecords (i.e., CDs, records, tapes, and certain digital configurations) . . . Simply stated, if you want to record and distribute a song that was written by someone else, or if your business requires the distribution of music that was written by others, you must obtain a mechanical license" (Harry Fox Agency 2010, 1). The largest mechanical licensing agency in the United States is Harry Fox (http:// www.harryfox.com).

## PERMISSIONS

Q   I work with a very creative music major. He wants to take a couple of recognizable bars from an Elton John song and make a new song out of it. His idea, then, is to perform the new song at his clarinet recital. Does he need any special permission to do this? After all, what he borrows is such a small piece that it should be fair use.

A   First of all, given that these are recognizable bars, it may be considered the "heart of the work," which means that, under the fair-use factors, borrowing it would be too much. Next, what your student is doing is called "sampling." It is essentially when someone borrows a small part of already existing music and uses that clip as the basis for new music (Home Recording Connection 2013). Sampling could violate copyright law for either the music's lyrics or the tune or both. Thus, your student needs to obtain permission from the owner of that particular Elton John song before creating his "new" song. Under no circumstances should this "new" song be played in a recital unless permissions for creating and performing the new song were granted to the student. (For your information, even superstars may sample. Both Lady Gaga and Jennifer Lopez have been in the news recently, charged with sampling from a Chicago musician's work [Schmadeke 2013].)

Q   Is it all right for our cheerleaders to perform routines to popular music at games and other public events? (They like to bring their own CDs and a boom box.)

A   In order to be sure that the use of the music your cheerleaders choose for their public performances is not a copyright infringement, your institution can purchase a license to use royalty-free music. Such music is obtained through clearinghouses and similar organizations (see chapter 4) or, more simply, from vendors who deal in this kind of music. These vendors either obtain permissions from copyright owners or find public-domain music. The vendors then put this music into collections, which they sell for a fee to schools and other groups who need public performance music. Often, these royalty-free music vendors have educational prices and sell blanket permissions to use the music any way an institution wishes, from public performances to multimedia productions (Royalty Free Music 2012). There are other options, as well, for obtaining the use of music for public performances, so check the U.S. Copyright Office's website (www.copyright.gov). For example, the college or university could directly contact one of the clearinghouses that deal in licenses for popular music performances. (Some of the organizations that represent such groups as songwriters, composers, music publishers, and recording labels are the American Society of Composers, Authors and Publishers [ASCAP], Broadcast Music, Inc. [BMI], the Harry Fox Agency, and the Recording Industry Association of America [RIAA].) See also figure 10-6 for guidance in making your decisions.

## FIGURE 10-6

**Performing Popular Music at Public Events**

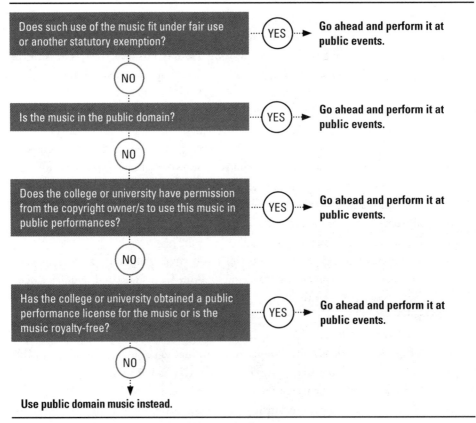

Does such use of the music fit under fair use or another statutory exemption? — YES → Go ahead and perform it at public events.

NO

Is the music in the public domain? — YES → Go ahead and perform it at public events.

NO

Does the college or university have permission from the copyright owner/s to use this music in public performances? — YES → Go ahead and perform it at public events.

NO

Has the college or university obtained a public performance license for the music or is the music royalty-free? — YES → Go ahead and perform it at public events.

NO

Use public domain music instead.

Q    Can my students print off the words to popular songs from an Internet site? They are using the lyrics as poetry examples for my English class.

A    Use the flow chart in figure 10-7 to guide your decision.

## FIGURE 10-7

**Printing Lyrics off the Internet**

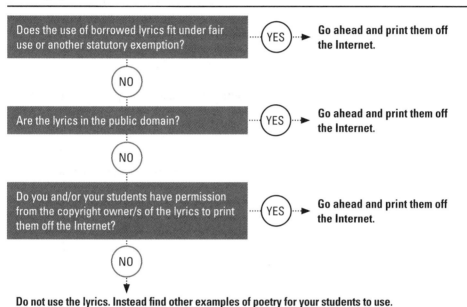

Does the use of borrowed lyrics fit under fair use or another statutory exemption? — YES → Go ahead and print them off the Internet.

NO

Are the lyrics in the public domain? — YES → Go ahead and print them off the Internet.

NO

Do you and/or your students have permission from the copyright owner/s of the lyrics to print them off the Internet? — YES → Go ahead and print them off the Internet.

NO

Do not use the lyrics. Instead find other examples of poetry for your students to use.

You may also check the website of the U.S. Copyright Office (www.copyright.gov) for possible exceptions.

## YOU CREATE IT, YOU OWN IT

Q    One of my students wrote and performed an original song for a college-wide holiday concert. She says that her parents told her about something called a "poor man's copyright." Should she use this to copyright her song?

A    It is a fallacy that sending a copy of your original work to yourself is a "poor man's copyright." This method of trying to protect your work has never stood up in court (Frankel 2009), and is meaningless under current copyright law because works are copyright-protected from the moment they are created. You can, however, officially register your work with the U.S. Copyright Office (see chapter 1).

## INFRINGEMENTS AND PENALTIES

Q   A group of students in a dairy science class wants to take the song "You're No Good" and create a satirical song about cheese entitled "You're No Gouda." Is this an infringement of copyright law?

A   No, if the use of the original song fits under the fair-use factors. Although it appears that they have created a derivative work, what they have done is to make fun of the original work. As long as such use fits under fair use, you don't need permission to make a parody. Section 107 of the U.S. Copyright law states that "the fair use of a copyrighted work . . . for purposes such as criticism [or] comment . . . is not an infringement" (U.S. Copyright Law 1976, sec. 107, 16).

Q   I have asked a technologically astute student to create a web page for our class. He wants to borrow music from another site and put it on our site. Is this an infringement of copyright law?

A   Use the flow chart in figure 10-8 to decide if this is an infringement of the law. For your information, always read the documentation on Internet sites. As can be seen from the flow chart (figure 10-8), it is possible that a specific site could provide a statement saying that works from that site could be used, with or without acknowledging the original site, on school or other educational web pages.

Q   Help! Part of the school sheet music collection was damaged in last night's rainstorm. The leak in the roof destroyed all but one piece of the altos' part. We have a concert tonight. Can we legally copy the altos' part several times for the concert?

A   Yes, it can be copied for the concert only. Include the copyright notice, found on the original sheet music, on the copy as well as any appropriate recognition to the sheet music source. Destroy the copies after the concert and purchase more originals, if they are available (Music Rights).

# FIGURE 10-8

**Borrowing Music from One Website for Another**

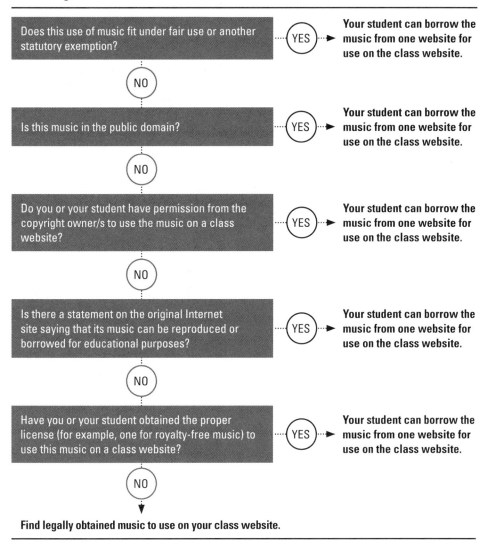

Does this use of music fit under fair use or another statutory exemption? — YES ► Your student can borrow the music from one website for use on the class website.

NO

Is this music in the public domain? — YES ► Your student can borrow the music from one website for use on the class website.

NO

Do you or your student have permission from the copyright owner/s to use the music on a class website? — YES ► Your student can borrow the music from one website for use on the class website.

NO

Is there a statement on the original Internet site saying that its music can be reproduced or borrowed for educational purposes? — YES ► Your student can borrow the music from one website for use on the class website.

NO

Have you or your student obtained the proper license (for example, one for royalty-free music) to use this music on a class website? — YES ► Your student can borrow the music from one website for use on the class website.

NO

Find legally obtained music to use on your class website.

Q   Can an associate professor download an e-book to his computer and play it aloud for
    the whole class to hear?

A   That actually depends on *how* he is going to use the e-book; for example, to support the
    curriculum or for entertainment or reward. See figure 10-9 for more information.

## FIGURE 10-9

**Playing an e-book Aloud for a Whole Class to Hear**

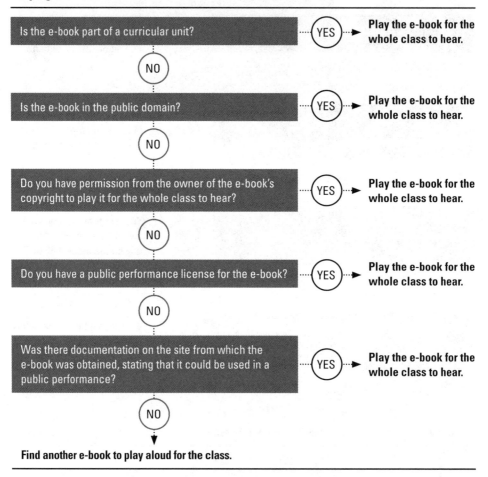

Is the e-book part of a curricular unit? — YES ▸ Play the e-book for the whole class to hear.

NO

Is the e-book in the public domain? — YES ▸ Play the e-book for the whole class to hear.

NO

Do you have permission from the owner of the e-book's copyright to play it for the whole class to hear? — YES ▸ Play the e-book for the whole class to hear.

NO

Do you have a public performance license for the e-book? — YES ▸ Play the e-book for the whole class to hear.

NO

Was there documentation on the site from which the e-book was obtained, stating that it could be used in a public performance? — YES ▸ Play the e-book for the whole class to hear.

NO

**Find another e-book to play aloud for the class.**

Q   I have been a librarian for a long time. Every year it seems that I once again need to re-mind administration, faculty, staff, and students about music copyright infringements and penalties. Comments I get include, "why does it matter—we do it all the time, and we don't get caught" and "everyone downloads music off the Web and copies off CDs and DVDs." How do I help them to understand copyright infringements can happen to—and be done by—anyone and that some infringers do get caught?

A   Perhaps one of the easiest ways to posit the notion that copyright law violations are recognized—at least part of the time—is to give popular culture examples, found in media sources ranging from trendy to more educational arenas. With that in mind, a few copyright infringement examples, all dealing with music or audio, are listed:

- Rush, a Canadian rock band, accused Rand Paul, U.S. senator from Kentucky, of playing two of their songs without permission in his recent Senate campaign (*The Courier-Journal* 2013).
- Burning CDs checked out from the library to your personal computer is a copy-right infringement (Caro 2009).
- Between 2003 and 2008, the U.S. music industry filed lawsuits against 35,000 alleged downloaders for copyright infringement (Skates 2008).
- In 2005, an Indiana songwriter accused Britney Spears of infringing on his copy-right with the song "Sometimes" (*People* 2005). The lawsuit was later dismissed; Spears was able to prove it had not been copied (Silverman 2013).
- George Harrison was sued for copyright infringement, because his song, "My Sweet Lord," allegedly infringed on the song, "He's so fine," as performed by the Chiffons (Copyright Website 2011).

Q   We are a small liberal arts college; we are also an online service provider—"a provider of online services or network access, or the operator of facilities therefor, including an entity offering the transmission, routing, or providing of connections for digital online communications, between or among points specified by a user, of material of the user's choosing, without modification to the content of the material as sent or received" (U.S. Copyright Office 2013, 1)—to our students, faculty, and staff. Right now, one of our worries is the fact that our users can upload anything they want to our server. What if something that is a copyright infringement is uploaded? Will we, as the college, be liable? Are there any ways that we can protect ourselves?

A   Yes, there is a way to reduce any liability that may occur from your users uploading illegal content: assign one of your employees to be the college copyright agent. With the passage of the Digital Millennium Copyright Act (DMCA) in 1998, Title 17 of the U.S. Code (the U.S. Copyright Act) was amended "to provide in part certain limitations on the liability of online service providers (OSPs) for copyright infringe-ment. Subsection 512(c) of the Copyright Act provides limitations on service provider liability for storage, at the direction of a user, of copyrighted material residing on a system or network controlled or operated by or for the service provider, if, among other things, the service provider has designated an agent to receive notifications of claimed infringement by providing contact information to the Copyright Office and by posting such information on the service provider's website in a location accessible to the public. The provision of information to the Copyright Office about the service provider's designated agent is a condition for reliance on the limitations on liability for service providers" (U.S. Copyright Office 2013, 1) Thus, as long as you designate an agent to collect copyright infringement information at your college, and provide the name and contact information of that agent to the U.S. Copyright Office, you will have done what you can to control any liability that may occur as a result of your users infringing on someone's copyright ownership.

## INTERNATIONAL COPYRIGHT LAW

Q   Let's assume you are a music librarian in the university library system. The university symphony conductor comes to you looking for a particular foreign score that he would like the symphony to perform during the spring concert series. He says he has used it in the past and it was free. You check and find that it is a score that was moved from the public domain back under U.S. copyright protection. Thus, there will be a hefty fee to obtain it for the spring concert series. What gives? How can this be? Don't things in the public domain *stay* in the public domain?

A   In this case, no. What happened is that a number of musical scores and other formerly copyrighted materials that were in the public domain were moved back under copyright protection when the United States Congress revised "U.S. copyright law to conform with an international copyright agreement. The new law reapplied copyright to millions of works that had long been free for anyone to use without permission" (Young 2012, 1). The U.S. Supreme Court, in *Golan v. Holder,* opined that "under unique circumstances" it is possible for such foreign works to lose public domain status and once again, become protected under copyright law (Hilden 2012, 1).

Q   For the all-college variety show, you have asked a student to dress up like Elvis, mimic his movements, and mouth the words to one of his songs. The student in question purchased a recording of Elvis's works when he backpacked in Europe last summer, and you notice that the recording has a European copyright on it. Can you use this recording in the variety show?

A   Much of Europe belongs to the same international copyright treaties and organizations as the United States. Thus, you should treat the Elvis recording purchased in Europe in the same manner that you would treat one purchased in the United States. See figure 10-10.

# FIGURE 10-10

**Using a Foreign Recording for a Public Performance**

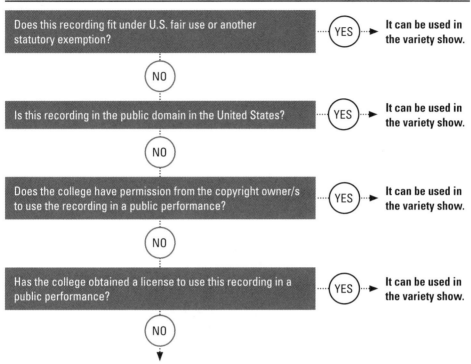

Does this recording fit under U.S. fair use or another statutory exemption? — YES → **It can be used in the variety show.**

NO

Is this recording in the public domain in the United States? — YES → **It can be used in the variety show.**

NO

Does the college have permission from the copyright owner/s to use the recording in a public performance? — YES → **It can be used in the variety show.**

NO

Has the college obtained a license to use this recording in a public performance? — YES → **It can be used in the variety show.**

NO

**Use a different song—one for which you have obtained the needed rights—in the variety show.**

Q   I purchased a CD of traditional Tibetan music when I was in China. Can I place it in the library for student checkout, when my class is studying international music?

A   Sure, this CD can be checked out from the library. This comes under the first sale doctrine; this piece of U.S. copyright law states that the owner of a legal copy of a phonorecord (sound recording) can use the copy as he or she sees fit (Lipinski 2006). This would include making the item available for circulation in a library.

Q   The director of the honors program found some popular music on the Web that she would like to download to her iPad. Her plan is that she will then play the music over the bus loudspeaker "for fun," when the honors students travel into Chicago for a university-sponsored outing. Her idea is that if she downloads the music from foreign websites, rather than U.S. ones, that she will not have to worry about U.S. copyright infringement. What do you think?

A   Be concerned about U.S. copyright law no matter where the download music was obtained from, given that "it is still illegal for someone in the United States to download a recording that is copyrighted in the United States, even if the download comes from an Internet server in a foreign country" (Fishman 2010, 122). Instead she needs to look for music to use on the bus trip that has a public performance license, is in the public domain, or for which she has obtained permission to use for entertainment.

## AVOIDING COPYRIGHT PROBLEMS

Q   Can the technology department tape multiple copies of an orchestra concert for distribution to participating students? (They will not charge for doing this.)

A   Use the flow chart in figure 10-11 to decide if such taping is allowed under copyright law. Consult the U.S. Copyright Office's site (www.copyright.gov) for exceptions and further information.

## FIGURE 10-11

**Free-of-Charge Taping of Concerts for Distribution**

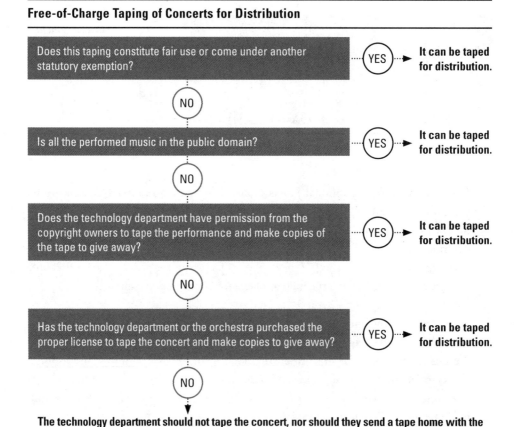

Does this taping constitute fair use or come under another statutory exemption? ···· YES ···▶ **It can be taped for distribution.**

NO

Is all the performed music in the public domain? ···· YES ···▶ **It can be taped for distribution.**

NO

Does the technology department have permission from the copyright owners to tape the performance and make copies of the tape to give away? ···· YES ···▶ **It can be taped for distribution.**

NO

Has the technology department or the orchestra purchased the proper license to tape the concert and make copies to give away? ···· YES ···▶ **It can be taped for distribution.**

NO

**The technology department should not tape the concert, nor should they send a tape home with the students, free of charge or otherwise.**

Q   Can a local business record a choral event, edit it, and sell it to the public?

A   In all probability, such a moneymaking scheme is a copyright infringement. Yet, there are some instances—however unusual—in which it would be possible for the local business to do this. (See figure 10-12.)

## FIGURE 10-12

**For-Profit Taping of University Concerts for Public Distribution**

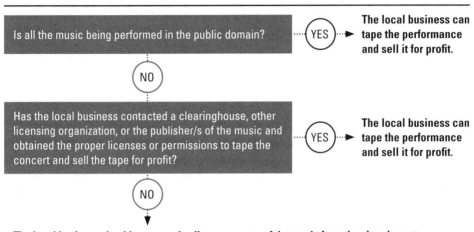

Is all the music being performed in the public domain? ····( YES )···▶ The local business can tape the performance and sell it for profit.

( NO )

Has the local business contacted a clearinghouse, other licensing organization, or the publisher/s of the music and obtained the proper licenses or permissions to tape the concert and sell the tape for profit? ····( YES )···▶ The local business can tape the performance and sell it for profit.

( NO )

The local business should not record, edit, or copy any of the music from the choral event.

Q   Admission is charged to all basketball games. Are we allowed to play popular music,
    over the loudspeaker, at intermission or before the game starts?

A   Use the flow chart in figure 10-13 to determine if the music may be played.

## FIGURE 10-13

**Playing Popular Music at University Athletic Events**

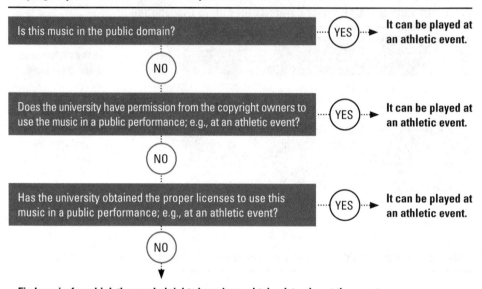

Find music, for which the needed rights have been obtained, to play at the event.
The easiest way to do this is to purchase the music royalty-free from a vendor.

Q   Lip dub videos have become very popular at our community college. A group of stu-
    dents from the vocational agriculture classes wants to create one, using a popular
    song, to focus on the American farmer. Once the video is created, they plan to put it
    up on the Web. Tell me, is this legal?

A   A lip dub video—"lip dub videos feature people lip-synching to a song before the
    original audio of that song is then dubbed over the final footage" (New York Times
    Company 2013, 1)—could be considered a public performance once it is available for
    public consumption via the Web. Therefore, apply figure 10-14 to determine whether
    placing lip dub videos, using popular songs, on the Web is a legal use.

# FIGURE 10-14

**Placing Lip Dub Videos, Using Popular Songs, on the Web**

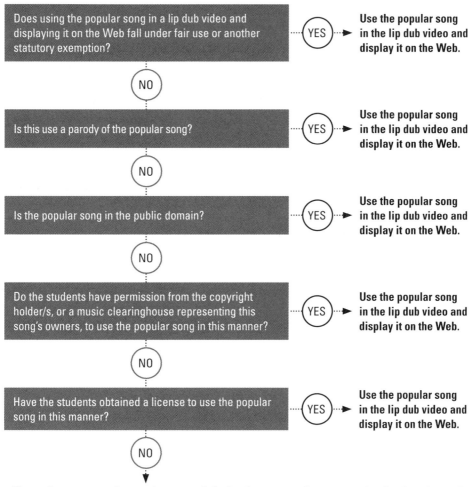

Does using the popular song in a lip dub video and displaying it on the Web fall under fair use or another statutory exemption? — YES → Use the popular song in the lip dub video and display it on the Web.

NO

Is this use a parody of the popular song? — YES → Use the popular song in the lip dub video and display it on the Web.

NO

Is the popular song in the public domain? — YES → Use the popular song in the lip dub video and display it on the Web.

NO

Do the students have permission from the copyright holder/s, or a music clearinghouse representing this song's owners, to use the popular song in this manner? — YES → Use the popular song in the lip dub video and display it on the Web.

NO

Have the students obtained a license to use the popular song in this manner? — YES → Use the popular song in the lip dub video and display it on the Web.

NO

The students may use the popular song only in the classroom to demonstrate that they have learned how to create lip dubs. For any other use, they should find another song with the needed rights.

Q    I am a technology educator in the college of education. I want to offer a class where I teach students how to use MovieMaker. My idea is that small groups of students will create an idea, develop a storyboard, videotape a short example, and add music to the final product—which will then be presented in class. I am concerned about adding the music piece. Copyright and music are so iffy. Can I do this?

A    As long as this use of music supports the curriculum (part of the lesson is teaching the students how to embed music into MovieMaker), then the students can legally do what you propose. Just make sure that this use of the music is for a curricular purpose, that project presentations stay in the classroom, and that the students understand the only other way they can use the project is for a portfolio.

Q    A faculty member at the university where I work says that students can legally put any songs they want into videos as long as they change them from an MP3 format to another format. I have never heard of this. What do you think?

A    Just like the question immediately above, if the use of the song supports the curriculum, it can be added to the video, even if the format is changed. However, if such use does not support the students' learning needs, then the derivative work made by changing the format is a violation of copyright law. See figure 10-15 for an illustration regarding this question.

# FIGURE 10-15

**Changing the Format of a Song**

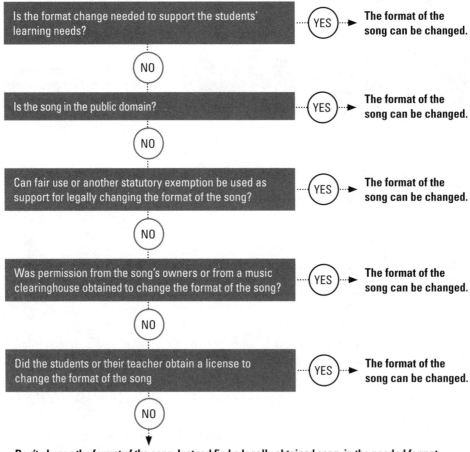

Don't change the format of the song. Instead find a legally obtained song, in the needed format, and add that to the student-produced video.

## CONCLUSION

When using audio formats—including musical recordings, sheet music, and copyright—the following are particularly important to investigate: fair use, public domain, permissions, documentation, licenses (for example, public performance), and royalty-free music companies. All, at one time or another, will help users employ sound materials without copyright infringements. Additionally, while purchasing royalty-free music from a vendor, obtaining licenses, or contacting clearinghouses may all involve spending a little money, pursuing these alternatives is usually worth it. All three are obtaining consent for you to use musical works in specific ways. Essentially, they are obtaining/providing permissions for you. Last, because confusion abounds in this area, if you have questions that this chapter does not cover or does not cover in the manner that you require, consult your college or university attorneys.

## REFERENCES

Apple. 2013. "Legal Information & Notices." www.apple.com/legal/terms/site.html.

Bell, Tom, W. 2004. "Music Copyrights Table." www.tomwbell.com/teaching/Music(C)s.html.

Bookshare. 2013. "Legal Information." www.bookshare.org/_/aboutUs/legalInformation.

Caro, Mark. 2009. "Crime Scene?" *Chicago Tribune*, October 28, 2009, section 3: 1, 5.

Classic Cat. 2011. "Classic Cat." www.classiccat.net.

Copyright Website. 2011. "Copyright Casebook: George Harrison and the Chiffons." www.benedict.com/Audio/Harrison/Harrison.aspx.

*The Courier-Journal.* 2013. "Rand Paul Accused by Rock Band of Violating Music Copyright Laws." www.huffingtonpost.com/2010/06/03/rand-paul-accused-by-rock_n_599372.html.

Fishman, Stephan. 2010. *The Public Domain: How to Find & Sue Copyright-Free Writings, Music, Art & More.* Berkeley, CA: Nolo.

Frankel, James. 2009. *The Teacher's Guide to Music, Media, and Copyright Law.* New York: Hal Leonard Books.

GMP Music. "Thank You for Selecting TEMP." http://www.gmpmusic.com/features.

Grooveshark. 2013. "Home." http://listen.grooveshark.com.

Harris, Mark. 2014. "File Sharing FAQ: An Explanation of File Sharing over the Internet." http://mp3.about.com/od/glossary/g/File-Sharing-Definition-An-Explanation-of-File-Sharing-Over-the-Internet.htm.

Harry Fox Agency. 2010. "General Information: F.A.Q.: What Is a Mechanical License?" http://www.harryfox.com/public/FAQ.jsp#12.

Hilden, Julie. 2012. "The Supreme Court's Decision in Golan V. Holder: Can the U.S. Government Constitutionally Pull Works Out of the Public Domain?" http://verdict.justia.com/2012/01/23/the-supreme-courts-decision-in-golan-v-holder.

Home Recording Connection. 2013. "Frequently Asked Questions." www.homerecordingconnection.com/faq.php#q13.

HowStuffWorks. 2013. "How Music Licensing Works." http://entertainment.howstuffworks.com/
    music-licensing3.htm.

Justia. *White-Smith Music Pub. Co. v. Apollo Co.*, 209 U.S. 1 (1908). http://supreme.justia.com/
    us/209/1/case.html.

Legal Information Institute. "Law about . . . Right of Publicity: An Overview." www.law.cornell
    .edu/topics/publicity.html.

Legislative Branch Appropriations Act of 1996. 1997. Public Law No. 104-197, sec. 110, 121.

Lipinski, Tomas A. 2006. *The Complete Copyright Liability Handbook for Librarians and Educators.*
    New York: Neal-Schuman Publishers.

Music Rights. http://www.iecc.edu/occ/lrc/musicrts.htm.

Musopen. "About." http://www.musopen.org/about.

National Association for Music Education. 2012. "Copyright Performance Licenses."
    http://musiced.nafme.org/resources/copyright-center/copyright-performance-licenses.

National Mustard Museum. 2012. *Official National Mustard Museum and Poupon U SongBook.*
    Middleton, WI: National Mustard Museum.

New York Times Company. 2013. "Schott's Vocab: Lip Dub." http://schott.blogs.nytimes.com/
    2011/05/06/lip-dub.

PD Info. 2013. "Public Domain Music: Royalty Free Music." www.pdinfo.com.

*People.* 2005. Passages. *People Magazine.* May 30, 2005: 101.

Royalty Free Music.com. 2012. "World's Largest Royalty-Free Stock Music Library."
    www.royaltyfreemusic.com.

Safari Books Online. "Innocent Intent." http://my.safaribooksonline.com/book/-/9781435459724/
    defenses-to-infringement/ch11lev1sec6.

Samuelson, Pamela. 2012. "Reforming Copyright Is Possible: And It's the Only Way to Create a
    National Digital Library." http://chronicle.com/article/Reforming-Copyright-Is/132751.

Schmadeke, Steve. 2013. "Lady Gaga Asks to Quash Courtroom Talk: Superstar Fights Suit by
    Chicago Artist Alleging Music Sample Stolen." *Chicago Tribune*, section 1, Wednesday,
    January 16, 2013, 10.

Silverman, Stephen M. 2013. "Judge: Britney Didn't Steal Song." www.people.com/people/
    article/0,,1127686,00.html.

Skates, Sara. 2008. "RIAA Changes Strategy in Fights Against Illegal Downloading."
    www.sesac.com/News/News_Details.aspx?id=882.

Sohn, David. 2008. "Music Download Warning List." www.cdt.org/copyright/warninglist.

Soundzabound. 2010. "Royalty Free Music for Schools." www.soundzabound.com.

U.S. Copyright Law. 1976. Public Law 94-553.

U.S. Copyright Office, Library of Congress. 2013. "Online Service Providers." http://www
    .copyright.gov/onlinesp.

———. 2009. "Circular 56: Copyright Registration for Sound Recordings." Washington, DC: U.S.
    Copyright Office.

———. 2009b. "Circular 56a: Copyright Registration of Musical Compositions and Sound Recordings." Washington, DC: U.S. Copyright Office.

———. 2008. "Circular 73: Compulsory License for Making and Distributing Phonorecords." Washington, DC: U.S. Copyright Office.

———. 2006. "Copyright in General." www.copyright.gov/help/faq/faq-general.html#register.

Young, Jeffrey R. 2012. "Supreme Court Upholds Law That Pulled Foreign Works Back Under Copyright." http://chronicle.com/article/Supreme-Court-Upholds -LawThat/130376/?sid=pm&utm_source=pm&utm_medium=en.

# 11

# Multimedia and Copyright Law
## Can You Borrow a Variety of Works for a Production You Are Creating?

**M**ultimedia is "interactive text, images, sound, and color. Multimedia can be anything from a simple PowerPoint slide show to a complex interactive simulation" (Utah Education Network, 1). Works can be used equally in face-to-face and/or online teaching (synchronous or asynchronous). Because multimedia productions may contain a number of separate items, each with its own copyright protection, multimedia is addressed in this book separately from the works that it may encompass. The questions that follow cover multimedia productions, higher education librarians and faculty, and copyright law. Questions with more than one answer are presented in flow-chart form. Remember, when you use the flow charts in this chapter, you are trying to find any criterion under which you may borrow a work. Therefore, you need only follow each flow chart until you come to that point where you satisfy one of the criteria. Once you reach that point, there is no need to go any further. For more information on each area discussed, refer to the chapter that covers that particular subject.

## FAIR USE

Q   A technology instructor assigns a multimedia production as a group project. One group borrows liberally for their multimedia assignment: a song from an online music source, a clip from a video, a cartoon from a newspaper Internet site, a poem from a print anthology, and a graphic from a website. Can they borrow these works under copyright law?

A   Yes, they can, if the use fits the flow chart in figure 11-1. Fair use is defined quite broadly when student projects are involved. Therefore, as long as the work borrowed is the smallest amount needed to cover the assignment, said work will come under fair use. However, if more than the minimum is borrowed, then public domain, permissions, and licenses may come into play. Thus remember, the smallest amount you need is the amount you should use. Additionally, such multimedia projects should be used for in-class presentations or student portfolios only.

## FIGURE 11-1

**Borrowing a Variety of Works for a Multimedia Production**

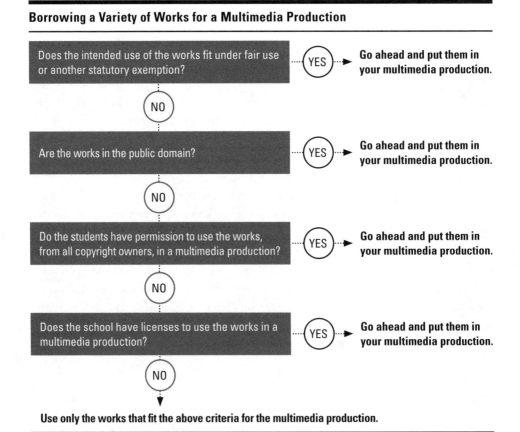

Q   Is it okay for my students to put photographs in their multimedia project?

A   Use the flow chart in figure 11-2 to determine if the students may use photographs. (For your information, obtaining permission from the subjects of a photograph is a privacy issue. This ethical matter, in addition to copyright, should be addressed when using photographs of human subjects for multimedia and other presentations, projects, and publications.)

## FIGURE 11-2

### Using Photographs in Multimedia Projects

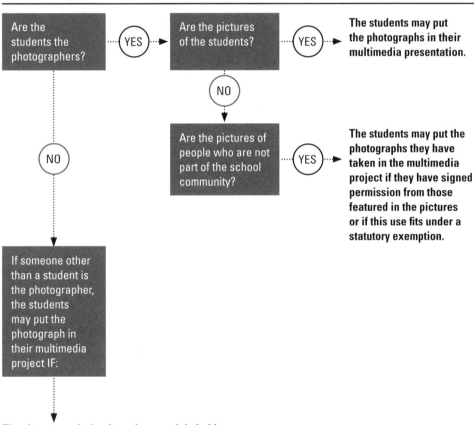

They have permission from the copyright holder.

**OR**—The photographs are in the public domain.

**OR**—Permissions or licenses for use have been obtained.

**OR**—The use of the photographs falls under fair use.

**Q**   When creating multimedia projects, do I have to use the Fair Use Guidelines for Educational Multimedia?

**A**   No. While some educators use the "Fair Use Guidelines for Educational Multimedia" (see chapter 2) to measure how much of protected works can be used in multimedia projects, in this chapter I primarily use the four fair use factors found under Section 107 of the 1976 copyright law (see also chapter 2). (Reminder: Under Section 107 of the U.S. Copyright Law [1976], the four fair use factors are "(1) the purpose and character of the use, including whether such use is of a commercial nature or is for nonprofit educational purposes; (2) the nature of the copyrighted work; (3) the amount and substantiality of the portion used in relation to the copyrighted work as a whole; and (4) the effect of the use upon the potential market for or value of the copyrighted work." You can find the law in a number of places, including the Copyright Office's website at www.copyright.gov. I do this because under fair use (U.S. Copyright Law, sec. 107) more can be borrowed than was allowed under the conservative interpretation of the four fair use factors, the "Fair Use Guidelines for Educational Multimedia." In addition, in the preamble to the "Fair Use Guidelines for Educational Multimedia" (2003), the authors made the following observations:

> While only the courts can authoritatively determine whether a particular use is fair use, these guidelines represent the participants' consensus of conditions under which fair use should generally apply and examples of when permission is required. Uses that exceed these guidelines neither may nor may not be fair use. . . . the more one exceeds these guidelines, the greater the risk that fair use does not apply. (*Copyright Crash Course* 2011, 1)

**Q**   Can I legally take recorded classical music, a film clip of a ballerina dancing, and a cartoon graphic representing a mayoral candidate and create a political parody on the elective process? I am going to a conference and think this would make a distinctive introduction to a presentation I am planning.

**A**   It is possible by doing this that you have created a transformative work. "When taking portions of copyrighted work, ask yourself the following questions: Has the material you have taken from the original work been transformed by adding new expression or meaning? Was value added to the original by creating new information, new aesthetics, new insights, and understandings?" (Stanford University Libraries 2010, 1). Transformative works can change the original media into something with new significance, which it sounds like your parody will do. Such use of copyrighted items can be legal through the first of the four fair use factors, purpose and character of use. (See chapter 2 for more information on this factor.)

## PUBLIC DOMAIN

Q   I found a multimedia work on the Web. There is no copyright notice on it. Therefore, it is in the public domain, and I can use it any way I want, correct?

A   No, that is not correct. It just means that the owner/creator did not put a copyright notice on it. Unless the website specifically states that the multimedia work is in the public domain, you must assume that it—and/or its pieces—is copyrighted and treat it accordingly.

Q   How do I put my multimedia work into the public domain?

A   If you are the owner of your multimedia work, and all contents of the multimedia product also belong to you, it is easy to transfer your rights (U.S. Copyright Office 2006). In the case of public domain, you just label your work, "public domain." If you have borrowed some or all of the contents of the multimedia work from others, then you cannot put it into public domain unless, or until, you obtain permission from the owners of the content pieces.

Q   Can a multimedia work, created entirely of public domain items, be copyright-protected and/or licensed?

A   Yes. The intermingling of the public domain items to make a new whole can be protected under copyright law and/or licensed. For example, the creator of "A Fair(y) Use Tale," a video made up entirely of clips from Disney movies, is licensed under a Creative Common license (Center for Internet and Society). However, the original public domain pieces are still public domain.

## DOCUMENTATION AND LICENSES

Q   I'm planning on giving credit to everyone from whom I borrow for my Inspiration project. I believe that since I am citing the owners and showcasing their work, I will not need to purchase any licenses or obtain permission for using these works. Am I right?

A   No! You are wrong! By giving credit, you will not be committing plagiarism. However, you could still be infringing on someone's copyright ownership. Thus, the same rules apply as for borrowing any copyrighted works.

Q   Can I, as a teacher, produce my own computer-based presentation for class instruction using a combination of student and commercial works?

A   Use the flow chart in figure 11-3 to determine which materials you can use in your presentation.

## FIGURE 11-3

### Using Student or Commercial Works in Computer-Based Presentations

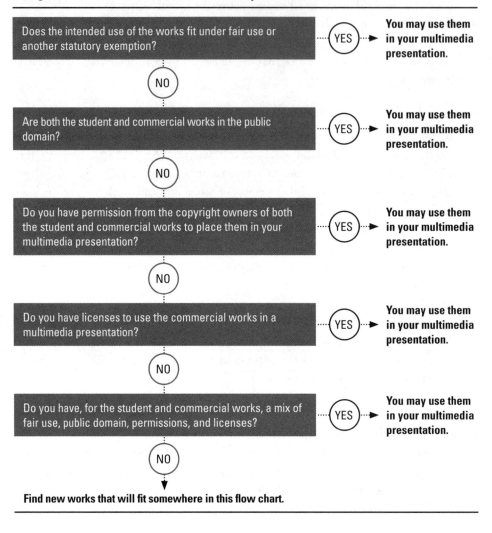

Does the intended use of the works fit under fair use or another statutory exemption? ····YES···▶ **You may use them in your multimedia presentation.**

**NO**

Are both the student and commercial works in the public domain? ····YES···▶ **You may use them in your multimedia presentation.**

**NO**

Do you have permission from the copyright owners of both the student and commercial works to place them in your multimedia presentation? ····YES···▶ **You may use them in your multimedia presentation.**

**NO**

Do you have licenses to use the commercial works in a multimedia presentation? ····YES···▶ **You may use them in your multimedia presentation.**

**NO**

Do you have, for the student and commercial works, a mix of fair use, public domain, permissions, and licenses? ····YES···▶ **You may use them in your multimedia presentation.**

**NO**

**Find new works that will fit somewhere in this flow chart.**

Q   What is the first sale doctrine? How does it affect multimedia works?

A   The first sale doctrine gives the owner of a particular copy of a work the right to dispose of that copy as she or he sees fit (Webopedia 2010). This means that someone who purchases a "lawfully made" computer-generated presentation has the right to display it, keep it, resell it, give it away, or toss it. However, the owner of the copy does not have the right to make copies of his or her one copy, prepare derivative works, permit other borrowing of the work, or place the original in the public domain. Such rights belong to the copyright holder of the original work.

Q   Imagine that you are an economics instructor for a class that is taught at two different liberal arts colleges, one site face-to-face and the other site via the Web. You find a film in a vendor's catalog that fits the subject area of one of your class units. What really is appealing about this film is the catalog statement, which says that this item has copyright clearance to be used in both online and televised distance-education classes. You purchase the film and insert it into a multimedia project that you created for your class. Within a week, you have been contacted by the film's copyright owner. This person states that you have violated copyright law and must pay royalties to him for using his work for distance education. You point out the statement in the vendor's catalog, and the copyright owner tells you that it is a misprint. Have you really infringed on copyright law? Are you liable?

A   Yes, even though you used the work in good faith and according to the documentation that you found, you are in copyright violation. Cease using the film for distance education.

Q   A student has come into the library with an interesting request. He wants to construct a video game, using music clips, poetry, graphics, and film. This is not for a class assignment; he is interested in gaming and wants to create one all on his own. His question to you is where can he get the media he needs without having to worry about copyright compliance?

A   You might direct him to a website that works with open-licensed media, such as Creative Commons (for information on Creative Commons, see chapter 5) or ClearBits, which "provides hosting and distribution for open licensed media" (ClearBits, 1).

## PERMISSIONS

Q   Can an instructor show students examples of multimedia projects to illustrate assessment concepts over a distance-education network?

A   Multimedia works can be used for face-to-face teaching, library reserve, and distance education (Harper 2007). While all multimedia works can be used in these ways, they have the same limitations that are placed on uses of works in general. For example, does the use of the work fit under fair use, is the work in the public domain, does the borrower have permission or a license for such use, and so on. For distance-education courses, certain criteria must be met, as illustrated in figure 11-4. Please also see discussion of the TEACH Act in chapter 13.

## FIGURE 11-4

**Using Student Examples in Distance Education**

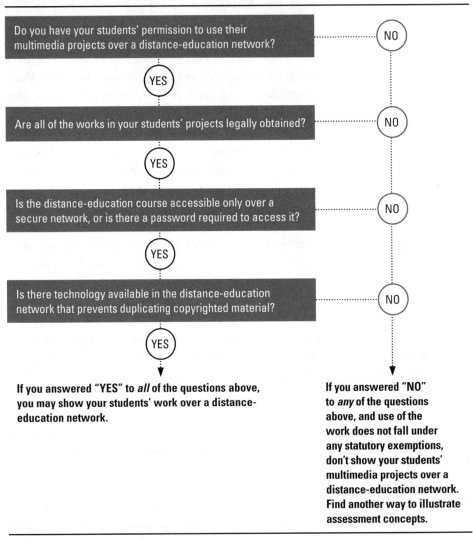

Do you have your students' permission to use their multimedia projects over a distance-education network? — NO

YES

Are all of the works in your students' projects legally obtained? — NO

YES

Is the distance-education course accessible only over a secure network, or is there a password required to access it? — NO

YES

Is there technology available in the distance-education network that prevents duplicating copyrighted material? — NO

YES

If you answered "YES" to *all* of the questions above, you may show your students' work over a distance-education network.

If you answered "NO" to *any* of the questions above, and use of the work does not fall under any statutory exemptions, don't show your students' multimedia projects over a distance-education network. Find another way to illustrate assessment concepts.

Q How can I get permission to use an animation for a multimedia presentation when the animation is credited "from the Internet"?

A You can't. Find another animation for which permission is available or the copyright owner identified, or both (and then ask for permission).

Q If you write for permission to use a newspaper cartoon in a multimedia presentation and don't get a response, can you use the cartoon in your project if you cite the work?

A No, you cannot legally do so. By citing the work, you will not have plagiarized, however.

Q Our undergraduate science students are required to create a professional portfolio during their senior year. With all the new technologies available, these portfolios have morphed from print only into multimedia products with PowerPoint, music, websites, video, you name it. What kinds of permissions do the students need to obtain as they put together their portfolios?

A That depends on how the students plan to use the portfolios they are creating. If they plan to use them for an assignment, as examples of their work for employment interviews, or as an unpaid presentation at a professional organization meeting or conference, then they do not need to get permissions for things they have borrowed from other sources (as long as they borrowed the least amount needed in each case). However, should they wish to earn money off their portfolio materials—for example, present the portfolio at a paid presentation—then any materials borrowed from sources other than those created by the seniors, themselves, need permissions or a license for use.

Q Three students and I have created a presentation using Prezi. We have a variety of things we move between: print, video, and images. A communications professor has approached me and asked if she might use this presentation. Two of my students have graduated, and I no longer have their addresses. Can the communications professor legally use our presentation with just my permission?

A "If there are multiple creators or authors of the work you wish to use, you must get permission from each individual" (Copyright Education & Consultation Program, 2).

## YOU CREATE IT, YOU OWN IT

Q Somebody already copyrighted the name that I wanted to use for my multimedia project. Can I still use it?

A Names cannot be copyrighted. Therefore, you can use a name, unless it is trademarked. For your information, "A *trademark* is a word, phrase, symbol or design, or a combination of words, phrases, symbols or designs, that identifies and distinguishes the source of the goods of one party from those of others" (United States Patent and Trademark Office 2010, 1).

Q   I created a very detailed multimedia project for a theater class that I teach. I am now moving to a new university, and I want to take my project with me. My current university says that I have to leave it with them. Who should get control of my multimedia project?

A   Use the flow chart in figure 11-5 to determine if you own the project or if it is a work for hire.

## FIGURE 11-5

**Who Owns Instructor-Created Multimedia?**

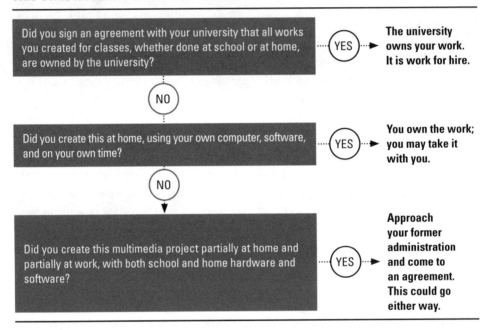

Did you sign an agreement with your university that all works you created for classes, whether done at school or at home, are owned by the university? ···· YES ···► The university owns your work. It is work for hire.

NO

Did you create this at home, using your own computer, software, and on your own time? ···· YES ···► You own the work; you may take it with you.

NO

Did you create this multimedia project partially at home and partially at work, with both school and home hardware and software? ···· YES ···► Approach your former administration and come to an agreement. This could go either way.

Q   I want to protect my ownership of a multimedia project that I created and presented over real-time television to a masters'-level class in another state. What do I need to do?

A   Register it with the U.S. Copyright Office. (See chapter 1.)

Q   Two of my English students—on their own time—created a PowerPoint (PPT) project on how to write a term paper, using material from print sources and the Web, as well as sound and video clips from popular media. It is really done very well. They are proud of their work and would like to post it to the Web. However, they are afraid, with the amount of information being added daily to the Web, that their work will not be easily found. Therefore, in addition to checking to ensure that they have obtained all necessary copyright permissions for their work, they want to give it a "catchy" domain name—one that others will want to access. They have chosen LifeofPiPaper as their domain name, even though the PPT has nothing to do with this popular book and movie. Does this matter, since they are not charging for use of the PPT?

A   Yes, it can matter. Make sure that a domain name fits the subject of the multimedia project; do not delude those who might access your work (Donaldson 2008).

## INFRINGEMENTS AND PENALTIES

Q   How do I know if I am allowed to use Internet clip art in my multimedia project?

A   Use the flow chart in figure 11-6 to answer this question.

## FIGURE 11-6

**Using Clip Art in Multimedia Projects**

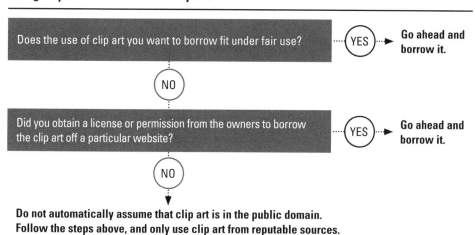

Do not automatically assume that clip art is in the public domain.
Follow the steps above, and only use clip art from reputable sources.

Remember: there are many instances in which web pages provide clip art to users. While clip art is most often in the form of images, animations and sound can also be clip art. The problem is that sometimes those creating or owning a web page borrow copyrighted images, and so on, from other sites, place these on their site, and then inform users that the site is in the public domain. Unless you know more about a piece of clip art, you might not know whether it is really in the public domain or not. Therefore, when using clip art that has been identified as public-domain material, it is best to obtain it from a site that you consider reputable, such as a prominent computer software site.

Q    I teach online. May I place an instructional video in my multimedia presentation for
     class?
A    Use the flow chart in figure 11-7 to determine if you are allowed to use the video.

## FIGURE 11-7

### Using Videos in Multimedia Projects

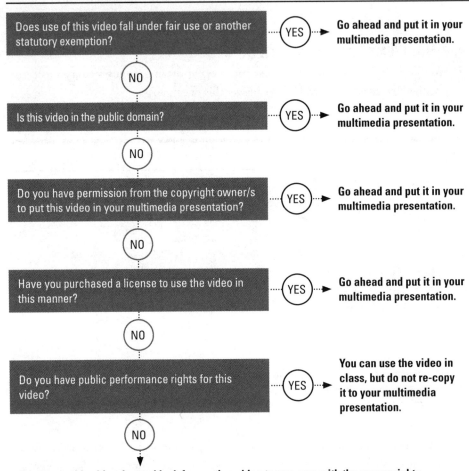

Does use of this video fall under fair use or another statutory exemption? ---- YES ----► **Go ahead and put it in your multimedia presentation.**

NO

Is this video in the public domain? ---- YES ----► **Go ahead and put it in your multimedia presentation.**

NO

Do you have permission from the copyright owner/s to put this video in your multimedia presentation? ---- YES ----► **Go ahead and put it in your multimedia presentation.**

NO

Have you purchased a license to use the video in this manner? ---- YES ----► **Go ahead and put it in your multimedia presentation.**

NO

Do you have public performance rights for this video? ---- YES ----► **You can use the video in class, but do not re-copy it to your multimedia presentation.**

NO

**Do not use this video. Instead look for another video to use, one with the proper rights or permissions.**

Q   Can I change a digitized image enough that it becomes my work, and can I place it in
    my multimedia production without worrying about copyright infringement?

A   No. A derivative work is a derivative work.


Q   Two of my freshman literature students are Harry Potter fanatics. They have created a
    Keynote presentation about the boy wizard, including a listing of links of Harry Pot-
    ter websites. I have heard that lists can violate copyright law, and I don't want them to
    get into any trouble. What's the deal here?

A   It is not a copyright violation if your students make their own list of Harry Potter
    links and put them in their Keynote presentation. It could be an infringement if they
    borrowed a listing of Harry Potter links created by someone else.


## INTERNATIONAL COPYRIGHT LAW

Q   I teach history at a large midwestern university. As part of a class multimedia presen-
    tation, I have created a list of links to historical sites worldwide. If I put the presenta-
    tion on my web page and make my links "live," will my students be copyright-compli-
    ant if they use the links?

A   Yes. However, it would be good "netiquette" to ask for permission from those sites
    before you provide their links to your students. (It may not always be practical, on the
    other hand, to ask for permission to link to others' Internet sites. You will need to use
    your own judgment on this issue.)


Q   Our college library has an extensive collection of foreign language tapes, DVDs,
    CDs, videos, and multimedia. Purchased in several foreign countries (we have a large
    population of foreign-born students at our college), we believe that all items were
    legally obtained. We would like to copy these to a server, in order to stream them into
    classrooms when they are needed for curricular support. Can we do so legally?

A   As we have discussed in earlier chapters, due to the number of international copyright
    conventions and organizations to which the United States belongs, it is best to treat
    foreign works as you would something created and published in the United States. See
    figure 11-8 for more information. Also remember, just because you have the ability
    and equipment/materials to copy something, that does not automatically make such
    copying legal.

## FIGURE 11-8

**Copying Media to a Server for Curricular Use**

Does copying the media to a server fit under fair use or another statutory exemption? ···(YES)➤ **You may copy the media to a server.**

(NO)

Is the media being copied to the server in the public domain? ···(YES)➤ **You may copy the media to a server.**

(NO)

Does the library have permission from the copyright owner/s of the media to copy it to a server? ···(YES)➤ **You may copy the media to a server.**

(NO)

Has the library purchased a license to copy the media to a server? ···(YES)➤ **You may copy the media to a server.**

(NO)

Is there documentation on the media's packaging that states it may be copied for curricular use? ···(YES)➤ **You may copy the media to a server.**

(NO)

**While some may argue that copying for curricular purposes is automatically legal, in actuality that is not the case. The first sale doctrine (see this chapter under "Documentation and Licenses") specifies that you have purchased an item, not the right to copy it indiscriminately.**

## AVOIDING COPYRIGHT PROBLEMS

Q   One of the undergraduates in the honors program wants to obtain copyright registration for the multimedia project he did in an art class. Can he do so, since he is still underage?

A   Sure he can. The U.S. Copyright Office "issues registrations to minors" as well as adults for copyright purposes (U.S. Copyright Office, 1).

Q   We are working on a parody unit in English class. I would like to collect a bunch of film and music parodies off the Web and from popular media, and string them together into one cohesive whole that I can then use with my class. Is this okay to do?

A   Well, by borrowing parodies from a number of websites and popular media and stringing them together, you are creating a derivative work. However, there is a way that you can use these parodies in class, as part of the classroom exemption—just link to each parody separately while you are teaching.

Q   The sorority I belong to is holding a variety show in a couple of weeks. Alumni members normally tape the whole show—songs, poetry readings, short skits, dances, and so on—and then use these tapes for sorority recruitment or just to watch at home. I think that they are creating a multimedia derivative work, and that this could be a copyright infringement. Should I warn my sorority sisters?

A   You have three different things going on here. First of all, is it legal for the sorority alumni to tape the variety show? Well, as with most things copyright, that depends. One might be able to argue that this is a type of personal fair use; that is, if the alumni members are taping the performance in order to watch it in their homes at a later time. (See figure 11-9 for information.) Secondly, have the alumni, by taping the acts that are performed one after another, created a derivative work? One could argue that, yes, a derivative work has been created. That said, one could again follow figure 11-9—there are some instances in which creating a derivative work would be fine (if the items in question were in the public domain or if the right permissions, licenses, or documentation had been obtained). Lastly, should you warn your sorority sisters? Well, this may put you in the uncomfortable position of becoming the "copyright police." We will discuss this in more depth in the last chapter. However, you might choose to inform them, in a nonconfrontational manner, that such a public taping may well be a copyright infringement.

## FIGURE 11-9

**Taping a Variety Show**

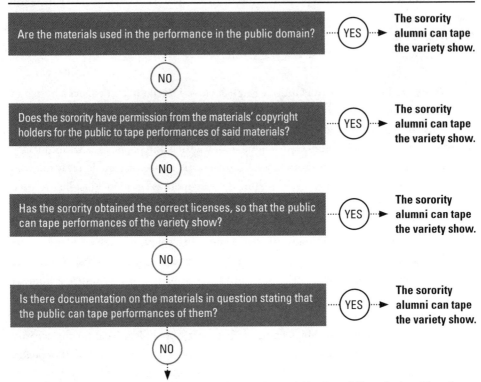

In all probability, there will be some things that can be taped by the public and other things for which there are no permissions, licenses, or documentation for public taping. If the sorority alumni keep the variety show tapes in their homes, for personal use only, one might be able to argue that such use is OK. Otherwise, it is best not to tape the variety show.

Q    I am an astronomy professor. As part of a unit on the planets, I plan to collect images, music, film—any media I can find that has been named after a planet. The final product will be a multimedia production that I will show to the class. One of my students has created an array of amazing sketches of Saturn. I would like to include several of these in my production. Since he drew them for my class, can I just take them and add them to the multimedia unit?

A    Original work—no matter the age of the individual creating it—is automatically copyright-protected. This means that your student's sketches are copyrighted, and you need to ask permission from him to use these drawings in your multimedia production. (Additionally, if he were a minor, it would be prudent to also check with his parents or guardian before using his work.) Finally, obtain the permission in writing, including the date and the signatures of the borrower (yourself) and those who are granting permission for use (in this case, the student and/or his parents/guardian).

## CONCLUSION

It is important to remember that the more you borrow without obtaining permission from the owner/creator of a work, the greater the likelihood that you might be in infringement of copyright law. Sometimes all that the owner/creator wants is recognition for his or her work. Therefore, on all your educational multimedia creations (and other creations as well), remember to include a reference section at the beginning, end, or in the body of your work where you cite those from whom you have obtained material. However, because a multimedia product may contain a number and variety of formats as part of its whole, obtaining the needed rights for use can, at times, be complicated and time-consuming.

## REFERENCES

The Center for Internet and Society. "A Fair(y) Use Tale." http://cyberlaw.stanford.edu/documentary-film-program/film/a-fair-y-use-tale.

ClearBits. "About Clearbits." http://www.clearbits.net/about.

Copyright Crash Course. 2011. "Building on Others' Creative Expression." http://copyright.lib.utexas.edu/ccmcguid.html.

Copyright Education & Consultation Program. http://blogs.cites.illinois.edu/library-copyright/getting-permission.

Donaldson, Michael C. 2008. *Clearance & Copyright: Everything You Need to Know for Film and Television*. 3rd ed. Los Angeles: Silman-James.

Fair Use Guidelines for Educational Multimedia. 2003.www.washington.edu/classroom/emc/fairuse.html.

Harper, Georgia. 2007. "Copyright Crash Course: Building on Others' Creative Expression: Fair Use Guidelines for Educational Multimedia." http://copyright.lib.utexas.edu/ccmcguid.html#3.

Stanford University Libraries. 2010. "Copyright & Fair Use: Measuring Fair Use: The Four Factors." http://fairuse.stanford.edu/Copyright_and_Fair_Use_Overview/chapter9/9-b.html.

U.S. Copyright Office. 2006. "FAQ: Assignment/Transfer of Copyright Ownership." www.copyright.gov/help/faq/faq-assignment.html.

———. FAQ: "Who Can Register?" www.copyright.gov/help/faq/faq-who.html.

United States Patent and Trademark Office. 2010. "Trademark, Copyright, or Patent?" www.uspto.gov/trademarks/basics/trade_defin.jsp.

Utah Education Network. "Ed Technology Glossary of Terms." www.uen.org/core/edtech/glossary.shtml#M.

Webopedia. 2010. First sale doctrine. www.webopedia.com/TERM/F/first_sale_doctrine.html.

# 12

# Print Works and Copyright Law
## Is It Legal to Copy Print Works for Class at the Last Minute?

Print, as a medium of communication, has been around for literally thousands of years. In the past, print forms included tomb encryptions, illuminated manuscripts, and codices. Today, common print items consist of books, newspapers, magazines, poetry, play scripts, cartoons, recipes, and more. In addition, the invention of computers; iPads, iPods, and handheld digital devices like Kindles and NOOKs; and even cell phones (when texting) has brought print into the digital world. Are issues of copyright a part of this new level of print? Although these new mediums may make copyright seem even more confusing than before, the answer to that question is "yes, definitely." So let's begin this chapter by taking a look at print and fair use (law and guidelines), both of which are very important for academic librarians and other higher education professionals.

When copying or borrowing from print sources, it is important to be aware not only of the fair use factors discussed in chapter 2 (U.S. law), but also of the brevity, spontaneity, and cumulative effect (three print) test. These three "tests" are guidelines, endorsed by the United States Congress, for purposes of educational and classroom copying (print), and interpreted from the 1976 Copyright Act. Basically, what they do is help decipher application of the fair use factors. "Brevity" means the least amount possible is to be copied. This amounts to a whole poem if the poem is less than 250 words or an excerpt from a poem of no more than 250 words; 2,500 words or less for an essay or article, or no more than 10 percent or 1,000 words for an excerpt; or one illustration per book or periodical. "Spontaneity" means that the copying is a "last minute" request for class, usually instigated by an individual instructor.

"Cumulative effect" means the amount of work that is copied over a class term. For print material this means: "(i) The copying of the material is for only one course in the school in which the copies are made. (ii) Not more than one short poem, article, story, essay, or two excerpts may be copied from the same author, nor more than three from the same collective work or periodical volume during one class term. [and] (iii) There shall not be more than nine instances of such multiple copying for one course during one class term" (U.S. Copyright Office 2009, 7). Be aware that it may be possible for print copying to fall under the fair use factors (law) but not under guidelines. Therefore, while both are addressed in this chapter, if your use of a work falls under the law, then you don't need to worry about guidelines.

Below are questions that cover print, academicians, and copyright. Questions with more than one answer are presented in flow-chart form. Remember, when you use the flow charts in this chapter, you are trying to find any criterion under which you may borrow a work. Therefore, you need only follow each flow chart until you come to that point where you satisfy one of the criteria. Once you reach that point, there is no need to go any further. For more information on each area discussed, please refer to the chapter (in part I) in which that particular subject is covered.

## FAIR USE

Q    I teach biology. I have a textbook that I wish to assign to my students. However, it is very expensive, and I feel guilty asking them to purchase it for my class. Can I photocopy parts of the book for each member of class?

A    Use the flow chart in figure 12-1 to determine if you are allowed to make these copies.

## FIGURE 12-1

**Photocopying Parts of a Book**

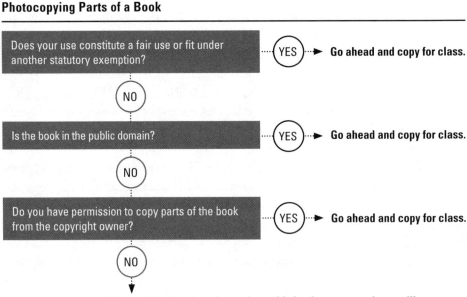

Q   I am a college librarian. A student with visual problems, and who can only read large
    print, wishes to use a specific book that the library has only in regular-sized font. Can
    the student copy this book using the enlarging feature on a copy machine?

A   In the twenty-first century, there are several possible answers to this question. If the
    book is not available in large print in a book format or on a device such as a Kindle,
    Nook, iPad, or other handheld appliance that can enlarge text—or in some other form
    that makes it usable by the visually impaired student, such as an audiobook—then
    copying it comes under fair use. However, there are a number of companies that make
    large-print copies of books, as well as any number of books now accessible via hand-
    held devices. There are also machines, such as closed-circuit television (CCTV) and
    small handheld magnifiers, which enlarge print. It is best to pursue all of these options
    before encouraging the student to enlarge the book using a copy machine. Also, if the
    library has purchased a large-print book and it is not yet available, check with the pub-
    lishing company to see if they will let the student make an enlarged copy to use until
    the commercial one arrives.

    For your information, although it does not apply to the specific situation in figure 12-2,
    section 121 of the U.S. Copyright Law is important to educators when working with
    blind and other students with disabilities. This section sets forth limits on the exclusive
    rights of copyright holders when reproducing works for people who are visually im-
    paired and people with other disabilities. (See section E of appendix A.)

Q   Does copying one illustration from a picture book fall under fair use?

A   Because it is a picture book, that is, there are many illustrations in the book, one copy
    of one illustration would fall under the fair use factors, unless each illustration is regis-
    tered for copyright separately. In that case, copying one illustration from a picture book
    could be an infringement. Check on the verso (back) of the title page. Information
    on the illustrations' copyright should be there. Remember, if the information you are
    looking for is not on the verso, or elsewhere in the book, you need to go through the
    basic steps we discuss in this book, including checking to see if the item is in the public
    domain, and if not, searching for permission to use it. In such a case, a clearinghouse
    for print materials (see chapter 4) could come in handy. Also be sure to check if any of
    the statutory exemptions for classrooms, libraries, or archives apply.

## FIGURE 12-2

**Copying Books for Visually Impaired Students**

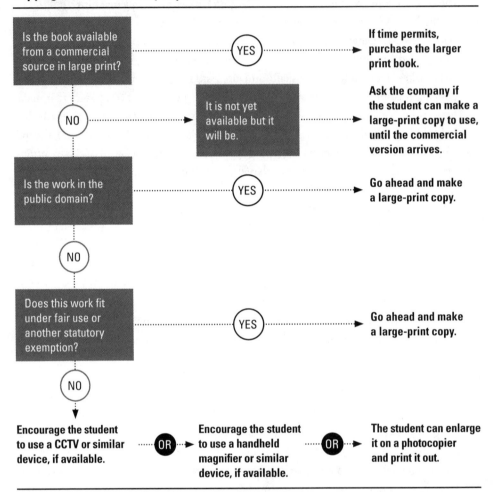

## PUBLIC DOMAIN

Q   There is a chapter in a book that I would really like to use in my class. I have tried
    contacting the publisher, but the company doesn't seem to exist anymore. Does that
    mean that this book is now in the public domain?

A   Use the flow chart in figure 12-3 to determine if the book is in the public domain.

# FIGURE 12-3

## Books in the Public Domain

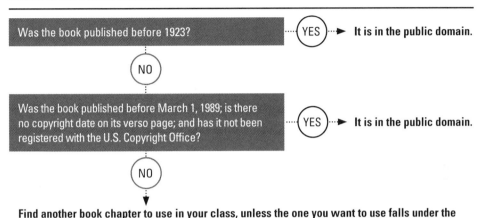

Was the book published before 1923? — YES ▶ **It is in the public domain.**

NO

Was the book published before March 1, 1989; is there no copyright date on its verso page; and has it not been registered with the U.S. Copyright Office? — YES ▶ **It is in the public domain.**

NO

**Find another book chapter to use in your class, unless the one you want to use falls under the fair use factors or another statutory exemption.**

Q   If a magazine is out of print, is it now in the public domain and thus, is it legal for a professor to make copies of one of the articles for his class?

A   It is important to recognize here that magazine articles can be (1) independently protected by their own copyright registrations or (2) part of the magazine's general copyright registration. How the article is copyright-protected depends on the agreement between the owner of the article and the magazine publisher at the time of publication. Thus, you must check copyright registration for the article you wish; that is, there is no one answer to this question. (See also the flow charts, figures 12-4-1 and 12-4-2.)

# FIGURE 12-4-1

## Magazine Articles in the Public Domain

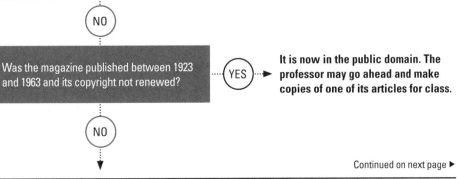

Was the magazine published before 1923? — YES ▶ **It is now in the public domain. The professor may go ahead and make copies of one of its articles for class.**

NO

Was the magazine published between 1923 and 1963 and its copyright not renewed? — YES ▶ **It is now in the public domain. The professor may go ahead and make copies of one of its articles for class.**

NO

Continued on next page ▶

## FIGURE 12-4-2

**Magazine Articles in the Public Domain**

The professor must assume that the magazine is still under copyright protection. However, it can still be legal for him to make copies of some of its articles for his class. To see how, continue:

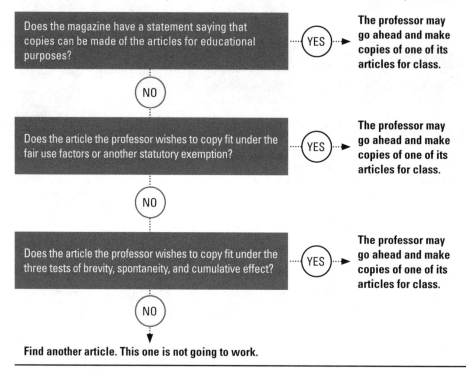

Find another article. This one is not going to work.

**Q** I teach technology courses in the engineering department. A student asked me if she could include information from a government document in a paper she is writing; and, if she did, if she needed to be concerned about copyright. What should I tell her?

**A** Tell her that yes, she can include such information in her paper; just remember to cite the documents, whether they are in the public domain or not. (Although many government documents are in the public domain, there are some that are not. It is best to treat all such items as you would any other information source.)

**Q** Can the theater department put on a Shakespeare play, in a public performance, without paying royalties to a clearinghouse or theater service? (After all, Shakespeare's plays *must* be in the public domain!)

**A** If the theater department uses an original Shakespeare play with no added directives, illustrations, or updates, then yes, they may put on a Shakespeare play in a public performance. If the script they use has any added components, however, then it may be back under copyright. In such a case, the department would need to get permission from the owner of the revisions or go through a theater clearinghouse in order to perform the play in public. See also figure 12-5.

# FIGURE 12-5

**Performing a Shakespeare Play in Public**

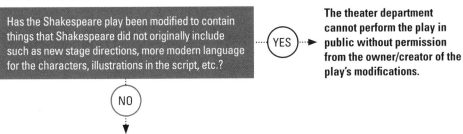

The original Shakespeare plays are in the public domain.

The theater department can perform the play in public. The original Shakespeare plays are in the public domain.

Q  Is an obituary from the 1930s in the public domain if the newspaper it was originally printed in is out of business?

A  No. The only materials automatically in the public domain are those published before 1923 or those that the owner/s have placed in the public domain (see chapter 3). It is possible that the defunct newspaper sold its archives to another individual or newspaper and that entity now owns the copyright.

## DOCUMENTATION AND LICENSES

Q  I am the advisor for a group of students studying to be school librarians. A question has come up: do school librarians need public performance rights to read a storybook to an elementary class? I know that they do this all the time. How should I advise these students?

A  Well, assuming the book is being used in a public performance, in a school setting, and that the school is nonprofit, the performance is occurring in the library or another place dedicated to instruction, and the storybook was legally obtained, then, yes, school librarians can read a book and not be infringing on someone's copyright (U.S. Copyright Law 1976). It is also possible that such a reading fits under the four fair use factors. Furthermore, "there are general practices that we have come to accept as OK. These practices have become so normalized that they actually affect the development and interpretation of the copyright law" (Russell 2003). Therefore, yes, school librarians can read a storybook to a class without public performance rights.

Q   A textbook publishing company sent me a teacher's guide that says its worksheets may be copied for student use. One of the worksheets is two pages long, with five activities listed. I only need activities one, two, and four. Can I scan the worksheet, remove the parts that the students do not need, and share that version electronically with my students?

A   In all likelihood, the action you are describing is an infringement; it appears to be creating a derivative work. Use figure 12-6, "Copying a Teacher's Guide Page," for more guidance.

## FIGURE 12-6

### Copying a Teacher's Guide Page

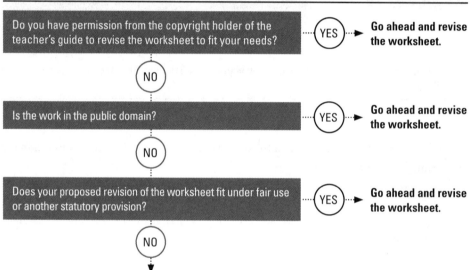

Do you have permission from the copyright holder of the teacher's guide to revise the worksheet to fit your needs? — **YES** → **Go ahead and revise the worksheet.**

**NO**

Is the work in the public domain? — **YES** → **Go ahead and revise the worksheet.**

**NO**

Does your proposed revision of the worksheet fit under fair use or another statutory provision? — **YES** → **Go ahead and revise the worksheet.**

**NO**

**Do not revise the worksheet. Instead, find another worksheet that meets your needs, create one of your own, or copy the entire worksheet, but direct your students to only use activities one, two, and four.**

Q   We do not have enough scripts for our play. Is there any problem with copying a couple more for the student directors?

A   Yes, there is a problem! The theater instructor or whoever is in charge of production of the play usually signs a contract with a licensing agency as to which rights have been purchased and which have not. The university/group producing the play then pays royalties to the agency for those rights purchased. Purchased rights can include the number of times the play may be put on in public, the dates between which the play may be put on, the amount and type of advertising that may be done, whether you can make changes to the script or not (most licenses exclude the making of script changes), or even the copying of scripts (Dramatists Play Service 2013). First check the terms of the license you have signed. Your question on copying the script a couple more times may be answered there. If it is not, it is best to ask the licensing agency for permission to copy the scripts, if more are needed.

Q   We are in the process of putting on a musical. How many times can we give public performances of it?

A   The contract the school signs with the licensing agency will determine how many times the musical may be performed in public.

Q   I want to copy a magazine article thirty times for a class reading assignment. Can I do this under copyright law?

A   Use the flow chart in figure 12-7 to determine if copyright law allows copying this article.

## FIGURE 12-7

**Making Multiple Copies of Articles**

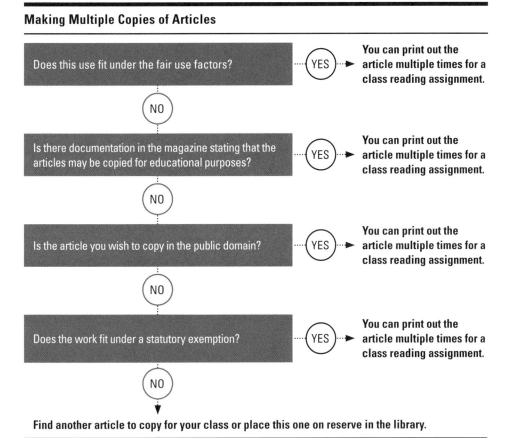

## PERMISSIONS

Q   I'd like to start my class computer-based presentation by digitizing a current political cartoon from the local newspaper and inserting it onto the first slide. Is doing this OK?

A   The flow chart in figure 12-8 will help you decide if you are allowed to use the cartoon this way. In addition, the following information may be useful:

- The copyright owner of a newspaper cartoon is usually a syndicate, such as United Media, which acts as a vendor for the cartoonist, contacting newspapers, handling royalties, and working with contracts and licenses. However, a few cartoonists may own their own cartoons, or the cartoons could be owned by the newspapers or magazines employing the cartoonist (Stim 2007).

- Section 110(1) of the Copyright Law says that it is not an infringement for a teacher to display a work in a nonprofit education setting (classroom) if the copy was lawfully made. Section 110(2) adds the following, which may affect the display if you are transmitting it: if the display is a regular part of the instructional activities; if the display is directly related/or material is of assistance to the teaching content of the transmission; and if the transmission of the work is made for classroom reception or for people with disabilities or other circumstances that prevent their attendance in the classroom; then—it is not an infringement to use it (U.S. Copyright Law 1976).

- While it may be impractical to purchase a copy of the cartoon for every student in class, that is a legal option in this case.

- In addition to following figure 12-8, you may want to consider the first sale doctrine. This doctrine gives those who obtain individual copies of a work the privilege of deciding how to use or dispose of said copies in any manner they wish (First Sale Doctrine 2010; Lipinski 2006). It does not give the individual copy owners the right to reproduce the work indiscriminately, however.

- This means that if you purchased the political cartoon legally, then you have the right to display it, keep it, resell it, give it away, or toss it. However, you do not have the right to make copies of your one copy, prepare derivative works, permit other borrowing of the work, or place the original in the public domain. Because in this instance, you wished to make a digital copy of the cartoon, the first sale doctrine, here, is "iffy" at best.

# FIGURE 12-8

**Digitizing Newspaper Cartoons**

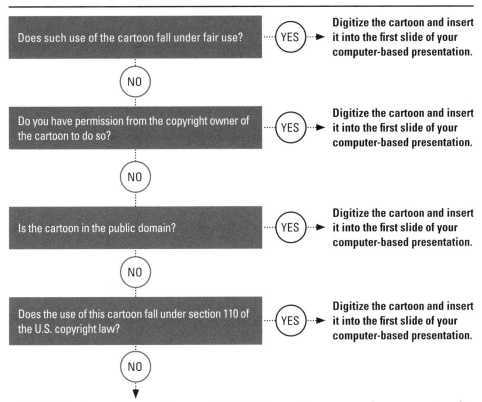

Don't digitize the cartoon or put it on your first slide. You may, however, purchase a newspaper for every student in class and ask them to look at the cartoon while you talk about it, use a document camera to project the image, or find another introduction to your computer-based presentation.

Q   A journalism class instructor wishes to create a course-pack for a newspaper seminar he is teaching. He includes newspaper articles, book chapters, clippings, and other readings that he feels his students need. While all the items have been obtained from other sources, he has been very diligent in remembering copyright law, and has received permission from all owners to copy their works for inclusion in the packet. Our dilemma is this: he wants to go digital and post these on a class website, instead of handing out print versions. Is this OK?

A   Unless the journalism instructor received permission to also digitize the readings when he contacted each copyright owner, scanning of the works represents creating derivatives. Thus, all owners again need to be contacted for their permissions.

Q    I am an instructional designer at a large university. I am in the midst of creating an on-line training module on privacy issues found in FERPA (Family Educational Rights and Privacy Act) and HIPPA (Health Insurance Portability and Accountability Act), for university faculty and staff. I have found a flow chart in a book at our main library that I would like to use in the online presentation. Do I need to contact the copyright holder for permission to use one flow chart (there are forty-five in the book)?

A    This can be a complicated answer. Use figures 12-9-1 and 12-9-2 for help with this question. Other queries to consider include: is the university public or private? Do you, as the instructional designer, want to borrow the flow chart "as is," change the words in the boxes, or take out all words (i.e., just use the basic flow chart design) and add your own words? Does the number of flow charts in the book make a difference as to whether or not you need to ask for permission? Does the book you wish to borrow from have one copyright or is each flow chart registered singly by the U.S. Copyright Office?

## FIGURE 12-9-1

### Copying a Flow Chart from a Book for Use in an Online Training Module

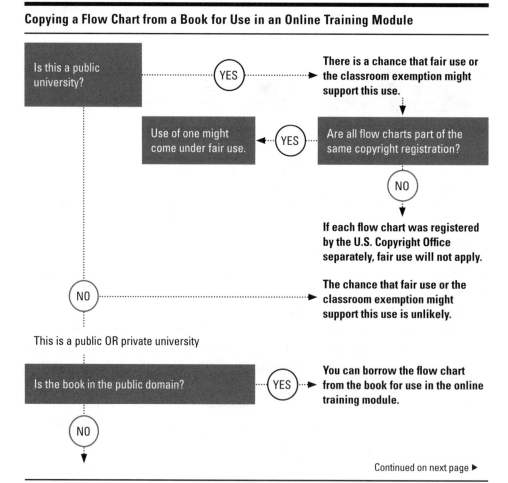

Continued on next page ▶

# FIGURE 12-9-2

## Copying a Flow Chart from a Book for Use in an Online Training Module

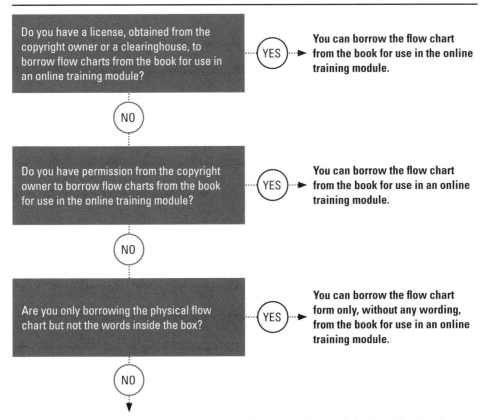

Do you have a license, obtained from the copyright owner or a clearinghouse, to borrow flow charts from the book for use in an online training module?

YES → You can borrow the flow chart from the book for use in the online training module.

NO

Do you have permission from the copyright owner to borrow flow charts from the book for use in the online training module?

YES → You can borrow the flow chart from the book for use in an online training module.

NO

Are you only borrowing the physical flow chart but not the words inside the box?

YES → You can borrow the flow chart form only, without any wording, from the book for use in an online training module.

NO

Find a flow chart to use for which you have permission or a license, is in the public domain, or create your own flow chart for use in the online training module.

Q   I chair a statewide children's literature conference. I would like to put part of an illustration from a well-known picture book on the front page of the conference handbook. Do I need permission to do so?

A   Probably. There are several questions to ask first. See figure 12-10 for help.

## FIGURE 12-10

**Borrowing Part of an Illustration for a Conference Handbook**

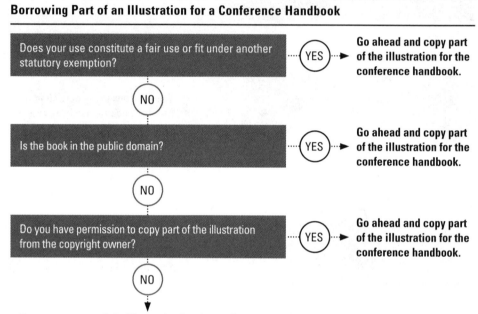

Does your use constitute a fair use or fit under another statutory exemption? — **YES** → Go ahead and copy part of the illustration for the conference handbook.

NO

Is the book in the public domain? — **YES** → Go ahead and copy part of the illustration for the conference handbook.

NO

Do you have permission to copy part of the illustration from the copyright owner? — **YES** → Go ahead and copy part of the illustration for the conference handbook.

NO

Do not copy part of the illustration for the conference handbook. Instead, find another illustration or create your own graphic to put on the front page of the conference handbook.

## YOU CREATE IT, WHO OWNS IT?

Q   The culinary arts program wants to do a cookbook as a fund-raiser. Students and faculty will share their favorite recipes, and these will be compiled into a purchasable cookbook. Are recipes copyright-protected?

A   According to the U.S. Copyright Office, "listings of ingredients as in recipes . . . are not subject to copyright protection. However, where a recipe is accompanied by substantial literary expression in the form of an explanation or directions, or when there is a combination of recipes, as in a cookbook, there may be a basis for copyright protection" (U.S. Copyright Office 2012). (This means that a compilation or collection of recipes, each recipe individually generic enough to be non-protected under copyright law, can be copyrighted. This is similar to the discussion in chapter 6 in which there is a conversation of how links can be in the public domain, but lists of links can be protected under copyright law.) What all this means for the culinary arts program is that recipes out of other cookbooks should not be used. Therefore, the recipes for the fund-raiser cookbook either need to be original to the students and faculty donating them or they need to be generic; that is, lists of ingredients and basic steps to putting them together—without any additional creativity or originality. Moreover, the culinary arts program can officially register the cookbook with the U.S. Copyright Office. (Remember, under U.S. copyright law the cookbook is copyright-protected even if it is not registered with the U.S. Copyright Office.)

Q  Who owns the photograph of a gourmet meal prepared by the culinary arts department, the photographer or the department?

A  The photographer; prepared dishes cannot be copyright-protected (Copyrightlaws .com 2013).

Q  A group of undergraduate science professors want to put together their own curriculum. Can they use flow charts and simple Venn diagrams obtained from a commercial manual?

A  Similar to recipes, flow charts and diagrams can only be protected by copyright law when they have a considerable amount of originality to them. Basically, the form—unless unusual enough to be considered a work of art—cannot be protected. Additionally, the content must convey original information in order for it to be copyright-protected. Flow charts and Venn diagrams that basically illustrate procedures or processes cannot be copyrighted (personal communication from U.S. Copyright Office 2003). If the flow charts and diagrams in the commercial manual are simple procedural works, the science professors can use them. However, the bottom line is that the science professors, themselves, will have to study the flow charts and Venn diagrams and make their own interpretations. If they determine that the flow charts and Venn diagrams are original enough to be copyright-protected, then they need to contact the copyright owners of the commercial manual and ask for permission to use these works.

Q  I am an art instructor at a community college. One of my students is amazingly talented. She won a state award for one of her paintings, which she then sold to a local business. The local business has created postcards of her painting, which they plan to sell. The business says that since they bought her painting, they own the copyright to it. I say that the student owns the copyright, and that the business must pay royalties if they print up postcards of that painting. Who is right?

A  You are. Unless the student consciously transferred the copyright to the painting to the local business, she still owns said copyright. (Remember, transfer of the copyright requires a written document/contract.) Thus, the local business owns the specific painting; it does not own the right to make derivatives of it or to make copies of it. In all likelihood, they have already infringed on her exclusive rights (copyright) by creating the postcards.

Q   I teach a course covering the foundations of educational technology. As one of the assignments, I have the students research the history of an early piece of technology and write a paper documenting what they have found. The university equipment archives, which provides the students access to its historical pieces for these student projects, would like to have a copy of all papers written to place in their collection along with the actual equipment. I have told the students that it is their choice as to whether they give a copy of their paper to the equipment archives or not, and if they do donate them to the archives, that they have the right to specify whether or not these papers are in print or digital formats, as well as to expect that the papers will stay in the format in which the archives received them. The archives' administrators would like, once the paper is donated, to have the right to change the format to meet current and future researchers' needs. Which is it?

A   If the students donate a paper, they have the right to specify the format of the donation. Only if the students give up their copyright ownership to their research papers are the university equipment archives' administrators entitled to change the format of the donation. (Here the argument is that the students are simply giving the archives a *copy* of the paper, not all ownership to the paper, itself.)

## INFRINGEMENTS AND PENALTIES

Q   Is it a copyright infringement if my class uses clip art off the Internet to design book covers for a class unit?

A   If this is a class assignment and part of the students' learning, then the answer is "No." It is best, however, to direct the class to use clip art from reputable Internet sites, such as sites for which the program, department, or college has purchased a license. Also instruct your students to follow the documentation found on the sites they use.

Q   Help! Class starts in ten minutes, and I need a poem! There is a poem that will work in one of my instructor's manuals. Can I copy it for all members of my class? After all, it is a last-minute thing.

A   The flow chart in figure 12-11 will help you determine if you can make the copies. (Please note that reading the poem to the class or passing it around for everyone to see is allowable under section 110 of the U.S. Copyright Law.)

# FIGURE 12-11

**Last Minute Copying**

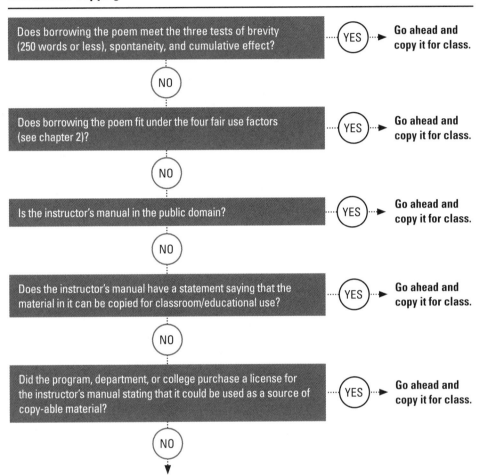

Does borrowing the poem meet the three tests of brevity (250 words or less), spontaneity, and cumulative effect? — **YES** → **Go ahead and copy it for class.**

NO ↓

Does borrowing the poem fit under the four fair use factors (see chapter 2)? — **YES** → **Go ahead and copy it for class.**

NO ↓

Is the instructor's manual in the public domain? — **YES** → **Go ahead and copy it for class.**

NO ↓

Does the instructor's manual have a statement saying that the material in it can be copied for classroom/educational use? — **YES** → **Go ahead and copy it for class.**

NO ↓

Did the program, department, or college purchase a license for the instructor's manual stating that it could be used as a source of copy-able material? — **YES** → **Go ahead and copy it for class.**

NO ↓

**Don't copy the poem out of the instructor's manual. Instead, read it to the class or let the class take turns reading it themselves from the manual.**

Q   Is a community college bookstore liable if it unwittingly obtains and sells books that were illegally obtained by the vendor they use?

A   Yes. Users (including commercial establishments and colleges, profit or nonprofit) are responsible for their own actions, whether they realized there was a copyright infringement or not.

Q   I am the learning center coordinator in a college of education. Last month, I pur-
    chased several kits dealing with the environment for the learning center. Each kit is
    composed of a DVD, a teacher's manual, several manipulatives, and a collection of
    activity sheets. The student teachers want me to laminate the activity sheets, so they
    can take them out to their student-teaching sites and use them time after time. I am
    concerned that the activity sheets are considered consumables, and as such, laminat-
    ing them would be a copyright infringement. What should I do?

A   Section 109 of the U.S. Copyright Act addresses a concept often called the "first sale
    doctrine." This doctrine "says that a copyright owner gets to control the first transfer of
    a particular physical copy of the copyrighted work. After that first transfer, the recipi-
    ent gets to control that physical copy. The copyright owner still owns the copyright, but
    the recipient owns the copy" (Bhat 2011, 1). What this means, in your case, is—unless
    there is a statement in the documentation of the kits that the activity sheets may not
    be laminated or in some other way preserved—that you may preserve these materials
    in your kits by laminating them, since you own these specific activity sheets.

## INTERNATIONAL COPYRIGHT LAW

Q   One of the freshman English classes is studying *Beowulf*. Mr. Smith, an English pro-
    fessor, has found an excellent article on this subject, published in a British journal,
    that he would like to share with his fellow faculty. How can he easily—and legally—
    provide his colleagues with a copy?

A   This answer can get complicated. Here are several possible solutions to consider. (1)
    If use of the article falls under fair use, the article is in the public domain, Mr. Smith
    has permission or a license from the copyright owner to copy the article, or there is a
    disclaimer in the magazine saying (something to the effect) that the articles in it can
    be copied "for educational purposes," (and his use fits the disclaimer), it will be easy for
    him to share the *Beowulf* article with other faculty. (Remember, since the United States
    belongs to several copyright treaty organizations, it is simplest to treat the work as you
    would under U.S. law.) (2) If none of the above is the case, he could ask the library to
    put his copy of the article on reserve, for other faculty to access. (3) In addition, the
    "Guidelines Conforming to Fair Use for Educational Purposes Agreement on Guide-
    lines for Classroom Copying" (these guidelines were made part of the *Congressional
    Record* in 1976) say that a teacher may make or have made a single copy of an article,
    chapter, short story, poem, essay (or a diagram or picture in any of the above works)
    (U.S. Copyright Office 2009). Thus, if following these guidelines, Mr. Smith could
    make one copy of the article for his use (or request that one copy of the article be made
    for him). (4) Moreover, under section 108(a) of the 1976 Copyright Act, a library may
    make one copy of a work if (a) there is no commercial advantage (direct or indirect)
    to making another copy; (b) the library collection is open to the public, especially re-

searchers; and (c) the copy of the original work includes on it either a copyright notice or a statement saying the work may be under copyright protection. Thus, each of the other English faculty could also either copy the article themselves or ask the library to make a copy for him or her. Are you getting confused yet? Well, all of the above may apply, depending on your situation. However, (5) the easiest way for Mr. Smith to get this information to his fellow English faculty is to route it (send it from faculty member to faculty member through inter-campus mail)!

Q   I would like to obtain an e-book on international politics to place on a handheld device that we have in the library. A statement on a web page, which has a copy of this book, says the book is out of print in the country of origin and that users need to check with their own countries' copyright laws before downloading it. What does this mean for me?

A   Since there is no one international copyright law (most countries have their own, and a few do not address copyright law), and the site directions tell you to check with your country's law, the easiest thing to do is to treat the book as if it were published in the United States. Could you legally obtain a digitized copy of it here? The flow chart in figure 12-12 will help you make this decision.

## FIGURE 12-12

**Placing an e-book on a Library Handheld Device**

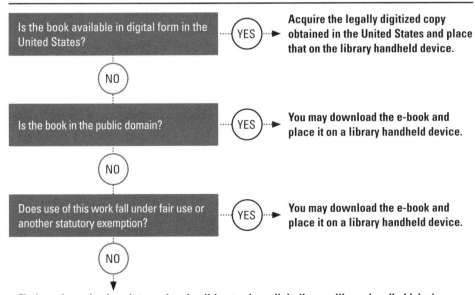

Is the book available in digital form in the United States? — YES → Acquire the legally digitized copy obtained in the United States and place that on the library handheld device.

NO

Is the book in the public domain? — YES → You may download the e-book and place it on a library handheld device.

NO

Does use of this work fall under fair use or another statutory exemption? — YES → You may download the e-book and place it on a library handheld device.

NO

**Find another e-book on international politics to place digitally on a library handheld device.**

## AVOIDING COPYRIGHT PROBLEMS

Q   Can educators use copied or scanned images of book covers on bulletin boards and in displays? After all, by doing so we're providing free advertising for the books.

A   This question has both a conservative and a liberal answer, and you, as the user, will need to decide which approach works best in your situation.

- **Conservative:** According to the basic interpretation of copyright law, this is an infringement. Why? Because it means that you may be copying works in an unauthorized manner. In other words, you need to obtain the proper permissions. Or you can put the actual book covers on your bulletin boards and in your displays.
- **Liberal:** The copying or scanning of book covers fits under the fair use factors. You may copy or scan them for use on bulletin boards and in displays. According to Carrie Russell (2002), the American Library Association's copyright specialist, this is another case in which, because the action is so commonplace, it changes how copyright law is understood. As long as no proceeds are obtained from the copied book cover displays, such displays become exceptions to the law; that is, they promote reading and have only a positive influence on the marketplace. Thus, such displays fit under the four fair use factors.

Q   How many articles can the library request through interlibrary loan from a single volume or issue of a professional journal in a given year?

A   Using the "Rule of Five" guideline (discussed in chapter 5), the library can request and receive up to five articles in any given year from a specific journal published in the last five years.

Q   I am a doctoral student, and I have a great research idea. I do not want anyone else to take it, so can I copyright it?

A   Ideas cannot be copyright-protected. Your best bet is to keep your idea a secret until such time as you start to research it.

Q   Let's assume that you are the history subject librarian at the main library. A faculty member in history comes to you and says he has heard that he cannot use any materials he privately owns to teach with, unless he only uses 10 percent of each of them (and that he can only use the 10 percent) for two years. He also says his understanding is that if the university owns the materials, then he can use any portion that he wants for as long as he wants, if said use is for an instructional purpose. Here is how you might respond (see below).

A   Guidelines often have the "10 percent rule." That means, if you borrow 10 percent or less, you are probably safe. Given personal or university-owned materials, there is no difference in how copyright law is interpreted. Therefore, it does not matter who owns the material. Last, there is no two-year limit on use of materials, unless you agreed with the owner to that in a contract. Bottom line: follow the law or guidelines and any contracts that you (or the university) signs. Remember that the classroom exemption 17 USC (110) lets you use media to teach with under certain parameters (see the classroom exemption discussion in chapter 5 of this book).

## CONCLUSION

While print has been around longer than many other formats, the same sorts of copyright questions keep popping up. How much copying or borrowing of another's work is too much? What is legal and what isn't? How can we copy and not be liable? Confusing? You bet! This chapter tries very hard to give you a definitive answer. However, in some cases, such a solution simply does not exist. Indeed, I hope that this chapter provides you with usable responses to some of your copyright questions.

## REFERENCES

Bhat, Anjali. 2011. "Protecting the First Sale Doctrine: PK Files Amicus Brief in Costco v. Omega." www.publicknowledge.org/blog/protecting-first-sale-doctrine-pk-files-amicu.

Copyrightlaws.com. 2013. "Copyright + Food: Photographing Food in Restaurants." http://www.copyrightlaws.com/creators/copyright-food-photographing-food-in-restaurants.

Dramatists Play Service, Inc. 2013. "Application for Nonprofessional Stage Performance Rights." www.dramatists.com/cgi-bin/db/secure/autonpa.asp.

First Sale Doctrine. 2010. www.tabberone.com/Trademarks/CopyrightLaw/FirstSaleDoctrine/FirstSale.shtml.

Lipinski, Tomas A. 2006. *The Complete Copyright Liability Handbook for Librarians and Educators.* New York: Neal-Schuman.

Russell, Carrie. 2002. "Is It a Crime to Copy?" *School Library Journal* 48, no. 1 (January): 41.

———. 2003. "A Get-Rich-Quick Scheme? Your School's Fund-Raiser May Not Qualify for a Copyright Exemption." *School Library Journal* 49, no. 2 (February): 43.

———. 2003b. "A More Manageable Harry: Is It Legal to Circulate Small Sections of the Latest 'Harry Potter'?" *School Library Journal* 49, no. 9 (September): 43.

———. 2003c. "A Tale of Two Formats: Is It Legal to Make DVD Copies of Instructional Videos?" *School Library Journal* 49, no. 4 (April): 45.

Simpson, Carol. 2001. *Copyright for Schools: A Practical Guide.* 3rd ed. Worthington, OH: Linworth.

Stim, Richard. 2007. *Getting Permission: How to License & Clear Copyrighted Materials Online and Off.* http://books.google.com

# 13

# Distance Learning and Copyright Law

## This Is Confusing! How Can We Share Materials with Our Students and Still Comply with the Law?

What is distance education? According to Wherry (2008, 59), distance education describes "classes that are delivered to a location distant from the originating . . . by any medium." When it comes to copyright law and learning in a non-face-to-face environment, there can be confusion and dissension. Today's distance education comprises digitized web-based delivery, asynchronous and synchronous communications, mobile (handheld) applications, television transmissions, and other forms of delivery (see previous chapters). Distance education must either rely on the fair use factors (discussed in chapter 2) or abide by Section 110(2), for which the Technology, Education and Copyright Harmonization Act (TEACH Act) is the current version (NC State University). The Digital Millennium Copyright Act (DMCA) also affects distance education (Wherry 2008). Unhappily for us as users, federal copyright legislation is often confusing. Therefore, the DMCA and TEACH Acts are subsequently briefly summarized, in terms of distance education, with a focus on higher education.

## DIGITAL MILLENNIUM COPYRIGHT ACT (DMCA)

Created by Congress in an attempt to move U.S. copyright law into the digital age, the DMCA is an add-on to the 1976 Copyright Act. It addressed libraries, copying, preservation, and reproduction of library materials; management of copyright; online service provider liabilities; the World Intellectual Property Organization (WIPO); the first sale doctrine; computer program exemptions; DVD issues; archival exemptions; and a range of other miscellaneous subjects dealing with digital communications and technologies and copyright (Peters, 2001). This last piece included a charge to submit to Congress recommendations on promoting digital technologies in distance education. The DMCA-collected recommendations originally were submitted to Congress in 1999 (Crews 2000; U.S. Copyright Office).

## TECHNOLOGY, EDUCATION, AND COPYRIGHT HARMONIZATION ACT (TEACH ACT)

Educators who apply the TEACH Act support a much more liberal interpretation of copyright use and access of lawfully obtained materials than old section 110(2) of the Copyright Act. (Old Section 110(2) of the Copyright Act: Instructional Broadcasting explains copyright coverage under the 1976 law. Covering classroom exemptions in light of face-to-face teaching, it was replaced by the TEACH Act. The old section is much more conservative than the TEACH Act, and much of it means little in light of digital transmissions [Gasaway 2002], which were not a consideration when this part of the copyright law was written.) The TEACH Act was written to update "the existing distance learning exception to the Copyright Act to accommodate the growth of digital age distance learning" (American Association of Community Colleges et al. 2002) or as Nelson (2009) states, to address "an imbalance between traditional and distance education classrooms" (p. 83). The TEACH Act is actually a "new" (as of November 2002) Section 110(2). This act opens up existing "face-to-face" teaching exemptions in the copyright law to allow educators at accredited, nonprofit educational institutions throughout the United States to use copyright-protected materials in distance education— including on websites and by other digital means—without prior permission from the copyright owner and without payment of royalties (Washington State University 2013). In order to use the TEACH Act, your educational organization needs to follow a long list of requirements (see below). *All* of these criteria must be met.

### Institutional Responsibilities

The institution must

- be an accredited nonprofit institution;
- have a copyright policy;
- provide copyright information to its faculty, students, and staff;
- provide notice to students that all distance education materials may be copyright-protected; and
- limit class access to students enrolled in it.

## Information Technology Responsibilities

Those who work with the information technologies that support distance education in your organization must

- limit access to students enrolled in a specific class;
- apply technological controls on storage and dissemination to prevent course students from retaining the material for longer than a class session;
- ensure that the distance education delivery systems used don't defeat technological measures used by copyright owners to keep their works under control;
- limit short-term retention of copies; and
- limit long-term copies' preservation.

## Instructor Responsibilities

The distance education course instructors must

- use only works exclusively permitted;
- not use works clearly disqualified;
- supervise all course materials' access;
- mediate all instructional activities;
- ensure that no digital versions of a work are available;
- corroborate the specific material and amount of said material to be digitized; and
- evaluate access control implications. (American Library Association 2013)

To explain more clearly the instructor responsibilities listed above: some copyright owners have been concerned with the idea that their analog materials could be converted to a digital format, thus making downloading and dissemination of their materials much easier. The concern is that owners' control over their materials would become much more difficult. Therefore, the TEACH Act includes a statement that prohibits digital conversion of analog materials, with some exceptions. The first exception is that "the amount that may be converted is limited to the amount of appropriate works that may be performed or displayed, pursuant to the revised section 110(2)" (American Library Association 2013, 1). What this means is that the distance education instructor needs to make sure that the material converted to digital format falls within the materials' scope and portion margins allowable under the TEACH Act. The second exception is that educators and other distance educators should check to make sure there is not already a copy of the work they want to utilize in a digitized format (American Library Association 2013). If such a copy is available for use, then users should obtain that copy.

In addition to the responsibilities of the administration, technology coordinators, support people, and the class instructors, librarians also find that they need to meet the TEACH Act requirements. Librarians are poised, because of their training, to develop and interpret copyright and other access policies; store distance-education course transmissions; find other sources of materials for non-face-to-face class use; and so on. However, librarians are not specifically listed in the TEACH Act.

Abiding by the numerous terms of the new Section 110(2) (the TEACH Act) can be difficult. Because of this, many institutions elect to simply follow the fair use factors instead. Either set of rules can be followed, just not both.

Working with distance-education copyright issues is extremely complicated and could be a whole book in its own right. However, the flow chart in figure 13-1 will give distance educators an idea of which set of rules they should abide by: new Section 110(2) (the TEACH Act) or the fair use factors.

## FIGURE 13-1

**Distance Educator's Flow Chart**

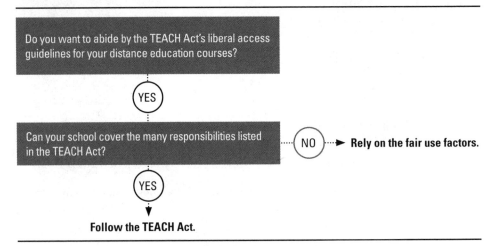

## FAIR USE

**Q**    Does fair use (see chapter 2) work with e-reserves?

**A**    It is possible. In a recent court case involving Georgia State University (GSU) and three publishing houses, the judge ruled in favor of the GSU library e-reserves' system in a majority of the claims. The judge found that the first and second fair use factors leaned toward the university, the third factor vacillated between the two parties, and the fourth factor tipped in favor of the publishing companies. She also observed, "because neither the authors nor the publishers have significant revenue from licensing, there was no real harm to the plaintiffs" (DuBoff and King 2013, 4). Libraries would be best served to determine such use on a case-by-case basis and also consider possible licensing agreements.

Q I work in the e-reserve section of our library. I am concerned I might mistakenly put something up on e-reserves—thinking it is in fair use, when in reality it is not—and that I will be found in copyright infringement and suffer the consequences. How can I safely do my job?

A Rest easy. The law actually addresses this in 17 USC 504 (c)(2) of the U.S. Copyright Act. This section "provides special protection to nonprofit libraries, educational institutions and their employees. When we act in good faith, reasonably believing that our actions are fair use, in the unlikely event we are actually sued over a use, we will not have to pay statutory damages even if a court finds that we were wrong. This demonstrates Congressional acknowledgement of the importance of fair use" (American Library Association 2013b, 4).

## PUBLIC DOMAIN

Q I teach lots of distance education classes and want to share only public domain materials with my students. How do I ensure that?

A You would need to make sure that all materials you used were labeled as public domain and from websites that you trusted (thus ensuring that the public domain statements were reliable). There are many such sites with agency, including Project Gutenberg (http://www.gutenberg.org) and Open Library (http://openlibrary.org).

Q A graduate teaching assistant in music walks into the library and asks if there are any music websites that he can share with his distance education students legally. Where do you send him?

A The easiest answer is to send him to sites that have public domain music available for download or as sheet music. Two examples are "Public Domain 4U" (http://public domain4u.com) and Public Domain Sherpa (http://www.publicdomainsherpa.com), which lists a number of sites for sound recordings and sheet music.

## DOCUMENTATION AND LICENSES

Q I am a student at a small southeastern college. There are many databases available on my college's library website. Sometimes I can print out an article, sometimes I cannot. What is going on?

A Your college library system has licenses with different databases or their vendors to provide students, faculty, and staff with full-text articles, abstracts, and so on. It all depends on each individual contract as to what you as the user can and cannot use.

Q The Instructional Technology Office at our university has put out a statement that we cannot upload music we personally purchased from iTunes or other music sites to support our distance education creative music courses. We feel, since we obtained these items ourselves, that we should be free to share them with our students. Who is right?

A  It depends on the agreement that you consented to when you obtained the music. Check back with the Internet source of the music and see what their policies state.

## PERMISSIONS

Q  I work in the reserves section of our college library. Sometimes professors teaching online ask me to provide access to an item in our e-reserve section. When I do so (as a link in our e-reserve site), as a courtesy, I also provide the professor with a PDF copy of the item so that he can attach it to his class management system. A law professor tells me that this is questionable under copyright law. I just thought that I was being helpful. What is the answer here?

A  See figures 13-2-1 and 13-2-2 for possible solutions.

## FIGURE 13-2-1

**Providing a Professor with a PDF Copy for Posting Online**

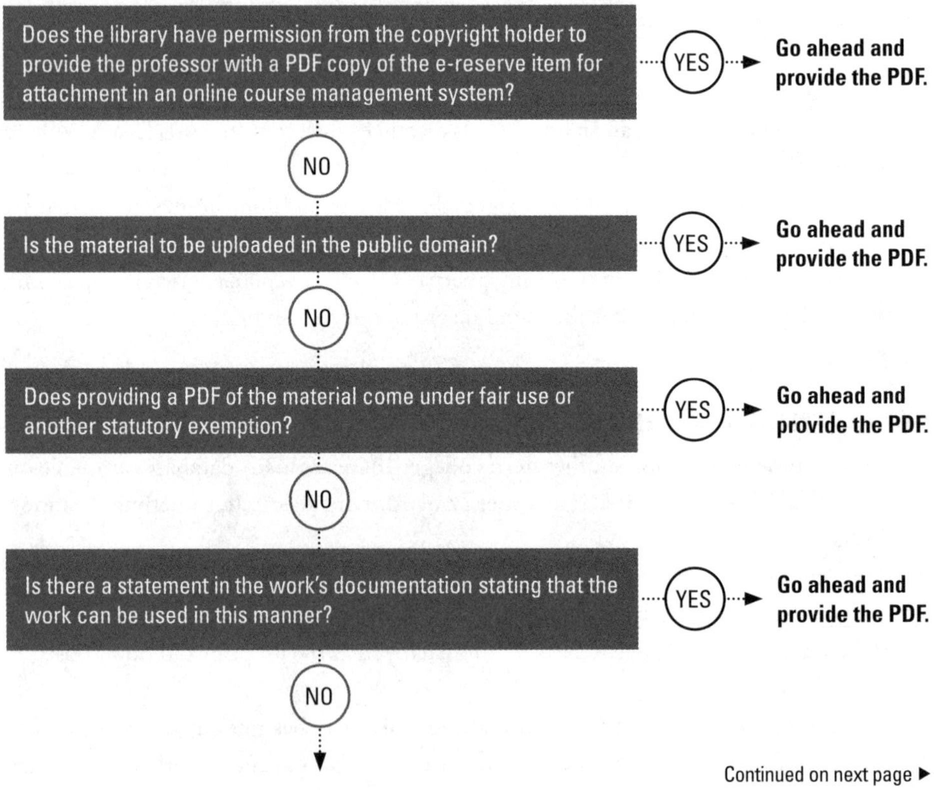

Does the library have permission from the copyright holder to provide the professor with a PDF copy of the e-reserve item for attachment in an online course management system? — YES → **Go ahead and provide the PDF.**

NO

Is the material to be uploaded in the public domain? — YES → **Go ahead and provide the PDF.**

NO

Does providing a PDF of the material come under fair use or another statutory exemption? — YES → **Go ahead and provide the PDF.**

NO

Is there a statement in the work's documentation stating that the work can be used in this manner? — YES → **Go ahead and provide the PDF.**

NO

Continued on next page ▶

## FIGURE 13-2-2

**Providing a Professor with a PDF Copy for Posting Online**

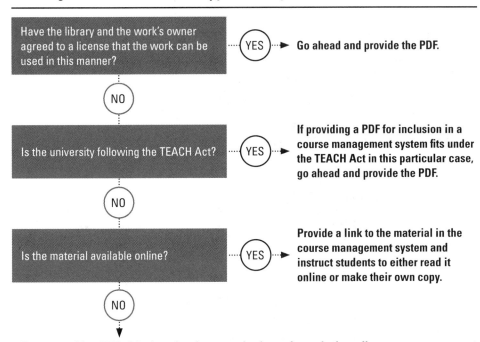

Have the library and the work's owner agreed to a license that the work can be used in this manner? ····YES···▶ Go ahead and provide the PDF.

NO

Is the university following the TEACH Act? ····YES···▶ If providing a PDF for inclusion in a course management system fits under the TEACH Act in this particular case, go ahead and provide the PDF.

NO

Is the material available online? ····YES···▶ Provide a link to the material in the course management system and instruct students to either read it online or make their own copy.

NO

Do not provide a PDF of the item for placement by the professor in the online course management system. Do, however, make sure that the professor has the e-reserve link available so that his/her students may access the item that way.

Q   I found a really neat graphic on a website featuring learning guidelines. I would like to add it to an online lesson that I am creating on state standards. One of my colleagues told me I could just "hotlink" to the graphic. What is hotlinking and would that work?

A   It might work, but don't do it. Hotlinking, "when content from your site is embedded on another site, using your bandwidth to serve the files" (cPanel 2013, 1) can be considered stealing, in terms of both bandwidth and intellectual property. Instead, contact the website moderator and ask for permission to either copy the graphic or link to the site.

## YOU CREATE IT, WHO OWNS IT?

Q   I am faculty at a technical school in the northwestern United States. Who owns the distance education class I have created (all work [lectures, PowerPoints, readings] is mine originally)—me, the technical school, or the technology support office that put my class into an online format? Oh, and by the way, I received a grant from an external agency to support my work in creating this course.

A   The answer to this can get complicated and includes contract as well as copyright law. Please see figure 13-3.

## FIGURE 13-3

**Ownership of an Online Class**

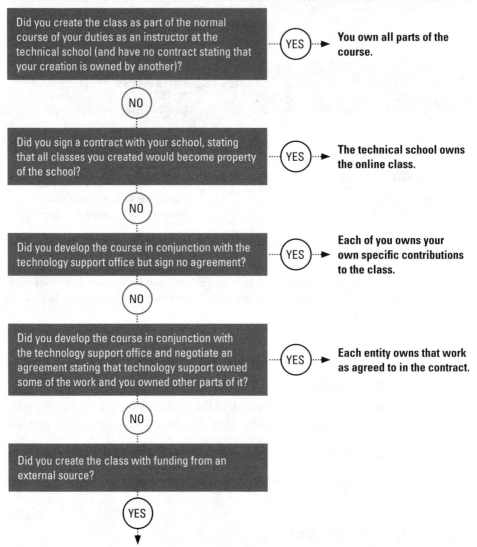

Q    How much of the course material I created for my online class am I required to share with my colleagues? I want to protect my intellectual property rights.

A    Unless your contract with your institution states that it owns all your work or that you are to share your course material with your institutional colleagues, what you have created is your intellectual property. This means that you alone own the copyright to that property and can do with it as you wish.

## INFRINGEMENTS AND PENALTIES

Q    A new faculty member in the Communications Department approaches you with a question. She is teaching a blended (partially online and partially face-to-face) class this coming spring. She has a very expensive book she wishes her students to read for the class, and has requested that you scan the book, so that she can place it in PDF form on Blackboard (a course management system). You tell her that you are very uncomfortable doing this and that to do so may be a copyright infringement. She stresses that she would rather stay within legal limits, but that she really wants that book available to her students. How do you react to this request?

A    There is more than one answer to this request. Please follow the flow charts in figures 13-4-1 and 13-4-2 for steps you might take to help this faculty member.

## FIGURE 13-4-1

**Scanning a Book to Put on Blackboard**

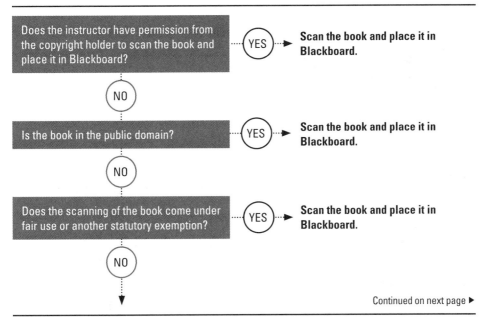

Continued on next page ▶

## FIGURE 13-4-2

**Scanning a Book to Put on Blackboard**

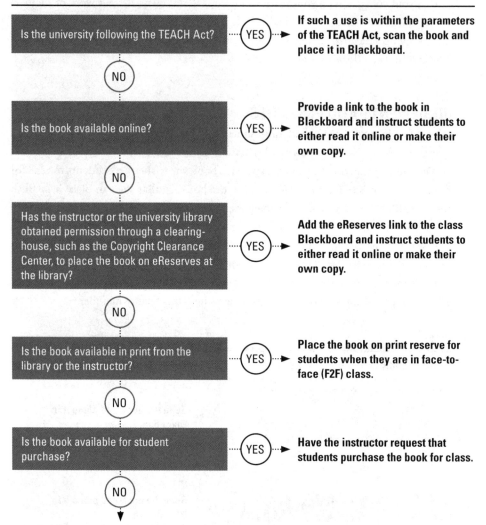

| | | |
|---|---|---|
| Is the university following the TEACH Act? | YES → | If such a use is within the parameters of the TEACH Act, scan the book and place it in Blackboard. |

NO

| | | |
|---|---|---|
| Is the book available online? | YES → | Provide a link to the book in Blackboard and instruct students to either read it online or make their own copy. |

NO

| | | |
|---|---|---|
| Has the instructor or the university library obtained permission through a clearing-house, such as the Copyright Clearance Center, to place the book on eReserves at the library? | YES → | Add the eReserves link to the class Blackboard and instruct students to either read it online or make their own copy. |

NO

| | | |
|---|---|---|
| Is the book available in print from the library or the instructor? | YES → | Place the book on print reserve for students when they are in face-to-face (F2F) class. |

NO

| | | |
|---|---|---|
| Is the book available for student purchase? | YES → | Have the instructor request that students purchase the book for class. |

NO ↓

**Find something else to take the place of the book; something you are able to obtain legal rights to use.**

Q   I am a student taking online classes at a college out-of-state. All of the materials from my professors are posted in Moodle (a course management system). I am concerned—if one of my professors posts a PDF of an article online that she has obtained in an illegal manner, if I print it out and use it, am I also violating copyright law?

A As a student, you may make one copy of an item for an educational purpose. Thus, even if the professor posted the PDF illegally, you should be able to print out a copy and use it to support the class curriculum. Just make sure that such use reinforces your learning, and remember: make only one copy.

## INTERNATIONAL COPYRIGHT LAW

Q You are scheduled to teach a synchronous online cohort with students in several countries. You wish to put some sort of copyright statement in your syllabus, but you are concerned, since different countries have different laws, and this could get complicated. What might such a copyright statement look like?

A Here is an example of a generic copyright statement that might work for such a course: "All materials provided for this online cohort class are for CLASS USE ONLY. Please do not share these materials with others outside of class; to do so may be a copyright infringement in your country and/or the country of origin."

Q I have been asked to teach a MOOC (massive open online course) for my university. What materials can I legally put in my course, since my students could be living and studying anywhere in the world?

A One could argue, because MOOCs are so new, that copyright law has not yet caught up to them. Use figures 13-5-1 and 13-5-2 to consider some ways to supply your MOOC students with course materials.

## FIGURE 13-5-1

**Posting Course Materials to MOOCs**

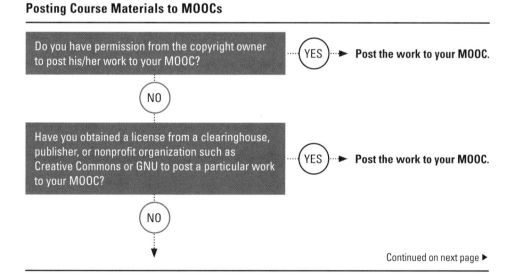

Continued on next page ▶

## FIGURE 13-5-2

**Posting Course Materials to MOOCs**

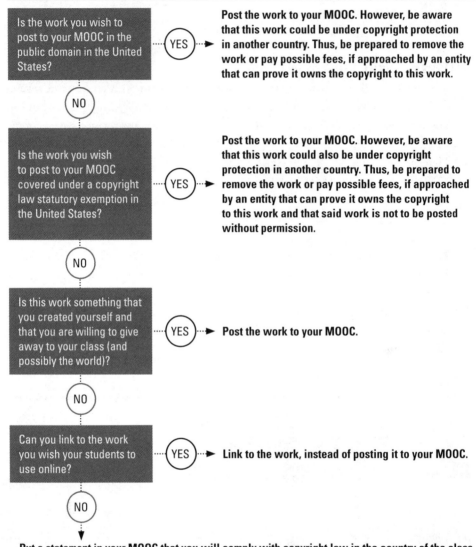

Is the work you wish to post to your MOOC in the public domain in the United States? — **YES** → Post the work to your MOOC. However, be aware that this work could be under copyright protection in another country. Thus, be prepared to remove the work or pay possible fees, if approached by an entity that can prove it owns the copyright to this work.

**NO**

Is the work you wish to post to your MOOC covered under a copyright law statutory exemption in the United States? — **YES** → Post the work to your MOOC. However, be aware that this work could also be under copyright protection in another country. Thus, be prepared to remove the work or pay possible fees, if approached by an entity that can prove it owns the copyright to this work and that said work is not to be posted without permission.

**NO**

Is this work something that you created yourself and that you are willing to give away to your class (and possibly the world)? — **YES** → Post the work to your MOOC.

**NO**

Can you link to the work you wish your students to use online? — **YES** → Link to the work, instead of posting it to your MOOC.

**NO**

↓

Put a statement in your MOOC that you will comply with copyright law in the country of the class origin (e.g., the United States), and if there is a problem with using the work in another country, that you will attempt to find a reasonable replacement. In addition, keep current in copyright law; given the newness of MOOCs, there is always the possibility of change.

## AVOIDING COPYRIGHT PROBLEMS

Q   I am confused. I teach online classes at a regional university. We use several course management systems, among them Blackboard and Moodle. I know that Moodle is free online and that the university pays for faculty and student use of Blackboard. So . . . does that mean that any materials we upload to Blackboard are automatically copyright-protected and any that we upload to Moodle are not?

A   It means nothing of the sort! What learning or course management system an instructor uses to teach online or blended courses does not make a difference as far as copyright protection for uploaded documents. There is, however, the legal or illegal use of materials uploaded to a particular course management system. As the course instructor you need to ask a number of questions of any material that you wish to upload. Figures 13-6-1 and 13-6-2 demonstrate this.

## FIGURE 13-6-1

**Questions to Ask of a Medium Being Uploaded to a Course Management System**

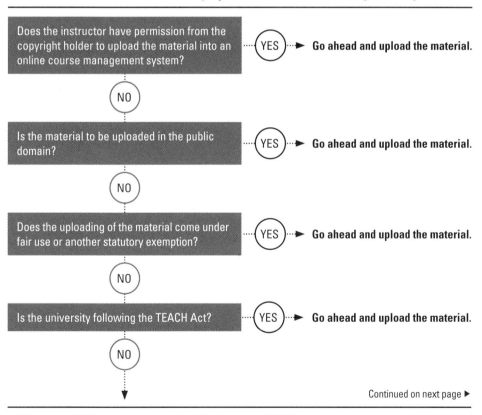

Continued on next page ▶

## FIGURE 13-6-2

**Questions to Ask of a Medium Being Uploaded to a Course Management System**

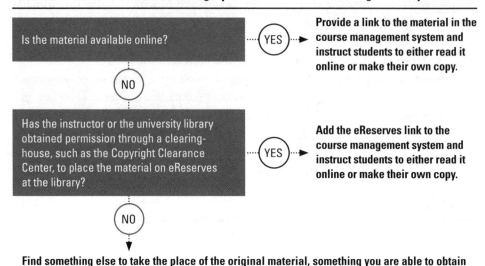

Find something else to take the place of the original material, something you are able to obtain legal rights to use.

## CONCLUSION

As more and more community colleges, four-year institutions, and universities use distance-delivery systems to support curriculum and student needs, copyright rules will be challenged and new limits set. The fact that "digital copyright law is built upon analogue copyright law" (Stokes 2009, 20) can make copyright law's intersection with distance education seem very complex. Some distance education "rules of thumb" that can be helpful—especially when addressing online education components—include:

- make sure all material used is lawfully obtained;
- take digital content off the Web after the class is over;
- include copyright notices;
- limit access to the class website:
  — students registered for a course,
  — closed, secure system,
  — password or pin number, and
  — students advised that they are not permitted to make copies of or distribute class materials to others;
- terminate access at the end of the class term;
- use as little of a copyrighted work as is needed; and
- apply the law.

With all of these things swirling around your head, a thought to consider is that "the intent of copyright law . . . is that creators deserve the right to be compensated for their work and have some control over how it is used" (Harris 2011, 110).

## REFERENCES

American Association of Community Colleges, et al. 2002. Letter to the Honorable Dennis J. Hastert, Speaker of the U.S. House of Representatives and the Honorable Richard A. Gephardt, Minority Leader, U.S. House of Representatives. www.educause.edu/ir/library/pdf/NET0319.pdf.

American Library Association. 2013. "Distance Education and the TEACH Act." www.ala.org/Template.cfm?Section=Distance_Education_and_the_TEACH_Act&Template=/ContentManagement/ContentDisplay.cfm&ContentID=25939.

———. 2013b. "Fair Use and Electronic Reserves." http://www.ala.org/advocacy/copyright/fairuse/fairuseandelectronicreserves#intro.

cPanel. 2013. "Documentation: Hotlink Protection." http://docs.cpanel.net/twiki/bin/view/AllDocumentation/CpanelDocs/HotLinkProtection.

Crews, Kenneth D. 2000. *Copyright Essentials for Librarians and Educators*. Chicago: American Library Association.

DuBoff, Leonard and Christy King. 2013. "Copyright and You: Survey of Recent Changes to Intellectual Property Law." *TechTrends* 57, no. 3: 3–4.

Gasaway, Laura N. 2002. "TEACH Act—Amended Section 110(2)." www.unc.edu/~unclng/TEACH.htm.

Harris, Frances Jacobson. 2011. *I Found It on the Internet: Coming of Age Online*. 2nd ed. Chicago: American Library Association.

Nelson, Erik. 2009. "Copyright and Distance Education: The Impact of the Technology, Education, and Copyright Harmonization Act." *Advancement of Computing in Education Journal* 17, no. 2: 83–101.

NC State University. "The TEACH Act: Section 110(2) of the Copyright Act." www.provost.ncsu.edu/copyright/toolkit.

Open Library. "Open Library." http://openlibrary.org/.

Peters, Marybeth. 2001. "Digital Millennium Copyright Act (DMCA) Section 104 Report." www.copyright.gov/docs/regstat121201.html.

Project Gutenberg. 2013. "Free e-Books—Project Gutenberg." http://www.gutenberg.org/.

Public Domain 4U. 2013. http://publicdomain4u.com.

Public Domain Sherpa. 2013. http://www.publicdomainsherpa.com/public-domain-recordings.html.

Stokes, Simon. 2009. *Digital Copyright: Law and Practice*. Portland, OR: Hart.

U.S. Copyright Act. 17 USC 504. "Remedies for Infringement: Damages and Profits."

U.S. Copyright Office. "Copyright and Digital Distance Education." www.copyright.gov/disted.

Washington State University. 2013. "Distance Education: Expanding the Classroom."
    http://publishing.wsu.edu/copyright/distanceeducation.html.
Wherry, Timothy Lee. 2008. *Intellectual Property: Everything the Digital-Age Librarian Needs to
    Know*. Chicago: American Library Association.

# 14

## Conclusion

### What Does All This Mean for Librarians and Other Higher Education Professionals?

The first five chapters of this book focus on defining the most important issues within copyright for higher education librarians, faculty, and other professionals. Chapters 6 through 13 reflect on how professors and instructors, librarians, technology coordinators, technology specialists, administrators, and others in colleges and universities can best apply copyright law in their particular educational environments. This, the final chapter, covers options for avoiding copyright problems as well as how we can best work with those who would have us infringe on others' copyrights.

### I'LL NEVER GET CAUGHT

Should you violate copyright law, it is possible that you will not be discovered. It is also possible that a software company, movie studio, or an organization representing whatever work you are copying will recognize that you are using their work illegally, and decide that it is not worth the time or money to prosecute. However, please be aware that "in some cases, software producers and distributors, as well as the organizations to which they belong, provide ways for consumers and concerned citizens to report cases of . . . piracy. Usually this can be done through the Internet or by phone, with the information kept confidential. In some cases, finders' fees may be available" (Butler 2002, 42). An example of a report template and FAQ (frequently asked questions) for reporting alleged software piracy is available from the Business Software Alliance (2013) at https://reporting.bsa.org/usa/report/add

.aspx?pr=1&intcmp=irphp000043b. Similar reporting models hold true for movie piracy (www.mpaa.org/contentprotection/report-piracy) and, depending on the organization, may also be applicable for other types of media. So, while you might not get caught, then again, you also might. Copyright infringement is enforced by the Federal Bureau of Investigation and can be a felony. However, whether the infringement is judged to be criminal or civil, it is punishable by law. Penalties can include sizeable fines, payment of attorneys' fees, and even prison (Scott). You must decide for yourself—is it worth the risk?

## WAYS TO AVOID COPYRIGHT PROBLEMS

How can we avoid copyright problems? The best ways are to understand copyright law and remain current as technology and law evolve. However, in real life, copyright is just one small part of our responsibilities as librarians and educators. Therefore, practicing these guidelines can be very difficult. Nevertheless, here are a few pointers to help you on your way to copyright compliance.

- Follow fair use and other statutory exemptions (i.e., the law); or follow copyright guidelines.
- Obtain permissions and licenses when necessary.
- Read documentation and other copyright information for each work you use or from which you borrow, and encourage others to do the same. This way you and other users will know what rights for a work are available.
- Pay royalties as required.
- Consult your organization's copyright policy or ethics code. If your institution does not have one, encourage your administration to develop one and follow its policies and procedures.
- Consult your institution's attorney when questions and problems occur.
- Put the purpose and intended use on all purchase orders. This way, the publisher/ vendor will know what you want the material for and can make sure that you obtain the permissions/licenses you need.
- Follow books, such as this one, that can help you answer copyright questions. Additionally, find and use materials that can support you and your school/district as you pursue copyright compliance (Butler 2008; 2009; 2009b).
- Consult copyright articles in print journals and on the Web to be as up-to-date as you possibly can.
- Do not attempt to profit from your copying.
- Cite what you quote. (Remember, citing is no substitute for permissions, licenses, etc. However, most copyright owners want credit for their works, and some—believe it or not—do not care as much about the monetary rewards. Thus, you can at least be careful not to plagiarize.)

- Participate in workshops, conferences, and in-service events that inform you about copyright law.
- Use material that you have created yourself.
- Observe and model responsible copyright practices.
- When in doubt, don't copy!

## HOW TO DEAL WITH THOSE WHO WOULD HAVE YOU BREAK THE LAW

Unfortunately, there will always be some who believe that they are above the law. They may be your administrators, fellow librarians or college professors and instructors, technology specialists, students, almost anyone. How do you deal with someone who asks you to infringe on another individual's or group's copyrights? (Remember that there are three types of infringement: [1] direct (where an individual knowingly violates a copyright owner's rights), [2] contributory or indirect (where someone helps or provides hardware or software used in the infringement), and [3] vicarious (where someone else, for example a supervisor, asks you to do the infringing or said supervisor obtains monetary gain from the infringement) (Simpson 2005). Below is an example involving faculty with a copying request/possible infringement.

Q   Imagine that you are an academic librarian who works with the College of Education (COE). You have just found an excellent article on teaching devices for handicapped students, which you point out to a COE faculty member. The faculty member asks you to photocopy this article twenty-five times, one for each of the instructors in his department. This way, he says, the whole department can obtain this information. You notice, on the inside front cover of the periodical from which the article came, a statement saying that no copying of material from the periodical is to occur without permission of the publishers. You point this out to the faculty member, who informs you that it doesn't matter. After all, you are a nonprofit higher education institution. Therefore, being nonprofit—and being in higher education, where "pushing the envelope" often happens—he feels no one will do anything if the copies are made. How do you respond without offending the COE faculty member?

A   Well, especially if you are new and untenured, you might consider (1) copying the article twenty-five times and giving it to all members of the department in question. Chances are that no one will be the wiser. You could also (2) choose to confront the faculty member on this issue and say "no," although this option might jeopardize your relationship with him. A better idea would be (3) to give this individual a brief rundown on copyright law and why it is important to not be in violation. You might also be able (4) to persuade him that routing the magazine from instructor to instructor instead is a much better option. However, assume that this faculty member is actually a dean and you are hesitant to cross this person. Now you are in a very sticky situation.

You are being asked to do something that you know is illegal, but you are afraid not to do it. You could copy the article as asked, but (5) document the occurrence, so that should some sort of retaliation transpire involving the copyright owners, you would have a record of your stance and actions; (6) place such documentation in your personnel files; (7) contact your ombudsman or faculty advocate, explain the situation, and ask for help and advice; (8) contact the university attorney, inform him or her of the situation, and request guidance; and/or (9) contact your professional organization(s) for support on what actions to take.

Other ways to deal with someone who asks you to violate copyright law include (10) encourage correct action; (11) provide examples of infringements and the actions taken against the infringers; (12) supply a copy of those parts of the law of importance in your specific instance; (13) remain composed and empathetic; (14) point out those parts of the work's documentation that list what the copyright owners consider infringement; (15) encourage records' keeping of all licenses, permissions, and so on; and (16) remind others that they will be held accountable for what they do (Butler, 2003). It is possible that some educators are simply not aware of how important copyright law is in their world. For example, many educators believe that in a nonprofit educational setting the borrowing of another's works is allowed indiscriminately. This is simply not true, as is shown in this book. (An interesting point to note here is that some administrators and faculty become so concerned about copyright issues that they choose to enforce a "no copy" rule or establish directives, such as one that allows for little or no use of videos in the classroom. Obviously, this is the "other" side of copyright in education—when the fear of disobeying the law becomes so paramount that nothing can be borrowed or copied.) Therefore, keeping copyright information at the forefront of educators' minds is imperative. Perhaps the best way to achieve compliance with copyright law is to educate—something that teachers and librarians have been trained to do.

## HOW AND WHY TO TEACH/TRAIN STUDENTS, COLLEAGUES, ADMINISTRATION, AND OTHERS ABOUT COPYRIGHT LAW

In our society, copyright and other intellectual property issues are not often taught in K–12 schools, community colleges and technical schools, or colleges and universities (unless they are taught as part of intellectual property law in those institutions with a law school). While one would argue that those in higher education should be training preservice educators, as well as school administrators and librarians, in the area of copyright law, since the likelihood of these individuals needing to use it in the future is very real, in actuality such information may or may not be provided. For some reason, once you become an adult, it is assumed that you will—by osmosis?—know when you are infringing on an owner's copyright and when you are not, as well as how to tell the difference. Obviously, nothing is further from the truth. Everyone needs to learn about copyright law, and this involves being educated as to its various components, concepts, and issues. A number of universities across the nation do offer classes which deal, all or partially, with copyright law, educators, and media. (For example, the author of this book, Dr. Rebecca P. Butler, teaches classes on copyright and technology at Northern Illinois University, DeKalb, Illinois.) Students, undergraduate and graduate, who take such courses will hopefully be better prepared in their professional lives and can also bring this information to those that they will work with in the future. Additionally, assuming that a college or university librarian or educator takes such a course, that person could return to his or her institution or library and offer in-services or faculty workshops on copyright law in higher education. Such workshops should ideally occur at the beginning of the school year and involve the administration as well. The workshop instructor should be prepared to (1) present copyright in terms of both law and ethics; (2) help others work through copyright problems; (3) use as many local examples of violations as possible; (4) have answers ready to promote copyright compliance versus noncompliance; and (5) explain fair use—the copyright concept that most educators and librarians believe they understand. Be aware that the Web contains any number of sites that can be used with, and by, educators and librarians for copyright information (American Library Association 2013; Brewer 2008; Brewer 2012; CampusDownloading; Desert Island Public Domain Film Library 2013; Jassin 2012; Open Source Initiative; Richmond School of Law 2013; Soundzabound 2010; Swank Motion Pictures; University of Minnesota 2010; and University of North Texas 2008). In addition, there are print sources, including multiple books, monographs, magazine and newspaper articles, and more with good copyright information (Association of Research Libraries 2007; Carmack 2005; Donaldson 2008; Fishman 2010; Frankel 2009; Ku and Rossen 2004; Lamoureux et al. 2009; Lipinski 2006; Littlejohn 2003; Russell 2012; Stokes 2009).

Where can preservice teachers (our current college students) as well as college and university librarians and other professionals find lessons and curricular support with which to teach their students about copyright and related issues? Units and activities often exist in library instructional manuals and books. In addition, the Internet is a veritable treasure trove of copyright information (ranging from fairly conservative to quite liberal), including lesson plans, activities, cartoons, and videos aimed at or that can be used with students of many different ages. (Often what is provided online—if not for the right age group—can also be redeveloped by an educator in order to apply to the audience that needs the information.) Activities on such websites range from making copyright web pages to YouTube videos to quizzes and tests to copyright activities to a copyright comic book (Aoki et al. 2006; Center for Social Media 2013; Common Craft 2013; Common Sense Media 2013; Copyright Alliance 2009; Granbery; Independent Lens 2013; Ishizuka 2013; Library of Congress; National Institute for the Defense of Competition. . . 2001; Teaching Copyright; and U-M Copyright Office 2010). It is important to remember, as you access books and websites on copyright, that because copyright is a gray area, not all authors agree. In addition, copyright law may change as new works or formats for works are developed and new ways of using works are created. Because of this, it is also important to be aware of the date of the material you consult; that is, what you seek advice from, ideally, should be as current as is possible. In addition, always look for reputable Internet sites, print sources, and other informational media.

## CONCLUSION

Fair use, public domain, permissions, licenses, documentation . . . these copyright terms are found throughout this book; without them, copyright and media usage in institutions of higher education would be a moot point. As can be seen, such terms overlap—sometimes one will work while another will not—sometimes two or more will help you as you copy or borrow others' work to support your curriculum and instruct your students. It varies exponentially. As Hobbs states, "copyright confusion affects the spread of innovative instructional practices, limits access to high-quality teaching materials, and perpetuates misinformation" (Hobbs 2010, 21). I hope that this book helps to clarify copyright in education and points you in the right direction when working with your students, fellow faculty, administrators, and others, as you instruct the new generations of copyright-compliant individuals.

## REFERENCES

American Library Association. 2013. "Copyright Tools." http://www.ala.org/advocacy/copyright
-tools#genie.

Aoki, Keith, et al. 2006. "Bound by Law?" www.law.duke.edu/cspd/comics/zoomcomic.html.

Association of Research Libraries. 2007. *Know Your Copy Rights: Using Works in Your Teaching—What You CAN Do: Tips for Faculty & Teaching Assistants in Higher Education*. Washington, DC: Association of Research Libraries.

Brewer, Michael. 2008. "Exceptions for Instructors in U.S. Copyright Law." http://librarycopyright
.net/resources/exemptions/index.php?startOver=true#.

Brewer, Michael. 2012. "Is It Protected by Copyright?" http://librarycopyright.net/digitalslider.

Business Software Alliance. 2013. "No Piracy: Report Piracy Now!" https://reporting.bsa.org/usa/
report/add.aspx?pr=1&intcmp=irphp000043b.

Butler, Rebecca P. 2002. "Software Piracy: Don't Let It Byte You." *Knowledge Quest* 31, no. 2
(November/December): 41–42.

———. 2003. "Copyright Law and Organizing the Internet." *Library Trends* 52, no. 2 (Fall): 307–17.

———. 2008. "Join the Copyright Compliance Team." *Knowledge Quest* 36(3): 66-68.

———. 2009. "Proactive Copyright: Workplace Compliance." *TechTrends* 53(3): 9-10.

———. 2009b. *Smart Copyright Compliance for Schools: A How-to-Do-It Manual*. New York:
Neal-Schuman.

CampusDownloading. "Legal Sites." http://campusdownloading.com/legal.htm.

Carmack, Sharon DeBartolo. 2005. *Carmack's Guide to Copyright & Contracts: A Primer for
Genealogists, Writers & Researchers*. Baltimore, MD: Genealogical Publishing.

Center for Social Media. 2013. "Fair Use." www.centerforsocialmedia.org/fair-use.

Common Craft. 2013. "Copyright and Creative Commons." http://www.commoncraft.com/video/copyright-and-creative-commons.

Common Sense Media. 2013. "Digital Literacy and Citizenship Classroom Curriculum." http://cybersmartcurriculum.org/mannersbullyingethics/lessons/6-8/considering_copying.

Copyright Alliance. 2009. "Copyright and the Classroom." www.copyrightfoundation.org.

Desert Island Public Domain Film Library. 2013. "The Oldest, Largest, and Highest Quality Public Domain Film Library in the World." http://desertislandfilms.com.

Donaldson, Michael C. 2008. *Clearance & Copyright: Everything You Need to Know for Film and Television*. 3rd ed. Los Angeles: Silman-James.

Fishman, Stephen. 2010. *The Public Domain: How to Find & Use Copyright-Free Writings, Music, Art & More*. 5th ed. Berkeley, CA: Nolo.

Frankel, James. 2009. *The Teacher's Guide to Music, Media, and Copyright Law*. New York: Hall Leonard Books.

Granbery, Margaret. "Copyright Education Study." http://copyrighteducation.weebly.com/quiz-answers.html.

Hobbs, Renee. 2010. *Copyright Clarity: How Fair Use Supports Digital Learning*. Thousand Oaks, CA: Corwin.

Independent Lens. 2013. "Copyright Criminals." www.pbs.org/independentlens/copyright-criminals/classroom.html.

Ishizuka, Kathy. 2013. "John Greene Tackles Copyright via YouTube." http://www.thedigitalshift.com/2013/02/copyright/copyright-john-green-explains-it-all.

Jassin, Lloyd J. 2012. "Locating Copyright Holders." www.copylaw.com/new_articles/permission.html.

Ku, Susan, and Steve Rossen. 2004. *Teaching Online: A Practical Guide*. 3rd ed. New York: Routledge.

Lamoureux, Edward Lee, et al. 2009. *Intellectual Property Law & Interactive Media: Free for a Fee*. New York: Peter Lang.

Library of Congress. "Taking the Mystery Out of Copyright." www.loc.gov/teachers/copyrightmystery.

Lipinski, Tomas A. 2006. *The Complete Copyright Liability Handbook for Librarians and Educators*. New York: Neal-Schuman.

Littlejohn, Allison, Ed. 2003. *Reusing Online Resources: A Sustainable Approach to e-Learning*. Sterling, VA: Kogan Page.

Motion Picture Association of America. 2013. "Report Piracy." www.mpaa.org/contentprotection/report-piracy.

National Institute for the Defense of Competition and Protection of Intellectual Property (INDECOPI) and the World Intellectual Property Organization (WIPO). 2001. "Copyright." http://www.wipo.int/freepublications/en/copyright/484/wipo_pub_484.pdf.

Open Source Initiative. "The Open Source Definition (annotated)." www.opensource.org/docs/definition.php.

Richmond School of Law. 2013. "Intellectual Property Institute." http://law.richmond.edu/centers/ipi/index.html.

Russell, Carrie. 2012. "Copyright for Librarians and Teachers, in a Nutshell." http://
    americanlibrariesmagazine.org/features/07022012/copyright-librarians-and-teachers
    -nutshell.

Scott, Brian. "The Penalties for Copyright Violation or Infringement." www.researchcopyright.com/
    article-penalties-for-copyright-infringement.php.

Simpson, Carol. 2005. *Copyright for Schools: A Practical Guide*. 4th ed. Worthington, OH: Linworth.

Soundzabound. 2010. "Royalty Free Music for Schools." www.soundzabound.com.

Stokes, Simon. 2009. *Digital Copyright: Law and Practice*. 3rd ed. Portland, OR: Hart.

Swank Motion Pictures. "Understanding Copyright." http://www.swank.com/college/copyright.html.

Teaching Copyright. www.teachingcopyright.org.

U-M Copyright Office. 2010. "A Graduate Student's Guide to Copyright: Open Access, Fair Use,
    and Permissions." http://www.lib.umich.edu/files/services/copyright/Dissertations.pdf.

University of Minnesota. 2010. "Copyright Information and Resources." https://www.lib.umn.edu/
    copyright.

University of North Texas. 2008. "UNT Copyright Resources." http://copyright.unt.edu/content/
    copyright-resources.

# APPENDIX A

## Selected Sections of the U.S. Copyright Law

The following appendix contains selected sections of the U.S. Copyright Law, 1976: Public Law 94-553 (Title 17 of the U.S. Code). These sections include important parts of the law for college and university librarians and faculty: rights of the copyright owner; the fair use provisions; statutory exemptions for libraries, educators, and people with disabilities; copyright ownership provisions; copyright duration; and damages for infringement. For the complete law, see http://www.copyright.gov/title17.

### § 106. Exclusive rights in copyrighted works

Subject to sections 107 through 122, the owner of copyright has the exclusive rights to do and to authorize any of the following:

(1) to reproduce the copyrighted work in copies or phonorecords;

(2) to prepare derivative works based upon the copyrighted work;

(3) to distribute copies or phonorecords of the copyrighted work to the public by sale or other transfer of ownership, or by rental, lease, or lending;

(4) in the case of literary, musical, dramatic, and choreographic works, pantomimes, and motion pictures and other audiovisual works, to perform the copyrighted work publicly;

(5) in the case of literary, musical, dramatic, and choreographic works, pantomimes, and pictorial, graphic, or sculptural works, including the individual images of a motion picture or other audiovisual work, to display the copyrighted work publicly; and

(6) in the case of sound recordings, to perform the copyrighted work publicly by means of a digital audio transmission.

### § 107. Limitations on exclusive rights: Fair use

Notwithstanding the provisions of sections 106 and 106A, the fair use of a copyrighted work, including such use by reproduction in copies or phonorecords or by any other means specified by that section, for purposes such as criticism, comment, news reporting, teaching (including multiple copies for classroom use), scholarship, or research, is not an infringement of copyright. In determining whether the use made of a work in any particular case is a fair use the factors to be considered shall include —

(1) the purpose and character of the use, including whether such use is of a commercial nature or is for nonprofit educational purposes;

(2) the nature of the copyrighted work;

(3) the amount and substantiality of the portion used in relation to the copyrighted work as a whole; and

(4) the effect of the use upon the potential market for or value of the copyrighted work.

The fact that a work is unpublished shall not itself bar a finding of fair use if such finding is made upon consideration of all the above factors.

### § 108. Limitations on exclusive rights: Reproduction by libraries and archives

(a) Except as otherwise provided in this title and notwithstanding the provisions of section 106, it is not an infringement of copyright for a library or archives, or any of its employees acting within the scope of their employment, to reproduce no more than one copy or phonorecord of a work, except as provided in subsections (b) and (c), or to distribute such copy or phonorecord, under the conditions specified by this section, if —

(1) the reproduction or distribution is made without any purpose of direct or indirect commercial advantage;

(2) the collections of the library or archives are (i) open to the public, or (ii) available not only to researchers affiliated with the library or archives or with the institution of which it is a part, but also to other persons doing research in a specialized field; and

(3) the reproduction or distribution of the work includes a notice of copyright that appears on the copy or phonorecord that is reproduced under the provisions of this section, or includes a legend stating that the work may be protected by copyright if no such notice can be found on the copy or phonorecord that is reproduced under the provisions of this section.

(b) The rights of reproduction and distribution under this section apply to three copies or phonorecords of an unpublished work duplicated solely for purposes of preservation and security or for deposit for research use in another library or archives of the type described by clause (2) of subsection (a), if —

(1) the copy or phonorecord reproduced is currently in the collections of the library or archives; and

(2) any such copy or phonorecord that is reproduced in digital format is not otherwise distributed in that format and is not made available to the public in that format outside the premises of the library or archives.

(c) The right of reproduction under this section applies to three copies or phonorecords of a published work duplicated solely for the purpose of replacement of a copy or phonorecord that is damaged, deteriorating, lost, or stolen, or if the existing format in which the work is stored has become obsolete, if —

(1) the library or archives has, after a reasonable effort, determined that an unused replacement cannot be obtained at a fair price; and

(2) any such copy or phonorecord that is reproduced in digital format is not made available to the public in that format outside the premises of the library or archives in lawful possession of such copy.

For purposes of this subsection, a format shall be considered obsolete if the machine or device necessary to render perceptible a work stored in that format is no longer manufactured or is no longer reasonably available in the commercial marketplace.

(d) The rights of reproduction and distribution under this section apply to a copy, made from the collection of a library or archives where the user makes his or her request or from that of another library or archives, of no more than one article or other contribution to a copyrighted collection or periodical issue, or to a copy or phonorecord of a small part of any other copyrighted work, if —

(1) the copy or phonorecord becomes the property of the user, and the library or archives has had no notice that the copy or phonorecord would be used for any purpose other than private study, scholarship, or research; and

(2) the library or archives displays prominently, at the place where orders are accepted, and includes on its order form, a warning of copyright in accordance with requirements that the Register of Copyrights shall prescribe by regulation.

(e) The rights of reproduction and distribution under this section apply to the entire work, or to a substantial part of it, made from the collection of a library or archives where the user makes his or her request or from that of another library or archives, if the library or archives has first determined, on the basis of a reasonable investigation, that a copy or phonorecord of the copyrighted work cannot be obtained at a fair price, if —

(1) the copy or phonorecord becomes the property of the user, and the library or archives has had no notice that the copy or phonorecord would be used for any purpose other than private study, scholarship, or research; and

(2) the library or archives displays prominently, at the place where orders are accepted, and includes on its order form, a warning of copyright in accordance with requirements that the Register of Copyrights shall prescribe by regulation.

(f) Nothing in this section —

(1) shall be construed to impose liability for copyright infringement upon a library or archives or its employees for the unsupervised use of reproducing equipment located on its premises: Provided, That such equipment displays a notice that the making of a copy may be subject to the copyright law;

(2) excuses a person who uses such reproducing equipment or who requests a copy or phonorecord under subsection (d) from liability for copyright infringement for

any such act, or for any later use of such copy or phonorecord, if it exceeds fair use as provided by section 107;

(3) shall be construed to limit the reproduction and distribution by lending of a limited number of copies and excerpts by a library or archives of an audiovisual news program, subject to clauses (1), (2), and (3) of subsection (a); or

(4) in any way affects the right of fair use as provided by section 107, or any contractual obligations assumed at any time by the library or archives when it obtained a copy or phonorecord of a work in its collections.

(g) The rights of reproduction and distribution under this section extend to the isolated and unrelated reproduction or distribution of a single copy or phonorecord of the same material on separate occasions, but do not extend to cases where the library or archives, or its employee —

(1) is aware or has substantial reason to believe that it is engaging in the related or concerted reproduction or distribution of multiple copies or phonorecords of the same material, whether made on one occasion or over a period of time, and whether intended for aggregate use by one or more individuals or for separate use by the individual members of a group; or

(2) engages in the systematic reproduction or distribution of single or multiple copies or phonorecords of material described in subsection (d): *Provided,* That nothing in this clause prevents a library or archives from participating in interlibrary arrangements that do not have, as their purpose or effect, that the library or archives receiving such copies or phonorecords for distribution does so in such aggregate quantities as to substitute for a subscription to or purchase of such work.

(h)(1) For purposes of this section, during the last 20 years of any term of copyright of a published work, a library or archives, including a nonprofit educational institution that functions as such, may reproduce, distribute, display, or perform in facsimile or digital form a copy or phonorecord of such work, or portions thereof, for purposes of preservation, scholarship, or research, if such library or archives has first determined, on the basis of a reasonable investigation, that none of the conditions set forth in subparagraphs (A), (B), and (C) of paragraph (2) apply.

(2) No reproduction, distribution, display, or performance is authorized under this subsection if —

(A) the work is subject to normal commercial exploitation;

(B) a copy or phonorecord of the work can be obtained at a reasonable price; or

(C) the copyright owner or its agent provides notice pursuant to regulations promulgated by the Register of Copyrights that either of the conditions set forth in subparagraphs (A) and (B) applies.

(3) The exemption provided in this subsection does not apply to any subsequent uses by users other than such library or archives.

(i) The rights of reproduction and distribution under this section do not apply to a musical work, a pictorial, graphic or sculptural work, or a motion picture or other audiovisual work other than an audiovisual work dealing with news, except that no such limitation shall apply with respect to rights granted by subsections (b) and (c), or with respect to pictorial or graphic works published as illustrations, diagrams, or similar adjuncts to works of which copies are reproduced or distributed in accordance with subsections (d) and (e).

## § 110. Limitations on exclusive rights: Exemption of certain performances and displays

Notwithstanding the provisions of section 106, the following are not infringements of copyright:

(1) performance or display of a work by instructors or pupils in the course of face-to-face teaching activities of a nonprofit educational institution, in a classroom or similar place devoted to instruction, unless, in the case of a motion picture or other audiovisual work, the performance, or the display of individual images, is given by means of a copy that was not lawfully made under this title, and that the person responsible for the performance knew or had reason to believe was not lawfully made;

(2) except with respect to a work produced or marketed primarily for performance or display as part of mediated instructional activities transmitted via digital networks, or a performance or display that is given by means of a copy or phonorecord that is not lawfully made and acquired under this title, and the transmitting government body or accredited nonprofit educational institution knew or had reason to believe was not lawfully made and acquired, the performance of a nondramatic literary or musical work or reasonable and limited portions of any other work, or display of a work in an amount comparable to that which is typically displayed in the course of a live classroom session, by or in the course of a transmission, if —

(A) the performance or display is made by, at the direction of, or under the actual supervision of an instructor as an integral part of a class session offered as a regular part of the systematic mediated instructional activities of a governmental body or an accredited nonprofit educational institution;

(B) the performance or display is directly related and of material assistance to the teaching content of the transmission;

(C) the transmission is made solely for, and, to the extent technologically feasible, the reception of such transmission is limited to —

(i) students officially enrolled in the course for which the transmission is made; or

(ii) officers or employees of governmental bodies as a part of their official duties or employment; and

(D) the transmitting body or institution —

(i) institutes policies regarding copyright, provides informational materials to faculty, students, and relevant staff members that accurately describe, and promote compliance with, the laws of the United States relating to copyright, and provides notice to students that materials used in connection with the course may be subject to copyright protection; and

(ii) in the case of digital transmissions —

(I) applies technological measures that reasonably prevent —

(aa) retention of the work in accessible form by recipients of the transmission from the transmitting body or institution for longer than the class session; and

(bb) unauthorized further dissemination of the work in accessible form by such recipients to others; and

(II) does not engage in conduct that could reasonably be expected to interfere with technological measures used by copyright owners to prevent such retention or unauthorized further dissemination;

(3) performance of a nondramatic literary or musical work or of a dramatico-musical work of a religious nature, or display of a work, in the course of services at a place of worship or other religious assembly;

(4) performance of a nondramatic literary or musical work otherwise than in a transmission to the public, without any purpose of direct or indirect commercial advantage and without payment of any fee or other compensation for the performance to any of its performers, promoters, or organizers, if —

(A) there is no direct or indirect admission charge; or

(B) the proceeds, after deducting the reasonable costs of producing the performance, are used exclusively for educational, religious, or charitable purposes and not for private financial gain, except where the copyright owner has served notice of objection to the performance under the following conditions:

(i) the notice shall be in writing and signed by the copyright owner or such owner's duly authorized agent; and

(ii) the notice shall be served on the person responsible for the performance at least seven days before the date of the performance, and shall state the reasons for the objection; and

(iii) the notice shall comply, in form, content, and manner of service, with requirements that the Register of Copyrights shall prescribe by regulation;

(5)(A) except as provided in subparagraph (B), communication of a transmission embodying a performance or display of a work by the public reception of the transmission on a single receiving apparatus of a kind commonly used in private homes, unless —

(i) a direct charge is made to see or hear the transmission; or

(ii) the transmission thus received is further transmitted to the public;

(B) communication by an establishment of a transmission or retransmission embodying a performance or display of a nondramatic musical work intended to be received by the general public, originated by a radio or television broadcast station licensed as such by the Federal Communications Commission, or, if an audiovisual transmission, by a cable system or satellite carrier, if —

(i) in the case of an establishment other than a food service or drinking establishment, either the establishment in which the communication occurs has less than 2,000 gross square feet of space (excluding space used for customer parking and for no other purpose), or the establishment in which the communication occurs has 2,000 or more gross square feet of space (excluding space used for customer parking and for no other purpose) and —

(I) if the performance is by audio means only, the performance is communicated by means of a total of not more than 6 loudspeakers, of which not more than 4 loudspeakers are located in any 1 room or adjoining outdoor space; or

(II) if the performance or display is by audiovisual means, any visual portion of the performance or display is communicated by means of a total of not more than 4 audiovisual devices, of which not more than 1 audiovisual device is located in any 1 room, and no such audiovisual device has a diagonal screen size greater than 55 inches, and any audio portion of the performance or display is communicated by means of a total of not more than 6 loudspeakers, of which not more than 4 loudspeakers are located in any 1 room or adjoining outdoor space;

(ii) in the case of a food service or drinking establishment, either the establishment in which the communication occurs has less than 3,750 gross square feet of space (excluding space used for customer parking and for no other purpose), or the establishment in which the communication occurs has 3,750 gross square feet of space or more (excluding space used for customer parking and for no other purpose) and —

(I) if the performance is by audio means only, the performance is communicated by means of a total of not more than 6 loudspeakers, of which not more than 4 loudspeakers are located in any 1 room or adjoining outdoor space; or

(II) if the performance or display is by audiovisual means, any visual portion of the performance or display is communicated by means of a total of not more than 4 audiovisual devices, of which not more than 1 audiovisual device is located in any 1 room, and no such audiovisual device has a diagonal screen size greater than 55 inches, and any audio portion of the performance or display is communicated by means of a total of not more than 6 loudspeakers, of which not more than 4 loudspeakers are located in any 1 room or adjoining outdoor space;

(iii) no direct charge is made to see or hear the transmission or retransmission;

(iv) the transmission or retransmission is not further transmitted beyond the establishment where it is received; and

(v) the transmission or retransmission is licensed by the copyright owner of the work so publicly performed or displayed;

(6) performance of a nondramatic musical work by a governmental body or a nonprofit agricultural or horticultural organization, in the course of an annual agricultural or horticultural fair or exhibition conducted by such body or organization; the

exemption provided by this clause shall extend to any liability for copyright infringe-ment that would otherwise be imposed on such body or organization, under doctrines of vicarious liability or related infringement, for a performance by a concessionnaire, business establishment, or other person at such fair or exhibition, but shall not excuse any such person from liability for the performance;

(7) performance of a nondramatic musical work by a vending establishment open to the public at large without any direct or indirect admission charge, where the sole purpose of the performance is to promote the retail sale of copies or phonorecords of the work, or of the audiovisual or other devices utilized in such performance, and the performance is not transmitted beyond the place where the establishment is located and is within the immediate area where the sale is occurring;

(8) performance of a nondramatic literary work, by or in the course of a trans-mission specifically designed for and primarily directed to blind or other handicapped persons who are unable to read normal printed material as a result of their handicap, or deaf or other handicapped persons who are unable to hear the aural signals accompa-nying a transmission of visual signals, if the performance is made without any purpose of direct or indirect commercial advantage and its transmission is made through the facilities of: (i) a governmental body; or (ii) a noncommercial educational broadcast station (as defined in section 397 of title 47); or (iii) a radio subcarrier authorization (as defined in 47 CFR 73.293–73.295 and 73.593–73.595); or (iv) a cable system (as defined in section 111 (f));

(9) performance on a single occasion of a dramatic literary work published at least ten years before the date of the performance, by or in the course of a transmission specifically designed for and primarily directed to blind or other handicapped persons who are unable to read normal printed material as a result of their handicap, if the performance is made without any purpose of direct or indirect commercial advantage and its transmission is made through the facilities of a radio subcarrier authorization referred to in clause (8) (iii), Provided, That the provisions of this clause shall not be applicable to more than one performance of the same work by the same performers or under the auspices of the same organization; and

(10) notwithstanding paragraph (4), the following is not an infringement of copyright: performance of a nondramatic literary or musical work in the course of a social function which is organized and promoted by a nonprofit veterans' organiza-tion or a nonprofit fraternal organization to which the general public is not invited, but not including the invitees of the organizations, if the proceeds from the perfor-mance, after deducting the reasonable costs of producing the performance, are used exclusively for charitable purposes and not for financial gain. For purposes of this section the social functions of any college or university fraternity or sorority shall not be included unless the social function is held solely to raise funds for a specific charitable purpose.

The exemptions provided under paragraph (5) shall not be taken into account in any administrative, judicial, or other governmental proceeding to set or adjust the royalties payable to copyright owners for the public performance or display of their works. Royalties payable to copyright owners for any public performance or display of their works other than such performances or displays as are exempted under paragraph (5) shall not be diminished in any respect as a result of such exemption.

In paragraph (2), the term "mediated instructional activities" with respect to the performance or display of a work by digital transmission under this section refers to activities that use such work as an integral part of the class experience, controlled by or under the actual supervision of the instructor and analogous to the type of performance or display that would take place in a live classroom setting. The term does not refer to activities that use, in 1 or more class sessions of a single course, such works as textbooks, course packs, or other material in any media, copies or phonorecords of which are typically purchased or acquired by the students in higher education for their independent use and retention or are typically purchased or acquired for elementary and secondary students for their possession and independent use.

For purposes of paragraph (2), accreditation —

(A) with respect to an institution providing post-secondary education, shall be as determined by a regional or national accrediting agency recognized by the Council on Higher Education Accreditation or the United States Department of Education; and

(B) with respect to an institution providing elementary or secondary education, shall be as recognized by the applicable state certification or licensing procedures. For purposes of paragraph (2), no governmental body or accredited nonprofit educational institution shall be liable for infringement by reason of the transient or temporary storage of material carried out through the automatic technical process of a digital transmission of the performance or display of that material as authorized under paragraph (2). No such material stored on the system or network controlled or operated by the transmitting body or institution under this paragraph shall be maintained on such system or network in a manner ordinarily accessible to anyone other than anticipated recipients. No such copy shall be maintained on the system or network in a manner ordinarily accessible to such anticipated recipients for a longer period than is reasonably necessary to facilitate the transmissions for which it was made.

## § 121. Limitations on exclusive rights: reproduction for blind or other people with disabilities

(a) Notwithstanding the provisions of section 106, it is not an infringement of copyright for an authorized entity to reproduce or to distribute copies or phonorecords of a previously published, nondramatic literary work if such copies or phonorecords are reproduced or distributed in specialized formats exclusively for use by blind or other persons with disabilities.

(b)(1) Copies or phonorecords to which this section applies shall —

(A) not be reproduced or distributed in a format other than a specialized format exclusively for use by blind or other persons with disabilities;

(B) bear a notice that any further reproduction or distribution in a format other than a specialized format is an infringement; and

(C) include a copyright notice identifying the copyright owner and the date of the original publication.

(2) The provisions of this subsection shall not apply to standardized, secure, or norm-referenced tests and related testing material, or to computer programs, except the portions thereof that are in conventional human language (including descriptions of pictorial works) and displayed to users in the ordinary course of using the computer programs.

(c) For purposes of this section, the term —

(1) "authorized entity" means a nonprofit organization or a governmental agency that has a primary mission to provide specialized services relating to training, education, or adaptive reading or information access needs of blind or other persons with disabilities;

(2) "blind or other persons with disabilities" means individuals who are eligible or who may qualify in accordance with the Act entitled "An Act to provide books for the adult blind," approved March 3, 1931 (2 U.S.C. 135a; 46 Stat. 1487) to receive books and other publications produced in specialized formats; and

(3) "specialized formats" means braille, audio, or digital text which is exclusively for use by blind or other persons with disabilities.

## § 201. Ownership of copyright

(a) Initial Ownership. — Copyright in a work protected under this title vests initially in the author or authors of the work. The authors of a joint work are coowner of copyright in the work.

(b) Works Made for Hire. — In the case of a work made for hire, the employer or other person for whom the work was prepared is considered the author for purposes of this title, and, unless the parties have expressly agreed otherwise in a written instrument signed by them, owns all of the rights comprised in the copyright.

(c) Contributions to Collective Works. — Copyright in each separate contribution to a collective work is distinct from copyright in the collective work as a whole, and vests initially in the author of the contribution. In the absence of an express transfer of the copyright or of any rights under it, the owner of copyright in the collective work is presumed to have acquired only the privilege of reproducing and distributing the contribution as part of that particular collective work, any revision of that collective work, and any later collective work in the same series.

(d) Transfer of Ownership. —

(1) The ownership of a copyright may be transferred in whole or in part by any means of conveyance or by operation of law, and may be bequeathed by will or pass as personal property by the applicable laws of intestate succession.

(2) Any of the exclusive rights comprised in a copyright, including any subdivision of any of the rights specified by section 106, may be transferred as provided by clause (1) and owned separately. The owner of any particular exclusive right is entitled, to the extent of that right, to all of the protection and remedies accorded to the copyright owner by this title.

(e) Involuntary Transfer. — When an individual author's ownership of a copyright, or of any of the exclusive rights under a copyright, has not previously been transferred voluntarily by that individual author, no action by any governmental body or other official or organization purporting to seize, expropriate, transfer, or exercise rights of ownership with respect to the copyright, or any of the exclusive rights under a copyright, shall be given effect under this title, except as provided under title 11.

## § 302. Duration of copyright: Works created on or after January 1, 1978

(a) In General. — Copyright in a work created on or after January 1, 1978, subsists from its creation and, except as provided by the following subsections, endures for a term consisting of the life of the author and 70 years after the author's death.

(b) Joint Works. — In the case of a joint work prepared by two or more authors who did not work for hire, the copyright endures for a term consisting of the life of the last surviving author and 70 years after such last surviving author's death.

(c) Anonymous Works, Pseudonymous Works, and Works Made for Hire. — In the case of an anonymous work, a pseudonymous work, or a work made for hire, the copyright endures for a term of 95 years from the year of its first publication, or a term of 120 years from the year of its creation, whichever expires first. If, before the end of such term, the identity of one or more of the authors of an anonymous or pseudonymous work is revealed in the records of a registration made for that work under subsections (a) or (d) of section 408, or in the records provided by this subsection, the copyright in the work endures for the term specified by subsection (a) or (b), based on the life of the author or authors whose identity has been revealed. Any person having an interest in the copyright in an anonymous or pseudonymous work may at any time record, in records to be maintained by the Copyright Office for that purpose, a statement identifying one or more authors of the work; the statement shall also identify the person filing it, the nature of that person's interest, the source of the information recorded, and the particular work affected, and shall comply in form and content with requirements that the Register of Copyrights shall prescribe by regulation.

(d) Records Relating to Death of Authors. — Any person having an interest in a copyright may at any time record in the Copyright Office a statement of the date of death of the author of the copyrighted work, or a statement that the author is still living on a particular date. The statement shall identify the person filing it, the nature of that person's interest, and the source of the information recorded, and shall comply in form and content with requirements that the Register of Copyrights shall prescribe by regulation. The Register shall maintain current records of information relating to the death of authors of copyrighted works, based on such recorded statements and, to the extent the Register considers practicable, on data contained in any of the records of the Copyright Office or in other reference sources.

(e) Presumption as to Author's Death. — After a period of 95 years from the year of first publication of a work, or a period of 120 years from the year of its creation, whichever expires first, any person who obtains from the Copyright Office a certified report that the records provided by subsection (d) disclose nothing to indicate that the author of the work is living, or died less than 70 years before, is entitled to the benefit of a presumption that the author has been dead for at least 70 years. Reliance in good faith upon this presumption shall be a complete defense to any action for infringement under this title.

## § 504. Remedies for infringement: Damages and profits

(a) In General. — Except as otherwise provided by this title, an infringer of copyright is liable for either —

(1) the copyright owner's actual damages and any additional profits of the infringer, as provided by subsection (b); or

(2) statutory damages, as provided by subsection (c).

(b) Actual Damages and Profits. — The copyright owner is entitled to recover the actual damages suffered by him or her as a result of the infringement, and any profits of the infringer that are attributable to the infringement and are not taken into account in computing the actual damages. In establishing the infringer's profits, the copyright owner is required to present proof only of the infringer's gross revenue, and the infringer is required to prove his or her deductible expenses and the elements of profit attributable to factors other than the copyrighted work.

(c) Statutory Damages. —

(1) Except as provided by clause (2) of this subsection, the copyright owner may elect, at any time before final judgment is rendered, to recover, instead of actual damages and profits, an award of statutory damages for all infringements involved in the action, with respect to any one work, for which any one infringer is liable individually, or for which any two or more infringers are liable jointly and severally, in a sum of not less than $750 or more than $30,000 as the court considers just. For the purposes of this subsection, all the parts of a compilation or derivative work constitute one work.

(2) In a case where the copyright owner sustains the burden of proving, and the court finds, that infringement was committed willfully, the court in its discretion may increase the award of statutory damages to a sum of not more than $150,000. In a case where the infringer sustains the burden of proving, and the court finds, that such infringer was not aware and had no reason to believe that his or her acts constituted an

infringement of copyright, the court in its discretion may reduce the award of statutory damages to a sum of not less than $200. The court shall remit statutory damages in any case where an infringer believed and had reasonable grounds for believing that his or her use of the copyrighted work was a fair use under section 107, if the infringer was: (i) an employee or agent of a nonprofit educational institution, library, or archives acting within the scope of his or her employment who, or such institution, library, or archives itself, which infringed by reproducing the work in copies or phonorecords; or (ii) a public broadcasting entity which or a person who, as a regular part of the non-profit activities of a public broadcasting entity (as defined in subsection (g) of section 118) infringed by performing a published nondramatic literary work or by reproducing a transmission program embodying a performance of such a work.

(d) Additional Damages in Certain Cases. — In any case in which the court finds that a defendant proprietor of an establishment who claims as a defense that its activities were exempt under section 110(5) did not have reasonable grounds to believe that its use of a copyrighted work was exempt under such section, the plaintiff shall be entitled to, in addition to any award of damages under this section, an additional award of two times the amount of the license fee that the proprietor of the establishment concerned should have paid the plaintiff for such use during the preceding period of up to 3 years.

# APPENDIX B

## Glossary for Chapter 6

**Definitions for all web terms in chapter 6 are below.**

**AdobeConnect**: AdobeConnect is Internet conferencing software (Adobe 2013).

**Animoto**: "Animoto is a web application that, with the click of a button, produces videos using images and music that a user selects" (Animoto, 1).

**Blackboard**: "The *Blackboard Learning System* is a comprehensive and flexible e-Learning software platform that delivers a complete course management system" (Blackboard 2004, 1).

**Blogs**: "A blog is a type of website, usually maintained by an individual with regular entries of commentary, descriptions of events, or other material such as graphics or video. Entries are commonly displayed in reverse-chronological order ... Many blogs provide commentary or news on a particular subject; others function as more personal online diaries. A typical blog combines text, images, and links to other blogs, Web pages, and other media related to its topic. The ability for readers to leave comments in an interactive format is an important part of many blogs" (Rhode 2010, 1).

**BrainPOP**: BrainPOP is an animated educational Internet site that "engages students, supports educators, and bolsters achievement. (It also features) . . . free lesson plans, video tutorials, professional development tools, graphic organizers, (and) best practices" (BrainPOP 2013, 1).

**BYOD**: "bring your own device: the policy of allowing employees or students to bring their own computing devices to work, college etc., and use them on the organization's network" (*Macmillan Dictionary* 2013, 1).

**Chatroulette**: A "social Web site (that) drops you into an unnerving world where you are connected through webcams to a random, fathomless succession of strangers from across the globe" (Bilton 2010, 1).

**Cloud Computing**: "Cloud computing is a general term for delivering hosted services over the Internet . . . these services can include blogs, YouTube videos, still-image slide shows, and a range of other applications" (Northern Illinois University 2010, 1).

**Computational Knowledge Engine**: Relatively new in the cloud computing realm, these "engines" can complement traditional search engines, such as Google, by providing computable answers to questions posed by users. At present, computational knowledge engines such as Wolfram Alpha are in the development stage (May 2009, 1).

**Concept-Mapping Tool**: Digital media used in the production of concept maps. (Concept maps are schema that demonstrate the relationships between and among concepts [Dictionary.com 2013].) Inspiration (www.inspiration.com/Inspiration) may be considered a concept-mapping software tool.

**Content Aggregator**: "A content aggregator is an individual or organization that gathers Web content (and/or sometimes applications) from different online sources for reuse or resale. There are two kinds of content aggregators: (1) those who simply gather material from various sources for their Web sites, and (2) those who gather and distribute content to suit their customer's needs" (SearchSOA 2013, 1). Aggregators, like Google Reader, bring desired information to one spot.

**Delicious**: "Delicious is a social bookmarking system, that . . . allows users to qualify content" (Housley 2013, 1). When using Delicious, the more often a website is bookmarked or identified with a tag, the more prominent it becomes.

**Diggo**: "a research and collaborative research tool. . . , and a knowledge-sharing community and social content site" (Diggo 2012, 1).

**Digital Rights Management (DRM):** "DRM refers to a collection of systems used to protect the copyrights of electronic media. These include digital music and movies . . . (and) . . . can be accomplished by using digital watermarks or proprietary file encryption" (Tech Terms.com 2013, 1).

**Dropbox**: "lets you easily sync files between computers, share with them others, and create backups . . . its contents are stored both locally and in the cloud" (CNET Editors Review 2012, 1).

**e-Reader**: "E-readers are a growing technology that allow users to read their favorite books, magazines, pdf and word files straight from a simple handheld mobile device" (Wishpot Inc. 2013, 1).

**Facebook**: "Facebook is a popular free social networking website that allows registered users to create profiles, upload photos and video, send messages and keep in touch with friends, family and colleagues" (WhatIs.com. 2013, 1).

**File Sharing**: "file sharing is the practice of making files available for other individuals to download. It can be as simple as sharing a file for general consumption via My Web-Space or enabling file sharing on your computer's operating system so that you can access your home computer files at work" (CIO... 2013, 1).

**Flickr**: "an online photo management and sharing application" (Turnbull 2005, 1).

**Goodreads**: "Goodreads is the largest social network for readers in the world . . . Goodreads members recommend books, compare what they are reading, keep track of what they've read and would like to read, form book clubs" (Goodreads 2013, 1).

**Google Wave**: One of many online Google tools, Google Wave was intended to encourage collaboration in the cloud (on the Web). However, because it has not been a popular product, Google will only maintain Google Wave through 2010. Its technology will be used in other Google products (Official Google Blog 2010).

**Hulu**: Hulu is a "free and legal" online video service that provides popular television shows, current movies, and more to its viewers "through an advertising supported model" (Hulu 2013, 1–2).

**Hyperlink**: "A hyperlink is a graphic or a piece of text in an Internet document that can connect readers to another webpage, or another portion of a document" (wiseGEEK 2013, 1).

**iPad**: A technological "gadget" whose function comes from the way the consumer uses it. Sometimes described as a big iPhone, the iPad can operate as an e-book reader; a provider of information, from recipes to star charts, via the Internet and a myriad of free and purchasable applications (apps); a video game player; a word processor; an iPod; and more (Phelan 2010).

**iTunes**: "iTunes is a free application for your Mac or PC. It organizes and plays your digital music and video on your computer. It keeps all your content in sync. And it's a store on your computer, iPod touch, iPhone, iPad" (Apple Inc. 2013).

**Kindle**: "A portable e-book device from Amazon.com that provides wireless connectivity to Amazon for e-book downloads as well as Wikipedia and search engines" (*Computer Desktop Encyclopedia* 2013, 1).

**LibriVox**: "provides free audiobooks from the public domain" (LibriVox: 1).

**Limewire**: Limewire is an example of a peer-to-peer (P2P) software that is used to obtain "free" music and videos by downloading files from the computers of others who have joined the network. Much file sharing using P2P software violates copyright law, because it involves the replication of copyrighted works (CIO. . . 2013, 1).

**LinkedIn**: LinkedIn is an online professional networking tool for business professionals (Linkedin 2013, 1).

**MediaCast**: "an open and interoperable digital content management and video streaming solution . . . provides you with tools to create, manage and deliver live and on-demand multimedia anytime, anywhere. From analog to digital encoding, to copyright compliance tools" (Inventive Technology 2013, 1).

**MOOC**: a "massive open online course"; "one of the newest trends in higher education. Universities offer classes online, for free, to anyone who wishes to take them" (Allen 2013, 29).

**Moodle**: "Moodle is a Course Management System (CMS), also known as a Learning Management System (LMS) or a Virtual Learning Environment (VLE). It is a free web application that educators can use to create effective online learning sites" (Moodle, 1 ).

**Mousebreaker**: This is an example of an online website with free online games (Mousebreaker 2005).

**MP3 Player**: An MP3 player is a portable digital audio device popular for playing music (Logan 2013).

**MySpace**: MySpace is a social networking website.

**myYearbook**: Started in 2005 by a high school sister-and-brother team, myYearbook is a social networking site where users play games and meet new people (myYearbook 2013).

**Netvibes**: "Founded in 2005, Netvibes pioneered the first personalized dashboard publishing platform for the Web." With Netvibes, users can pull onto one access point all of their digital communications (Netvibes 2013, 1).

**Ning**: "Based in Palo Alto, Calif., Ning offers an easy-to-use service that enables people to create custom branded social networks" (Ning 2013, 1)

**Nook**: The Nook is an e-book reader available from Barnes and Noble (Barnes and Noble 2013, 1).

**OverDrive**: "free software that allows you to download and enjoy audiobooks, music, and video on a computer, or e-books and audiobooks on a mobile device" (OverDrive 2012, 1).

**Pageflakes**: "Pageflakes allows you to put all your web favorites, including news, email and search engines, onto one personalized page using "flakes," or widgets" (Crunchbase 2013, 1).

**Pinterest**: Pinterest is a "social networking service that lets users 'pin' images they like on the web to boards they can share with friends and publish to the world at large" (Patel 2012, 1).

**Plurk**: Plurk is a social network, which defines itself as "a social journal for your life" (Plurk 2013, 1).

**Podcasts and Vodcasts**: "Podcasting is the process of capturing an audio event, song, speech, or mix of sounds and then posting that digital sound object to a Web site or "blog" (Meng 2005, 1). Vodcasting "is almost identical to podcasting. The difference is that the content is video versus audio" (Meng 2005, 1).

**Prezi**: Somewhat similar to PowerPoint (PPT), Prezi uses a canvas concept instead of the slides of PPT. Items such as text, audio, video, etc., can be dragged, tilted, zoomed in or out and connected to create an animation effect (Northern Illinois University 2010).

**Protopage:** This is a web application that can be used to combine personal RSS feeds, sticky notes, and Internet bookmarks into one package (Pash 2013, 1).

**QR Codes**: "stands for 'quick response,' as the codes are designed to be read quickly . . . two-dimensional barcodes that can be read by many cell phones and smartphones. The codes, which are small squares with black and white patterns, appear in a variety of places, such as magazine and newspaper ads. A QR code is used to encode some sort of information, such as text or a URL" (About.com 2013, 1).

**RSS Feeds**: "Short for Really Simple Syndication or Rich Site Summary . . . They're basically simple text files that, once submitted to feed directories, will allow subscribers to see content within a very short time after it's updated" (Boswell 2013, 1). With an RSS feed, the user can access only that information in which s/he is interested; that is, one can receive only news about sports.

**Scribd**: "On Scribd, you can easily turn any file—such as PDF, Word and PowerPoint—into a web document and immediately connect with passionate readers and information-seekers . . . through connected sites such as Facebook or Twitter and search engines such as Google" (Scribd 2013, 1).

**Second Life**: Second Life is an example of a 3-D virtual world, where participants create avatars in order to go to school and libraries, attend conferences, shop, visit, and so on.

**Shelfari**: "a gathering place for authors, aspiring authors, publishers, and readers . . . has many tools and features to help these groups connect with each other in a fun and engaging way" (Le Penske 2006, 1).

**Skype**: "Skype is an IP telephony service provider that offers free calling between subscribers and low-cost calling to people who don't use the service. In addition to standard telephone calls, Skype enables file transfers, texting, video chat and videoconferencing. The service is available for desktop computers, notebook and tablet computers and other mobile devices, including mobile phones" (Glushakow-Smith 2013, 1).

**Slideshare**: "SlideShare is a business media site for sharing presentations, documents and pdfs." On Slideshare, you can "embed slideshows into your own blog or website . . . share slideshows publicly or privately . . . synch audio to your slides . . . market your own event . . . join groups to connect with SlideShare members who share your interests . . . download the original file" (Slideshare 2013, 1).

**Social Gaming Network**: "The category has its roots in casual gaming, where users played alone and titles cost a fee to download. Social games . . . are built to be enjoyed and shared with friends through existing social networks and platforms like the iPhone. The games don't necessarily involve real-time competition or interaction. Many are asynchronous, meaning players can play on their own time while checking in at various points in the day. But because they tap into existing connections in one form or another, they heighten the sense of camaraderie, competition and pride found in gaming" (Kim 2009, 1).

**Social Media**: "a website that doesn't just give you information, but interacts with you while giving you that information" (Nations 2013, 1). It can allow users to communicate or interact with others also involved in a particular social media.

**TeacherTube**: "an online community for sharing instructional videos . . . professional development with teachers teaching teachers . . . (and) . . . a site where teachers can post videos designed for students to view in order to learn a concept or skill" (TeacherTube 2010, 1).

**Twitter**: Twitter is an example of a microblog (Rhode 2010). Microblogging is "blogging done with severe space or size constraints typically by posting frequent brief messages" (Merriam-Webster 2014, 1).

**Video Games**: "an electronic game played by means of images on a video screen and often emphasizing fast action" (*Merriam-Webster* 2013, 1).

**Video Streaming**: "Streaming video is a sequence of 'moving images' that are sent in compressed form over the Internet and displayed by the viewer as they arrive. Streaming media is streaming video with sound. With streaming video or streaming media, a Web user does not have to wait to download a large file before seeing the video or hearing the sound. Instead, the media is sent in a continuous stream and is played as it arrives. The user needs a player, which is a special program that uncompresses and sends video data to the display and audio data to speakers. A player can be either an integral part of a browser or downloaded from the software maker's Web site" (Arndt 2005, 1).

**Web 2.0**: Web 2.0 technologies include blogs, wikis, social media, mobile learning, and cloud computing (Secker, 2010, 125). Essentially Web 2.0 "is participatory as users are encouraged to create and upload content often in a collaborative manner" (Stokes 2009, 172).

**Web Feed**: A web feed or RSS feed "is a content delivery vehicle. It is the format used when you want to syndicate news and other web content. When it distributes the content it is called a feed. You could think of RSS as your own personal wire service" (Pressfeed 2010, 1).

**Web Syndication**: "A syndicate is a group that forms an association for the sake of a common interest. Starting in print journalism, syndication was an approach to widening the market for a comic strip or a columnist by allowing simultaneous publication in multiple venues. Web syndication can refer to either this strategy adapted to the Internet or to a format that allows readers to gather updates from their favorite websites into one place" (Elizabeth 2013, 1).

**Wikis**: "A wiki is a Web site that allows users to add and update content on the site using their own Web browser" (TechTerms.com 2013, 1).

**Wordles**: Wordles are "word clouds" that are generated "from text that you provide. The clouds give greater prominence to words that appear more frequently in the source text. You can tweak your clouds with different fonts, layouts, and color schemes. The images you create with Wordle are yours to use however you like" (Feinberg 2013, 1).

**Xanga**: "Xanga is a social blogging website ... a combination of a social network and a blog host" (About.com: WebTrends 2013, 1).

**YouTube**: YouTube is a popular website for sharing videos.

## REFERENCES

About.com: Cell Phones. 2013. "QR Codes: A Definition." http://cellphones.about.com/od/ phoneglossary/g/Qr-Codes.htm.

About.com: Web Trends. 2013. "What Is Xanga?" http://webtrends.about.com/od/pro5/fr/ what-is-xanga.htm.

Adobe. 2013. "Adobe Connect: The Next Best Thing to Meeting in Person." www.adobe.com/ products/acrobatconnectpro.

Allen, John. 2013. "The ABCs of MOOCs." *On Wisconsin* 111, no. 2: 28–31.

Animoto Production Inc. "Animoto's Channel." www.youtube.com/user/Animoto.

Apple Inc. 2013. What Is iTunes? www.apple.com/itunes/what-is.

Arndt, Ole. 2005. "Streaming Video on Your Website—Convert Visitors into Customers." http://ezinearticles.com/?Streaming-Video-on-Your-Website—Convert-Visitors-into -Customers&id=40805.

Barnes and Noble. 2013. "Nook." www.barnesandnoble.com/nook/index.asp?r=1&cds2Pid=30919.

Bilton, Nick. 2010. "The Surreal World of Chatroulette." www.nytimes.com/2010/02/21/ weekinreview/21bilton.html.

Blackboard Inc. 2004. "About the Blackboard Academic Suite (Release 6.1) Instructor Manual." http://library.blackboard.com/docs/r6/6_1/instructor/bbls_r6_1_instructor.

Boswell, Wendy. 2013. "RSS Feeds." http://websearch.about.com/od/rsssocialbookmarks/f/rss.htm.

BrainPOP. 2013. About Us: Who We Are." www.brainpop.com/about.

CIO and Vice Provost for Information Technology. 2013. "Understanding File Sharing." www.cio.wisc.edu/security/filesharing.aspx.

CNET Editors Review. 2012. "Dropbox." http://download.cnet.com/Dropbox/3000-18500_4 -10903856.html.

*Computer Desktop Encyclopedia*. 2013. "Kindle." http://computer.yourdictionary.com/kindle.

Crunchbase. 2013. "Pageflakes." www.crunchbase.com/company/pageflakes.

Dictionary.com. 2013. "Concept Map." http://dictionary.reference.com/browse/concept map.

Diggo. 2012. "About Diggo." https://www.diigo.com/about.

Elizabeth, Mary. 2013. "What Is Web Syndication?" www.wisegeek.com/what-is-web-syndication.htm.

Feinberg, Jonathan. 2013. "Wordle—Beautiful Word Clouds." www.wordle.net.

Glushakow-Smith, Steve. 2013. "What Is Skype?—Definition." http:// searchunifiedcommunications.techtarget.com/sDefinition/0,,sid186_gci1050583,00.html.

Goodreads. 2013. "About Us: What Is Goodreads?" www.goodreads.com/about/us.

Housley, S. 2013. "What Is Delicious Understanding Social Bookmarking." www.small-business -software.net/using-delicious.htm.

Hulu. 2013. "Hulu." www.hulu.com/about.

Inventive Technology. 2013. "MediaCast." http://www.inventivetec.com.

Kim, Ryan. 2009. "Social Networking Is Next Big Thing for Gaming." http://articles.sfgate.
    com/2009-08-03/business/17178226_1_casual-gaming-mafia-wars-social-gaming.

Le Penske, Cherie. 2006. "Press Release: Shelfari Launches World's First Social Media Site for
    Books." www.shelfari.com/Shelfari/Press/10-11-06.aspx.

LibriVox. "Listen." http://librivox.org.

Linkedin. 2013. "About Us." http://press.linkedin.com/about.

Logan, Gail. 2013. "Define MP3 Players." www.ehow.com/facts_5447652_define-mp-players.html.

*Macmillan Dictionary.* 2013. "Buzzword: BYOD." http://www.macmillandictionary.com/us/
    buzzword/entries/byod.html.

May, Simon Mackie. 2009. "Wolfram Alpha: Impressive, But Not the Future of Search, Yet." http://
    gigaom.com/collaboration/wolfram-alpha-impressive-but-not-the-future-of-search-yet.

Meng, Peter. 2005. "Podcasting and Vodcasting: A White Paper." Columbia: University of Missouri.

*Merriam-Webster.* 2014. "Microblogging." http://www.merriam-webster.com/dictionary/
    microblogging.

*Merriam-Webster.* 2013. "Video Game." www.merriam-webster.com/dictionary/video+game.

Moodle. "Welcome to the Moodle Community!" http://moodle.org.

Mousebreaker. 2005. "Welcome to Mousebreaker." www.mousebreaker.co.uk.

myYearbook. 2013. "Our Story." www.myyearbook.com/our_story.php.

Nations, Daniel. 2013. "What Is Social Media?" http://webtrends.about.com/od/web20/a/
    social-media.htm.

Netvibes. 2013. "About Netvibes." http://about.netvibes.com/.

Ning. 2013. "About Ning." http://about.ning.com.

Northern Illinois University. 2010. "Teaching with Technology Institute." DeKalb, IL: Northern
    Illinois University.

The Official Google Blog. 2010. "Update on Google Wave." http://googleblog.blogspot
    .com/2010/08/update-on-google-wave.html.

OverDrive. 2012. "OverDrive Media Console." http://help.overdrive.com/overdrive-media-console.

Pash, Adam. 2013. "Create a Personalized Homepage with Protopage.
    http://lifehacker.com/141588/create-a-personalized-homepage-with-protopage.

Patel, Nilay. 2012. "Pinterest's Uneasy Relationship with Copyright Law: What Happens Next."
    http://www.theverge.com/2012/2/22/2806473/pinterest-copyright-law-and-the-power-of
    -money.

Phelan, David. 2010. "The iPad: What Is It Good for?" www.independent.co.uk/life-style/
    gadgets-and-tech/features/the-ipad-what-is-it-good-for-1982635.html.

Plurk. 2013. "Plurk is a Social Journal for Your Life." www.plurk.com.

Pressfeed Co. 2010. "RSS Feeds, a Tutorial." www.press-feed.com/howitworks/rss_tutorial
    .php#whatarewebfeeds.

Rhode, Jason. 2010. "Writing in the Cloud: What Are Blogs?" writinginthecloud.blogspot.com.

Scribd. 2013. "About Scribd." www.scribd.com/about.

SearchSOA. 2013. "Look Up Tech Terms: Content Aggregator." http://searchsoa.techtarget.com/sDefinition/0,,sid26_gci815047,00.html.

Secker, Jane. 2010. *Copyright and e-Learning: A Guide for Practitioners*. London: Facet.

Slideshare. 2013. "Why Should You Use SlideShare?" www.slideshare.net/about.

Stokes, Simon. 2009. *Digital Copyright: Law and Practice*. 3rd ed. Portland: Hart.

TeacherTube. 2010. "About Us." www.teachertube.com/staticPage.php?pg=about.

Tech Terms.com. 2013. "DRM: Digital Rights Management." www.techterms.com/definition/drm.

Tech Terms.com. 2013. "Wiki." http://www.techterms.com/definition/wiki.

Turnbull, Giles. 2005. "What Is Flickr (and Hot Tips for Using It)." http://oreilly.com/pub/a/mac/2005/08/02/flickr.html.

WhatIs.com. 2013. "Facebook." http://whatis.techtarget.com/definition/Facebook.

wiseGEEK. 2013. "What Is a Hyperlink?" www.wisegeek.com/what-is-a-hyperlink.htm.

Wishpot Inc. 2013. "Latest e-Reader Reviews." www.ereaders.net.

# INDEX